CONTENTS

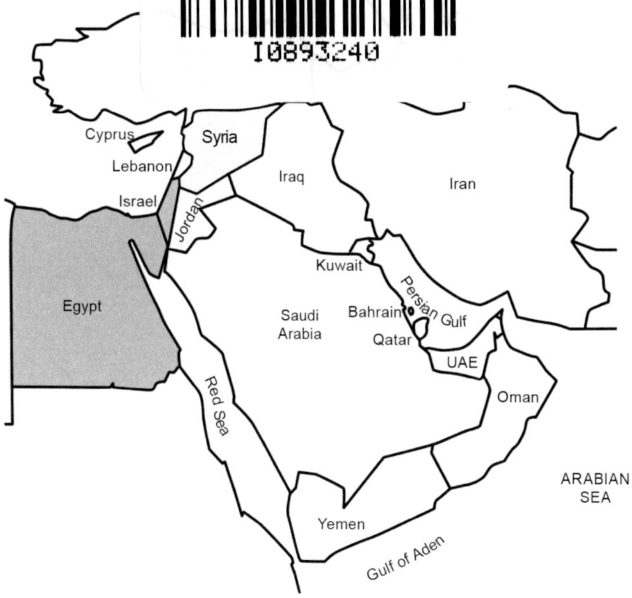

Note

In order to simplify the use of this book, all names, locations and geographic designations are as provided in *The Times World Atlas*, or other traditionally accepted major sources of reference, as of the time of the described events. Similarly, Arabic names are romanised and transcripted rather than transliterated and the spelling usually follows that in Wikipedia. Metric standards are used for length, volume, weight and area but Imperial feet are also used for altitude, as they are more accurate, and nautical miles for naval distances.

Helion & Company Limited
Unit 8 Amherst Business Centre, Budbrooke Road, Warwick CV34 5WE, England
Tel. 01926 499 619
Email: info@helion.co.uk Website: www.helion.co.uk Twitter: @helionbooks Visit our blog http://blog.helion.co.uk/

Published by Helion & Company 2024
Designed and typeset by Farr out Publications, Wokingham, Berkshire
Cover designed by Paul Hewitt, Battlefield Design (www.battlefield-design.co.uk)

Front cover artwork: On 5 June 1967, around 08.45hrs local time, just as the sun burned away the last traces of the morning mist, a formation of Dassault MD.450 Ouragan straight-wing fighter-bombers of the Israeli Defence Force/Air Force attacked the Meliz Air Base (better known as 'Bir Gifgafa' in the West), in northern central Sinai. The four MiG-21F-13s of No. 45 Squadron, United Arab Republic Air Force – which were on alert – were scrambled as the Israelis bombed the sole runway. However, two MIGs were destroyed before they could take- off. The other two involved a pair of Ouragans in a fierce air combat, in the course of which one of the Egyptian jets disappeared, whilst one of the Israeli craft then crashed into an air defence position on the ground. (Artwork by Elena Stanilevich © Helion & Company 2023)

ISBN 978-1-915070-77-7

British Library Cataloguing-in-Publication Data.
A catalogue record for this book is available from the British Library.

ABBREVIATIONS

AAA	Anti-Aircraft Artillery
AB	Air Base
AMAN	Israeli Military Intelligence
CIA	Central Intelligence Agency
DM1	Main Directorate of Military Intelligence (Egypt)
DMZ	De-militarised Zone
IAP	International Airport
IDF	Israel Defense Force (referred to as both *Israel* and *Israeli* Defense Force in various sources)
IDF/AF	Israel Defense Force/Air Force
Mossad	Israeli national intelligence organisation
NWC	National Water Carrier
PBP	Palestinian Border Police
PLA	Palestine Liberation Army
PLO	Palestine Liberation Organization
SAM	surface-to-air missile
UAC	United Arab Command
UAR	United Arab Republic
UARAF	United Arab Republic Air Force
UN	United Nations
UNEF	United Nations Emergency Force
UNTSO	United Nations Truce Supervision Organisation
USA/US	United States of America/United States

INTRODUCTION AND ACKNOWLEDGEMENTS

Researching the military history of the Arab-Israeli conflict – an activity supposed to be exercised with distance and objectivity – leads to many ironic conclusions, and sometimes it is outright disturbing.

My 'involvement' began at a very young age, with reading articles, and then books describing the fascinating achievements of the Israel Defense Force/Air Force (IDF/AF). The most memorable part of the stories from back in the 1970s and 1980s was that its fantastically trained pilots were flying French-made, delta-winged, silver-and-red-coloured Dassault Mirage III interceptors, and that they were shooting down Soviet-made jets designed by Mikoyan i Gurevich (MiG), 'at will', and how, during the 'Six-Day War', back in June 1967, they destroyed three Arab air forces within a few hours. I clearly recall descriptions leaving the impression of the Israelis throwing a fistful of bullets at their (*always* numerically superior) enemies – and still shooting them down – and there remain a few old articles in my library describing Arab MiG pilots 'nicely positioning' their jets so the Israelis could better shoot at them. Before long, I wanted to know more. Initially, this 'more' was little other than a wish to know what MiGs, and what jets of other Soviet design – such as those of the Sukhoi design bureau – had the Israelis shot down. What did they look like? What was their equipment, and armament? Why were the Israelis as successful as they claimed to be, and why – for example – were US pilots nowhere near as successful in 'their' air war of the same time, the one over North Vietnam? Finally, in the light of reading about distinguished Israeli pilots, I wanted to find out: who were the pilots flying these 'Arab' fighter-bombers?

Back then in the 1970s and 1980s, finding out about such details resulted in…little more than the sound made by crickets. There were simply no sources of reference about the Arab air forces: maybe two or perhaps three sentences strewn over dozens of different magazines, describing them, generally, as 'Soviet clients', 'Soviet trained', 'flying and fighting like Soviets', even as 'Soviet puppets'. Often enough, publications stated that, actually, it was not even 'Arabs' flying the jets shot down by the Israelis, but 'Soviet volunteers'. Because Arab air forces, 'in general', had 'too few of their own pilots', and these were 'poorly trained, undisciplined, and had no idea how to use their aircraft in combat'. Foremost, according to the accounts in question, they were all – and there were outright 'hordes' of 'them' – poised to destroy Israel, any time of the day.

From that point onwards, it took decades of research just to establish contacts to people who might know, if not directly to those MiG and Sukhoi pilots in question. Over time, this passion became a profession, resulting in numerous articles, and then books about the Arab air forces, and about specific aircraft types in service in the Middle East. To my big surprise, early publishing efforts were all turned down. None of the publishers I contacted complained about the content or the quality of my research: rather, the editors in question were providing explanations that they doubted there was sufficient interest in aerial warfare over the Middle East to validate investment into such a publication. At least as stunning were answers from two others, who explained, in no uncertain terms, that there was no way they would ever publish any book describing any kind of an Arab air force as a coherent and professional military service.

My experiences became even more estranging once the first few of my books were published: in addition to interest from some readers, they resulted in a lot of hostility – and from people who had never met me in person. Beside that, every single encounter with an Israeli that ever approached the stand where I was signing my books would start with their commentary that, 'Arabs always lie': a prolific Israeli military aviation writer wrote to a British colleague that I am (quote), '….an Austrian and everybody knows who was an Austrian' – hinting, obviously, at Adolf Hitler. When we met in person for the first time, another prolific Israeli military aviation writer – indeed, somebody claiming to have better knowledge of which particular pilot of the IDF/AF had shot down what Arab aircraft in air combat, when and where, than the service itself – 'greeted' me with the observation that I was something like disgusting, because I (quote) 'consider them [Arabs] for equal to us [Israelis]'. A few weeks later, his publisher openly announced on its website that my books were all based on hearsay – although I have quoted all my sources of reference, at least 50 percent of these were of Israeli origin, and based on official Israeli documentation.

Perhaps I am naïve, and perhaps unusual, but this only made me even more curious: why was there such animosity? Where was all that hatred coming from? As people researching and writing about history, do we not all share a common passion? After all, I experienced only responsiveness and curiosity while working with Arabs, and thus expected the Israelis to be at least curious. With a handful of exceptions, this was not the case, and thus I began to busy myself with yet more research, this time into the backgrounds of the Arab-Israeli conflict. The more publications I read, the more interesting it became, because it led to a growing number of surprising conclusions: foremost that the story of this war is the story of blatant, never-ending, and institutionalised mythology, of intentional ignorance and blind arrogance causing one tragedy after another; a story of most outrageous forms of racism and religious fanaticism, and stubborn disregard for even the most rudimentary human rights of multiple cultures and hundreds of millions of people; a story of atrocities executed with the complicity – or at least token support, but also due to massive mistakes – of multiple local and foreign powers, all of which pride themselves as 'civilised cultures'; and a story of despicable crimes only few of which were ever properly investigated, not to talk about sanctioned. Unsurprisingly, this story leaves nobody indifferent, and is massively loaded.

All of this is particularly valid for the June 1967 Arab-Israeli War.

The mass of accounts of this specific conflict start with the tragic tale of Israel being subjected to hundreds and thousands of terrorist attacks by Palestinian militants with the support of Egypt, Jordan, and Syria, all exclusively targeting peaceful Jewish settlers; survivors of the Holocaust that never meant any harm, but only to work their farms. Curiously, next to none explained why there were Palestinian militants around – although these obviously came from the territory on which Israel was established. On the contrary, such stories usually go on to stress that on 7 April 1967, Syrian artillery savaged numerous peaceful settlements. That this was just one out of 'hundreds' of such outrages, and that it left the Israel Defense Force (IDF/AF) 'without a choice but to silence the assailants'. When MiG-21 interceptors of the Syrian Arab Air Force (SyAAF) then 'approached Israel', Dassault Mirage IIICJ interceptors of the IDF/AF shot down seven jets piloted by – to quote a veteran pilot of the IDF/AF – 'turban wearers'. Aghast at this defeat, the leadership of the Union of Soviet Socialist Republics (USSR, colloquially 'Soviet Union') – widely considered to be in control of Egypt and Syria (as if the two were neither sovereign countries, nor had their own politicians capable of making their own decisions) – then lied to Egypt that Israel was preparing an all out invasion of Syria. Indeed, according to specific Israeli historians, the USSR was already plotting a military intervention and destruction of Israel, and had its – at the time – super-secret MiG-25R (ASCC/NATO-codename 'Foxbat') reconnaissance fighters not only deployed there, but also flying reconnaissance missions over unsuspecting and defenceless Israel.

Alternatively, and if it is not Syria and the USSR to blame, then it was Egypt, and especially its contemporary president, Gamal Abdel Nasser. Accordingly, during the Suez War of 1956, Israel invaded Egypt in order to force a reopening of the Straits of Tiran, which had been blocked for Israeli shipping since 1949. Indeed, Israel then withdrew its troops from the Sinai Peninsula, but only on condition that the Straits remain open. Therefore, any renewed blocking of Tiran would have been a 'red line': a 'just' reason for Israel to launch a 'war of self-defence' through 'pre-empting' an aggression by unified Arab armed forces.

With or without the Foxbats and the blockade of the Straits of Tiran, so the usual story runs, the Soviet warning then prompted Nasser – variously described as anywhere between a 'vitriolic anti-Semite' (although an Arab, and thus a Semite) and 'having Israel not very high on his priority list' – to mobilise his armed forces and order their deployment on the Sinai Peninsula, on 16 May 1967. Two days later, Nasser ('brazenly') ordered the withdrawal of the United Nations (UN) peacekeepers tasked with preventing terror attacks on Israel from that direction, and then blocked the Straits of Tiran to Israeli shipping. If this was not aggressive enough, then Israel's other immediate neighbours took up a belligerent stance, rallied to support Nasser, calling 'to drive the Jews into the sea', and even declaring a *Jihad* (Holy War). All of this eventually left the Zionist state without a choice but to launch a 'pre-emptive war', i.e. to exercise its right to self-defence, granted by the UN Charter.

'Miraculously', on 5 June 1967, on the verge of the entire nation being 'exterminated', the IDF/AF managed to achieve a 'flawless surprise' and, in a 'masterfully orchestrated' and 'perfectly executed' – yet 'pre-emptive' – operation, 'completely' destroyed the air forces of Egypt, Jordan, Syria, Lebanon, and Iraq. All of this in a matter of hours, and so precisely that the list of Arab aircraft claimed as destroyed by the IDF/AF and published for the first time in *The Jerusalem Post* newspaper on 11 June 1967, has not been updated by a single dot ever since, regardless how often re-published.

Free from the threat of enemy air power, the ground forces of the IDF then successively conquered the Sinai Peninsula in Egypt, the West Bank (a part of Palestine illegally annexed by Jordan), the Gaza Strip (another part of Palestine, but officially under Egyptian military administration), and the Golan Heights in Syria. All in a matter of just six days – which is why this conflict went down in history as the 'Six-Day War' (and not only in the English language).

Considering this version, it took me by surprise that the title page of the English-language issue of the *Jerusalem Post* newspaper for 5 June 1967 carried a large headline indicating it was Egypt that started the war with an attack on Israel. A mistake? Perhaps, but the author of that article was quoting official Israeli sources, and his article – including the title – was subject to Israeli military censorship. Something was not adding up.

Certainly enough, such mythology is not reserved for Israel or the West: on the contrary, there are no end of similar legends spread around the Arab world, all over Europe, in the former USSR, and elsewhere. Depending on the area in question, they are spiced with all sorts of conspiracy theories, ranging from rivalries between different Arab statesmen, via the direct involvement of aircraft carriers of the Royal Navy and the US Navy, even reconnaissance aircraft of the US Air Force, to 'Soviet treachery' – or complete military incompetence of the Arabs. Of particular irony is that, in regards of the topic of 'Arab military incompetence', even former allies of the Arabs, like the Russians or Indians, are in full agreement with Israel and the West.

Amid this avalanche of tales, and considering how heavily charged this topic is, the fundamental questions in a project of this kind are therefore: how to address all of this, and where to start?

My methodology was what eventually led to this project: for the introduction to this mini-series and the coverage of the air war, I have used publications by a number of Israeli and US researchers, based on their research in official archives of their countries, and those of several countries of the former Warsaw Pact. In other cases, Egyptian and US researchers have collected biographies of the major decision makers in Cairo. I am not going to guess why the works of the historians in question – nearly all premiered in notable scientific quarterlies – remain essentially unknown amongst the wider public: this is a topic somebody else might prefer to busy themself with. Instead, I have completed my work on this project with the help of a book written by a Syrian defector to Egypt, while contacts in Cairo have provided transcriptions of Document 44: the results of the official Egyptian investigation into the reasons and circumstances of the catastrophic defeat the country suffered in June 1967. Rounding up, there are also the results of interviews with dozens of participants, undertaken by Dr David Nicolle, by Lon Nordeen, by a few other colleagues, and by myself, over the last 40 years. Other sources of reference will be used in subsequent volumes. The result is a 'version' that is likely to appear at least 'unusual' if not 'outrageous' and 'anti-Semitic' to many: one that is significantly different from the usual story served up by the Western mainstream media in particular but also significantly different even to the one served in the Arab world.

Obviously, this book is a product of decades of research with often amazing degrees of help from dozens of persons. Foremost amongst them are veterans of the armed forces of (in alphabetic order) Egypt, Iraq, Israel, and Syria. Those I would like to thank for help in the creation of this first volume include late Air Marshal Alaa Barakat (EAF, ret.), Air Marshal Mustafa Shalabi el-Hinnawy (EAF), Air Marshal Farouq el-Ghazzawy (EAF, ret.), Air Marshal Badr Domair (EAF, ret.), late Lieutenant General Arif Abd ar-Razzaq (IrAF, ret.), late Air Marshal Tahir Zaki (EAF), Air Vice Marshal Ahmed Abbas (EAF, ret.), Major General Alwan Hassan al-Abossi (IrAF, ret.), Major General Ahabadin Ayman (ADC, ret.), Air Vice Marshal Qadri Abd el-Hamid (EAF, ret.), Air Vice Marshal Zia el-Hefnawi (EAF, ret.), Air Vice Marshal Mamdouh Heshmat (EAF, ret.), Air Vice Marshal Reda el-Iraqi (EAF, ret.), Air Vice Marshal Hussein el-Kfass (EAF, ret.), Air Vice Marshal Ahmed Kilany (EAF, ret.), Air Vice Marshal Mustafa Nabil al-Masri (EAF, ret.), Air Vice Marshal Abd al-Moneim Mikaati (EAF, ret.), Major General Makki (Iraqi Army, ret.), Air Vice Marshal Samir Aziz Mikhail (EAF, ret.), Major General Nassr Moussa (EAF, ret.), Major General Mohammed Naji (IrAF, ret.), Major General Salim Saffar (IrAF, ret.), Air Vice Marshal Siad Shalash (EAF, ret.), Air Vice Marshal Sa'ad ad-Din Sherif (EAF, ret.), late Air Vice Marshal Mohammed Abdel Moneim Zaki Okasha (EAF), Air Vice Marshal Nabil el-Shuwakri/Shoukry (EAF, ret.), Air Vice Marshal Mamdouh Taliba (EAF, ret.), Major General Ihsan Shurdom (RJAF, ret.), Major General Medhat Zaki (EAF, ret.), Major General Ahmed Yusuf (EAF, ret.), Air Vice Marshal Tahsin Zaki (EAF/ADC, ret.), late Brigadier General Ahmad Sadik Rushdie al-Astrabadi (IrAF Intelligence Department), Brigadier General Iftach Spector (IDF/AF, ret.), Brigadier General Faysal Abdul Mohsen (IrAF, ret.), Brigadier General Farouk Abdeen (RJAF, ret.), Air Commodore Tamim Fahmi Abdullah (EAF, ret.), late Air Commodore Gabr Ali Gabr (EAF, ret.), Air Commodore Fikry el-Gahramy (EAF, ret.), Air Commodore Fikry el-Gindy (EAF, ret.), late Air Commodore Mustafa Mohammed Hassan (EAF), late Air Commodore Mustafa Hafez (EAF), Air Commodore Fuad Kamal (EAF ret.), Air Commodore Abdel Moneim el-Tawil (EAF ret.), Air Commodore Ibrahim Gazerine (EAF ret.), Group Captain Kapil Bhargava (IAF, ret.), late Group Captain Saif-ul-Azam (PAF/BAF), Wing Commander Talaat Louca (EAF, ret.), Wing Commander Usama Sidqi (EAF, ret.), Wing Commander Kamal Zaki (EAF ret.), Squadron Leader Wagdi Hafez (EAF ret.), Captain Abdelmajid Tayyari (LAAF, ret.).

Furthermore, I would like to express my gratitude to Dr David Nicolle, from Great Britain, whom I consider my mentor, and – via him – to Mr Tarek el-Shennawy (pilot of Egypt Air and son of late Air Vice Marshal Abdel Moneim el-Shennawy); also to, Mr Ahmad Keraidy (pilot of Egypt Air and son of late Air Vice Marshal Abdel Wahhab el-Keraidy); to dear Mrs Patricia Salti (leading historian of the Royal Jordanian Air Force), and to Mr Paul Jackson (former Editor of *Jane's All the World's Aircraft*) for sharing precious details from their own research and private archives.

Last – but by no means least – I would also like to express my special thanks to Martin Smisek from the Czech Republic for working through the Czech National Archive for many years; Milos Sipos from the Slovak Republic for his help in research about the Iraqi and Syrian air forces; to Dmitry Zubkov from the Russian Federation for information on certain aspects of the Soviet involvement; to Nour Bardai, Dr Abdallah Emran, and Sherif Sharmi from Egypt; to Ali Tobchi from Iraq, Albert Grandolini and Antoine Pierre from France, and Holger Müller from Germany for conducting additional interviews and kindly providing many precious bits and pieces of information over the years. I must thank Jens Heidel for help with additional photographs of the United Arab Republic Air Force and Army from the 1950s and 1960s; to Jean-Marie Langeron from France for his help with precise performance comparisons between the primary fighter-bomber types discussed in this study; to Tomislav Mesaric from Croatia for his additional tips on this topic; and Ass'aad Dib in Lebanon for translations of Ali Muhammad Labib's history of the Egyptian Air Force; to Jeroen Nijmeijer from the Netherlands for his help with research about deliveries of Soviet aircraft; and to Lon Nordeen in the USA, for permission to use some of his research including interviews with a number of Egyptian participants. Last, but not least, my thanks go to Farzin Nadimi for his research in the archives of the Air Ministry in Great Britain, and to Hicham Honeini from Lebanon for his patience and kind help with translations of various publications and documentation from Arabic.

1

BACKGROUND

Officially, at least, the years between the First Arab-Israeli War of 1947–1949, and the Second Arab-Israeli War of 1956 – better known as the 'Suez Crisis' or 'Suez War' – were 'peaceful'. Generally, the same is true for the 'peaceful decade' between 1956 and 1967. Actually, relations between Israel and her neighbours were all the time little short of at boiling point, and at least twice, 'just hours short' of another war, for a myriad of reasons that were ultimately to provoke the showdown in June 1967.

LOTS OF LINES IN THE GRAVEL

For thousands of years, the ports of the eastern Mediterranean, and thus what became Syria, Lebanon, and Israel between 1946 and 1949 – such as (from north to south) Ugarit/Latakia, Banias, Tartus, Tripoli, Biblos, Sidon, Tyre, Acre, and Gaza – flourished thanks to their position at the literal 'crossroads between the Occident and the Orient', the 'West and the East', respectively: they were in the middle of commercial routes connecting Europe in the west, with merchants of Aleppo and Damascus, with traders in Palmyra and Petra, Baghdad and Basra, with seafarers of the Persian Gulf, with sources of commodities in southern Asia and the Far East. Through the first half of the twentieth century, all such ages-old commercial links were systematically blocked, and populations separated at the discretion of people who were complete foreigners to the area.

For about 400 years before Israel was officially established, the entire Middle East was a part of the Ottoman Empire. Between 1918 and 1928, the area was conquered by the British and French, who – in complete ignorance of the circumstances and demands of the local population, yet acting according to the Sykes-Picot Treaty of 1916 – diligently divided it into multiple artificial states under their colonial control, and with intention of 'teaching civilisation' to the local 'barbarians'.

In Palestine, the British mandatory authorities created such massive problems that the entire Middle East is troubled by them to this very day: in 1916, and almost simultaneously, the government in London promised a 'national home' to the followers of the ideology of Zionism and the same territory (plus most of modern-day Syria, Lebanon, Iraq, Jordan and southern Turkey/Türkye) to the Shariff of Mecca, as part of a kingdom he was to rule. Unsurprisingly, between 1920 and 1947, the area experienced successive waves of Jewish immigration and resulting revolts by the local population, before it was mercilessly conquered and ethnically cleansed by Zionists, with at least the tacit support of all the foreign powers of the time – and with multiple mass-murders and the deployment of biological weapons – in 1947–1949, and declared the State of Israel.[1]

Elsewhere, and once they had established themselves in control of 'their portion' of the Middle East, in 1920, the French split most of the Mediterranean coast to create two footholds: an Alawite state in the north, and a Christian state in the south. Amid multiple uprisings and fierce political resistance, the former was soon abandoned. However, the latter survived and resulted in the creation of Lebanon, and even before achieving independence in 1943, politically defined as a country dominated by Christian minority over a Sunni Arab minority in complete ignorance of its Shi'a and other populations. The conclusion that a failed state was an unsurprising result is likely to sound entirely wrong: for decades, Western media painted the picture of Lebanon as the 'Switzerland of the Middle East'. In reality, cut off from its traditional sources of income – Aleppo, Hama, Homs, and Damascus – only a minor part of the country's economy was doing well, and the state was all the time on the verge of a 'civil' war between its numerous ethnic and religious groups, all of which maintained private militias. Unsurprisingly considering such circumstances, the country rarely fought against Israel: through the 1960s, at least some of its Christian factions maintained secret ties to the new neighbour in the south.

North and east of Lebanon was Syria. Traditionally one of the major cultural centres and one of three power-brokers of the Middle East, and because its population never ceased challenging the military occupation, this territory was repeatedly savaged during the times of the French 'mandate' from 1920 until 1946. Indeed, thanks to the widespread French terror and oppression of the Sunni Arab majority of population, and preference for the 'warlike Alawite race', which was recruited for their colonial armed forces – post-independence, this potentially rich and powerful country was, essentially, ripped apart by no fewer than three interrelated conflicts. The first was the competition between the Hashemite dynasty and its Arab rivals, in progress since the early twentieth century; the second the Arab-Zionist struggle for control of Palestine; and the third the rivalry between superpowers – initially between Great Britain and France, but later between the US-led West and the Soviet-led East. A scene of continuous political intrigue and an outright secret war between intelligence agencies, Syria gradually grew into a police state maintained by its own armed forces: the rank and file of these being Alawites, and they were constantly at odds with traditional Sunni Arab leaders. Not only because much of Palestine had been in the possession of landowners from Damascus, Syria was – and remains – fiercely anti Zionist, and constantly at odds with its new neighbour.

East of Israel and south of Syria another artificial creation came into being: in 1921, enraged at both the British enthroning his younger brother as the king of Iraq and the Anglo-French carve-up of Arab lands, the eldest son of the Shariff of Mecca marched north from the family home in the Hijaz to re-take Damascus. Eventually, he halted in Amman, capital of the British mandate of Transjordan and was then recognised as the ruler over the territory east of the River Jordan, in return for his pledge to respect the French Mandate of Syria. Achieving independence and renamed as Jordan in 1946, the country remained heavily dependent on sponsorship from London for decades longer. Nevertheless, its British-commanded Arab Legion – the army of the Hashemite dynasty – fought fiercely against Israel in 1948, and late that year Amman annexed the West Bank in Palestine: a part of the territory it managed to secure during the First Arab-Israeli War of 1947–1949. This resulted in a particularly explosive combination, for by 1967 wholly two thirds of Jordan's population were Palestinians and the West Bank was the country's economic centre.

Further south, the arch rival of the Hashemites, the Sauds, forced the elder Hashemite, Husayn, to abdicate the throne of the Hijaz in 1924, and a year later forced his son Ali out of Jeddah. Logically, the emerging Kingdom of Saudi Arabia dominated everything from the eastern shores of the Red Sea to the Persian Gulf. It shared no direct border with Israel, however it was at odds with the Hashemite kingdoms of Iraq and Transjordan, constantly warry that – if they could assume control over Syria – this would provide them with the resources necessary to counterattack and recover the territories they had lost.

South and west from Israel was Egypt – the second traditional powerhouse and the breadbasket of countless empires that had controlled the Middle East: this ancient culture was now largely Arabized and had been subjected to British colonial rule from 1882 until 1922: indeed, it managed to completely liberate itself from foreign influence only through a series of intensive negotiations with London between 1952 and 1954. Egypt adopted Arab nationalism foremost due to domestic political rivalries, but also in an attempt to counter the Muslim Brotherhood, a religious movement agitating for the adoption of strict Islamic social practices and the establishment of an Islamist government. Keen to counter both the influence of the Hashemites and the Saudis, Cairo became crucial for the creation of the Arab League Charter of 1944: recognising the post-Mandate system of sovereign and independent states carved out by the British and the French, in March 1945 this became the Arab League.

Like the Kingdom of Saudi Arabia, the third powerhouse of the Middle East and thus the Arab world of the 1950s and 1960s, did not share any borders with Israel: this was the area formerly known as Mesopotamia, but renamed as Iraq in 1921. In this country, and despite vicious resistance of the population, the British imposed another member of the Hashemite dynasty as the king – supported by a Sunni Arab minority – to rule over the Shi'a Arab majority and a significant Kurdish minority.

Considering this complex of circumstances, it is unsurprising that all the governments of what were now Israel's neighbours, were at least as busy with themselves, and with building-up their own mythology and powerbases, as with the Arab-Israeli conflict.

PALESTINIAN REFUGEES

The creation of the State of Israel was achieved at the price of an unknown number of massacred Palestinian civilians, and at least 700,000 – perhaps up to 1 million – Palestinians (Christians and Muslims alike) expelled from their homes and prohibited from ever returning; and the complete eradication of at least 418 of their towns and villages. Just 150,000 Palestinians remained inside Israel as of late 1948, but another 20,000–30,000 were expelled over the next eight months.[2]

That said, it is amazing that ever since 1949 next to nobody appears to care about the people expelled from their homeland: essentially, the Palestinian refugees were left to vegetate in refugee camps, often only metres away from ceasefire lines with Israel that, gradually, became its borders. Arguably, those still in Palestine and formally registered were granted Israeli citizenship in 1952 and permitted to vote, but those without legal status were left vulnerable to deportation – and all were placed under military administration and subjected to martial law. Under a 'family reunification scheme' introduced by the Israeli authorities during the 1950s, about 40,000 Palestinians were allowed to return. However, the majority were not. On the contrary, the Absentees' Property Law of 1950 permanently denied the legal status of all Palestinians that had left – including those who only took temporary refuge in nearby villages or hills – and declared their land (something like 90 percent of the territory of Israel) to be owned by the Development Authority of the Israeli government. The overall result of this and about 60 subsequent legislations was an apartheid system: while officially enjoying equality with Jews, in reality, Palestinian citizens of Israel had (and still have) less than equal status in terms of all legal, civil, and political matters, and very limited access to social benefits or posts in state agencies: they were treated as foreigners with regards to employment, investment, and land ownership. For all practical purposes, Jews were granted the monopoly over all assets and politics, while Palestinian political activity was curbed through withholding travel permits for known nationalists, or prohibition of the establishment of associations and publications: the official line currently remains at the time of writing that 'Palestinians' are 'immigrants', and 'Palestine', de facto, never existed....

Another irony is that, on the international level, and instead of compelling Israel to respect the UN Charter and other relevant international laws and regulations, the United Nations then went as far as to create the United Nations Relief and Works Agency for Palestine Refugees in the Near East (UNRWA): while this agency kept the mass of refugees alive through the provision of basic aid, it was never authorised to prevent the traumatised, impoverished, and chronically hungry people in question from being misused for all the possible excuses for the worst sorts of misguided politics and aggressive wars, human rights violations, and atrocities, haunting the Middle East up to the present day.

About 100,000–130,000 Palestinians fled to Lebanon. Although welcomed initially, subsequently they were subjected to a haphazard and constantly changing mix of rules and regulations regarding their legal residence, freedom to travel and employment, and treated as foreigners. About 85,000–100,000 Palestinians fled to Syria in 1947–1948, and this number grew to 300,000 by 1950: they were offered both material and moral support and, over the following years, a series of laws effectively made them equal to Syrian nationals. That said, to maintain better control over them, and prevent them from provoking problems, and while building housing and schools for them instead of keeping them in refugee camps, the Syrian authorities preferred to move them away from the armistice lines with Israel. Thus, the mass of refugees was settled in newly-constructed neighbourhoods of Damascus and Aleppo. Egypt received around 7,000 Palestinian refugees, but transferred most of them to the Gaza Strip, where the local population of around 88,000 was already struggling to care for another 200,000 displaced people. From 1949 until 1962, the Strip was subjected to an emergency law, and virtually all local affairs controlled by an Egyptian governor-general: Palestinians were granted permission to enrol in Egyptian universities and, from 1962 onwards, a limited number were granted permission to take up state employment. The situation was fundamentally different in Jordan, where for the next 50 years the Hashemite monarchy refused to completely abandon the ambition of ruling the whole of Palestine. Correspondingly, Amman annexed all the Palestinian territory held by the Arab Legion as of 1948, and officially added all the 800,000 Palestinians of the West Bank – including 425,000 original residents and between 360,000 and 450,000 refugees, as well as another 30,000 residents and 100,000 refugees in the East Bank – to its population. However, while the Palestinians thus nominally enjoyed the same rights and privileges as the native population, and a few rose to senior government positions, essentially: they were left politically powerless. Indeed, in 1950 a decree was issued prohibiting even the use of the word 'Palestine' in any official documentation, while all men that did not own any land property – which was true for the mass of Palestinians – were excluded from parliamentary elections.

Such politics of oppression and ignorance – *vis-à-vis* the Palestinians and *vis-à-vis* the mass of Arabs of the Middle East – were the actual backdrop against which the June 1967 Arab-Israeli War was fought, even if all the leaders of the most important parties involved – whether Israeli, Lebanese, Syrian, Jordanian, or Egyptian – did their best to intentionally ignore such issues and explain their actions with all sorts of other reasons. From that point of view, one might easily draw the conclusion that the decision makers in Tel Aviv, Beirut, Damascus, Amman, and Cairo – or, and more precisely: the armed forces under their command – had no trace of an idea what they were fighting for. Without doubt, some of the politicians and military commanders involved were arrogant, egoistic, and extremist enough to be described as 'ignorant'. However, thinking that way would be a mistake: there is little doubt that there were enough decision makers that knew very well what they were doing, and why.

DE-MILITARISED ZONES

In the course of the ceasefire negotiations of 1949, several 'de-militarised zones' (DMZs) were created along the ceasefire lines between Israel, Egypt and Syria: the areas in question consisted of parts of Palestine occupied by non-Palestinian Arab forces at the end of hostilities. In a fashion typical for the mid-twentieth century, there was no ultimate arbitration, but the decision was left for sometime in the future: related agreements merely stipulated that all the involved parties were to withdraw their armed forces from the DMZs and none was to redeploy there again. Officially at least, the ground within the zones did not belong to any of the three countries but was under UN control: specifically, under the control of the United Nations Truce Supervision Organisation (UNTSO). Notably: although the country was the only one in the Middle East explicitly created by the UN and its Partition Plan for Palestine of 1947, Israel was the only country (and member of the UN) to resist the stationing of the UNTSO contingent on its territory, and especially on its side of the DMZs. As a consequence, UNTSO inspectors were only able to monitor the other side of the lines.

Equally official was that Israel was always insistent on 'peace and peaceful coexistence', and there is no doubt the majority of its population wished nothing else but to be left on its own. However, at least as official was the deployment of bulldozers and military units of the IDF into the central of the three DMZs opposite Syria – in spite of protests by UNTSO – in 1951, and the fact that the crews of these repeatedly opened fire at nearby Syrian villages, before starting to drain Lake Hula: a mosquito- and malaria-infested part of the Jordan River system. The Syrian Arab Army moved its units closer to the DMZ, but refrained from firing back: perfectly aware of its military inferiority *vis-à-vis* Israel, Damascus did its utmost to avoid an escalation although, as observed by one of the UNTSO observers, Major General A. R. Bolling of the US Army, 'Israel is prepared to risk military operations against any of the Arab States, and several recent Israeli actions appear to have been designed, at least in part, to provoke Arab initiation of hostilities.'

ISRAEL'S AGGRESSIVE EXPANSIONISM

Israel's occupation of nearly all of Palestine during the First Arab-Israel War – except for the West Bank and the Gaza Strip – followed by the deployment of the IDF into the DMZ near Lake Hula, did not come out of nothing. Certainly enough, considering myths about the 'small, weak and vulnerable Israel', a nation 'created by

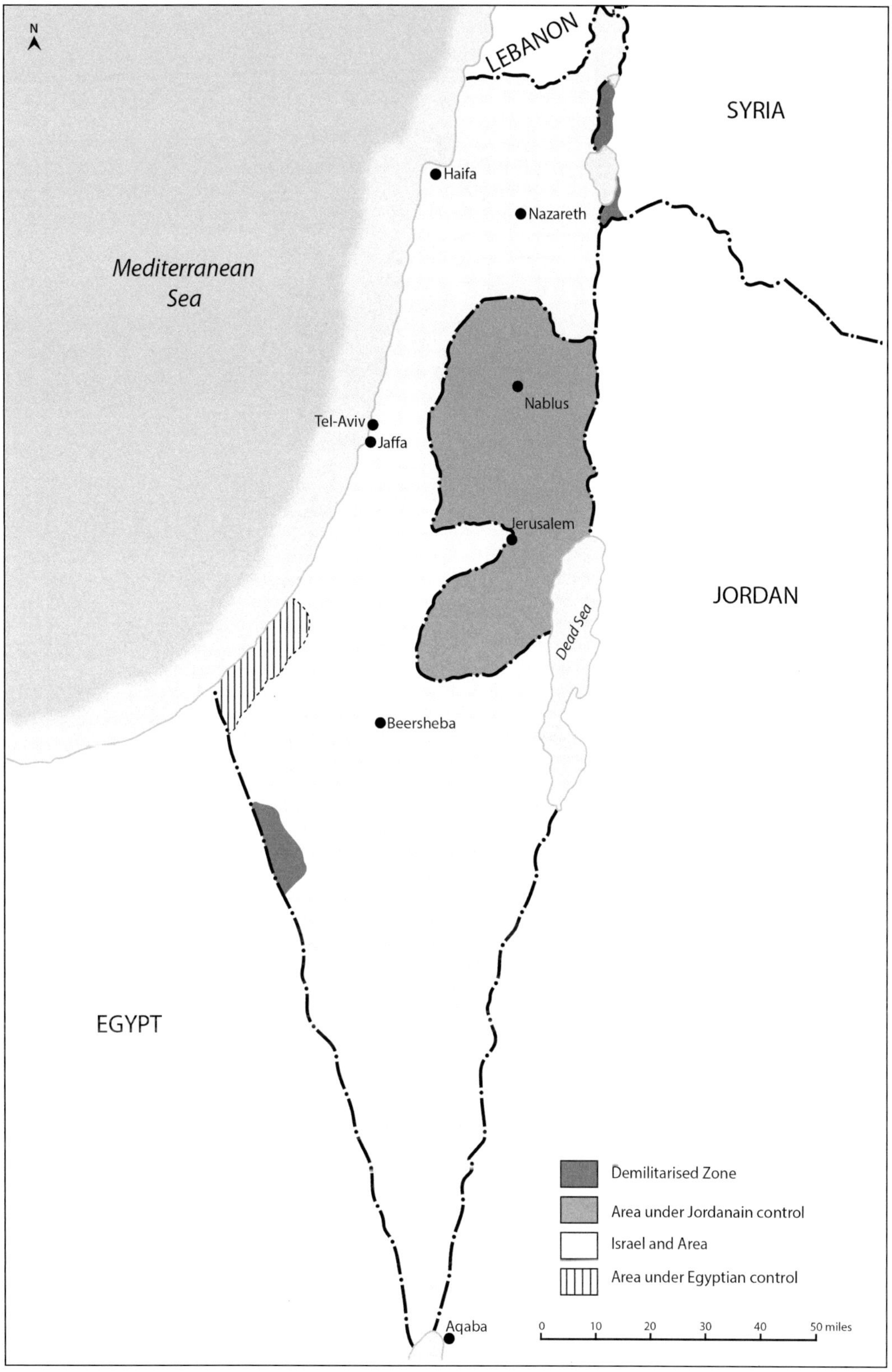

The DMZs as demarked through the UN-mediated ceasefire negotiations between Israel, Lebanon, Syria, Jordan, and Egypt of 1949. (Map by George Anderson)

the then leaders of the Jewish Organisation to US military intelligence officers before the State of Israel officially came into being, and summarised in a report filled by the Joint Chiefs of Staff of the US Armed Forces to the US President Harry S Truman, in March 1948, as follows:

A) initial Jewish sovereignty over a portion of Palestine;
B) acceptance by great powers of the right to unlimited immigration;
C) the extension of Jewish sovereignty over all of Palestine;
D) the expansion of 'Erez Israel' into Transjordan and into portions of Lebanon and Syria, and
E) the establishment of Jewish military and economic hegemony over the entire Middle East.[3]

In other words, before 15 May 1948 – and not 'only in reaction to an Arab invasion' – the leaders in Tel Aviv were aiming to establish themselves in control over all of Palestine. Moreover, they were aiming to secure the so-called 'Greater Israel' – including southern Lebanon, south-western Syria (including the Golan Heights), western Jordan, and all of the Sinai Peninsula in Egypt. These designs were to dominate the Israeli strategy for the next 30 years, to no small degree because the same leaders of the Jewish Organisation that developed them, subsequently served as the top political and military decision makers of the country.[4]

No doubt, many are certain to conclude that this was an exception and something irrelevant: after all, why should anything stated by Jewish leaders in Palestine of early 1948 to US intelligence operatives involved in the preparation of a major report for the Joint Chiefs of Staff of the US Armed Forces be of any historical relevance, or indicative of Israeli intentions once the country officially came into being?

According to Israeli historian Guy Laron, it was very much so that this plan was systematically pursued all the time after the establishment of Israel – at least by the General Staff of the IDF: ever since 1949, members of this body had been systematically

the UN for survivors of the Holocaust' but 'surrounded by hordes of blood-thirsty Islamist fanatics intending to destroy it', such a blatant violation of a UN-mediated ceasefire agreement with Syria is certain to appear strange, even unlikely. However, in the light of what the top political and military leaders of Israel had on their minds even before the country was officially established, it was nothing but *certain*. Not only had Israel became rooted in ideologies of racialism and militarism: on the international level, it followed the policy of expansionism. The related aims had been openly declared by

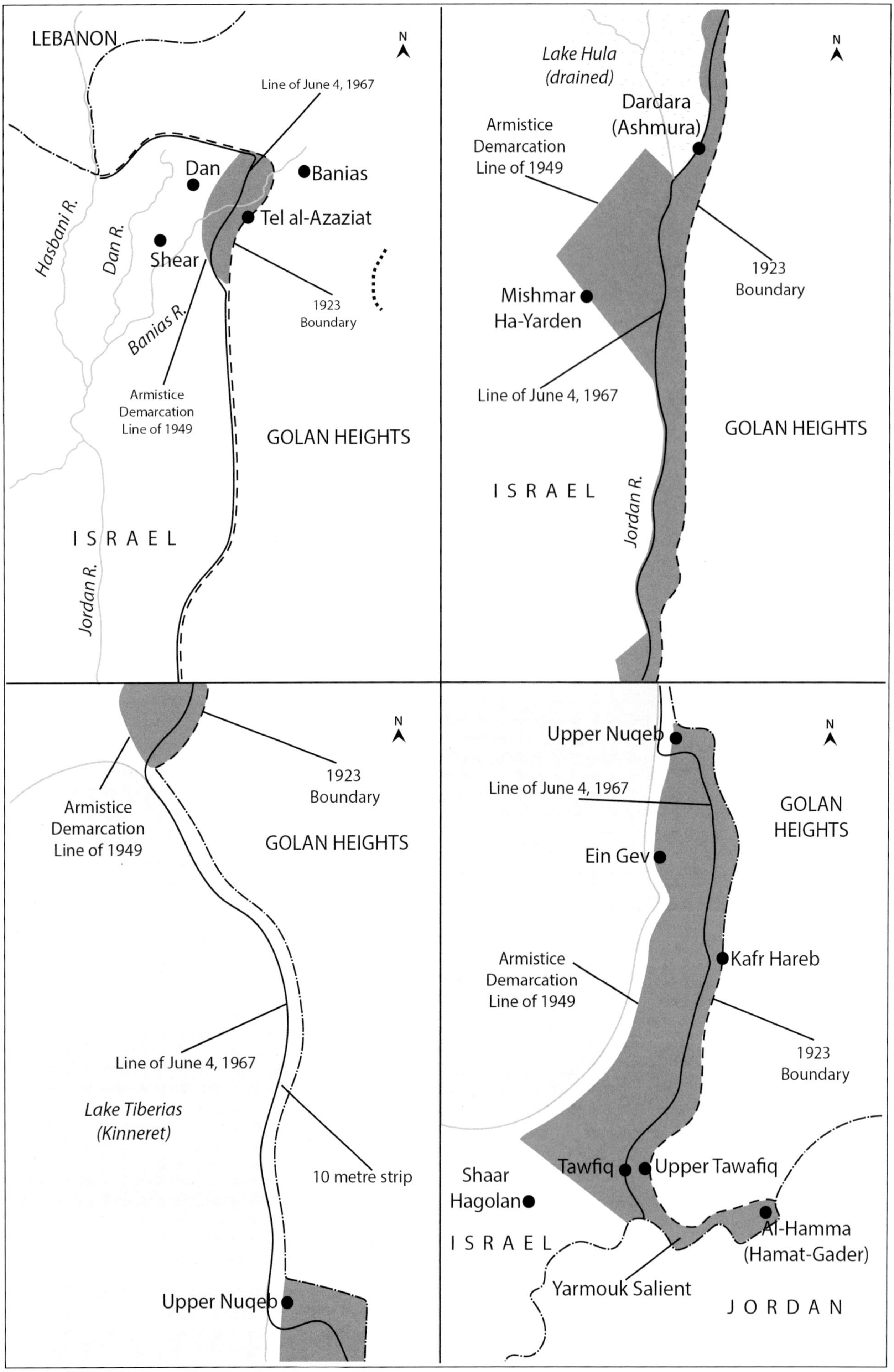

The three DMZs along the Israeli-Syrian armistice line of 1949. (Map by George Anderson)

indoctrinated that the 'borders' resulting from the ceasefire agreements of 1949 were 'unbearable'. Correspondingly, the Planning Department of the IDF was given the task of designing operations to establish 'different, safer borders'. The result was a number of contingency plans aiming to capture southern Lebanon up to the River Litani, secure the Golan Heights in Syria, reach the full length of the River Jordan: from 1953, the Sinai Peninsula was added to the list, to provide Israel, '...with oil and mineral ore', while by 1955, the contemporary Chief-of-Staff IDF, Moshe Dayan, expanded potential aims all the way to Cairo and Damascus. The designs for 'finishing the job' left undone during the First Arab-Israeli War – especially through seizing the Gaza Strip and the West Bank – went well beyond what could be described as the 'routine work' of every planning department of any professional armed force: it was accompanied with political and doctrinal preparations, including drawing up a code of law applied on conquered territories, and provision of courses in the military administration to officers of the IDF. Unsurprisingly, in 1963, during one of the first meetings between the newly-elected Prime Minister of Israel, Levy Eshkol with the contemporary Chief-of-Staff IDF, Lieutenant General Tzvi Tzur, the latter explained that the armed forces must be built-up to complete the conquest of Sinai, the West Bank, and southern Lebanon. Major General Yitzhak Rabin, then Tzur's deputy and later his successor, confirmed this, while the Chief-of-Staff IDF/AF, Ezer Weizman stressed that Israel, '...has to expand borders, whether it fits the government's approach or not'.[5]

WATER WAR, TAKE 1

In the late 1930s and through the 1940s, at least two scientific studies had concluded that the naturally available water sources of the Middle East were insufficient to sustain – for example – a mass Jewish immigration to Palestine.[6] Indeed, the available water could neither support the population nor economic growth of most of the neighbouring countries. Unsurprisingly, during the early 1950s governments in Amman, Damascus and Tel Aviv all drew separate plans for the development of the Jordan River system. Under the immense pressure of the hundreds of thousands of Palestinian refugees that had settled down east of the Jordan River, and still heavily dependent on financial aid from its creator, Great Britain, Jordan made the first move: in June 1952 it finalised the so-called 'Bunger Plan': a plan to dam the Yarmouk River – a tributary to the Jordan – near Maqarin, and utilise its waters to irrigate Jordanian territory, before letting the residue water flow to Lake Tiberias (known as the Sea of Galilee, or Kinneret, in Israel). The government in Amman convinced the USA and UNRWA to earmark funds for the construction works. Israel promptly objected to this plan because – via the Jordan River – it was the lower riparian state on the Yarmouk. Logically, the allocation of the US and UN funds was 'postponed'.[7]

Understanding that the water supply was one of the most critical issues troubling the Middle East, the administration of US President Dwight D. Eisenhower urged the UN to take the lead and develop a unified plan that would be acceptable to *all* the countries in question. Indeed, Eisenhower went as far as to authorise the Tennessee Valley Authority (TVA) to prepare a desk study that would synthesise the essential features of both the Arab and the Israeli schemes.

In July 1952, Israel officially endorsed regional cooperation and the US and UN efforts, and thus Eisenhower granted permission for the USA to fund several minor water-related projects in the country, and to assist in developing a national plan for its future water requirements. However, in 1952, the IDF deployed its troops not only to occupy the central DMZ with Syria, like a year before, but also to launch rapid construction work on a canal that was to divert the water of the Jordan River from the Daughters of Jacob Jordan Bridge. With this being against the armistice agreement from 1949, and all the agreements related to Eisenhower and the UN's plans because the construction was actually taking place outside Israel, and because no non-Israeli officials were ever informed about this development, nobody ever realised what was going on until early September 1953, when the Chief-of-Staff of the UNTSO, Major General Vagn Bennike, demanded an explanation from the Israeli government. Tel Aviv replied that it was 'only a small diversion to provide waterpower for an electricity-generating station on the shore of Lake Tiberias'. Unconvinced, Bennike went to see the work himself: he found bulldozers and other pieces of heavy equipment at work constructing a canal large enough to divert a substantial portion of the Jordan's waters into Israeli territory. In his own words, it would in fact divert, 'far more than what would be necessary for a hydroelectricity project'.[8]

Dutifully, the American demanded that the government of Israel stop the work, citing all the violations of various agreements. The Israelis flatly rejected this and accelerated their work. Syria then brought the matter to the UN Security Council – finally – causing a reaction from the US administration, which now found itself in a particularly unpleasant situation: after all, it was Eisenhower who had forced Jordan to stop its work, while the Israelis not only ignored his and UN requests to do the same, but also used US aid to finance their works, then occupied the DMZ and opened fire upon Syrian civilians on Syrian territory, thus violating the UN-mediated ceasefire agreement of 1949. Without a satisfactory response from Tel Aviv, on 18 September 1953, Eisenhower stopped all US economic aid to Israel.[9]

When the president of the USA proved unmoved by all the possible Israeli protests – and protests from Zionists and sympathisers in the USA – one month later, the government in Tel Aviv agreed to stop working on the diversion project: indeed, it promised it would cooperate with the UN efforts to reach a solution concerning the Jordan River – provided the UN would consider the legitimate rights of all riparian states. Correspondingly, Eisenhower appointed Eric Johnson as a special ambassador and tasked him with mediating a comprehensive plan for the regional development of the Jordan River system. As a starting point, Johnson used the project proposal commissioned by UNRWA from the consulting company Chas T Main, which in turn utilised the same principle employed by the TVA, and aimed to reduce the potential for conflict by promoting cooperation and economic stability. Both Israel and Jordan complained, necessitating negotiations that went on into 1954 and then 1955: gradually, differences were eliminated and the Jordan Valley Unified Water Plan was 'accepted' – or at least so the legend goes. Ironically, regardless of how often (mis)used to argue that Israel was right to continue its construction work – because, supposedly, its plan was accepted by Jordan – in reality: the Jordan Valley Unified Water Plan was *never officially ratified by anybody*. On 11 October 1955, the Arab League Council refused to ratify it, even if, in Johnson's opinion, this was, 'no total rejection': he concluded that the Arab League could not officially recognise Israel, but 'did commit itself to adhere to its technical details'.[10] In other words: the Jordan Valley Unified Water Plan was no solution, but another dispute added to an a continuously expanding list.

NATIONAL WATER CARRIER

The Jordan Valley Unified Water Plan had meanwhile been rendered irrelevant by another unilateral action by Israel. In autumn 1953, using German reparations for the Holocaust, initial payments of which were transferred in autumn 1953 – money that saved it from bankruptcy when Eisenhower stopped the US funding – Israel re-launched its construction work. To avoid provoking Eisenhower, instead of the Daughter of Jacob Jordan Bridge, the construction site was re-located to the – economically inferior – new position at Lake Tiberias. The first section of what eventually became known as the National Water Carrier (NWC) – including a pumping station and a several-hundred-metres-long, nine-pipe pipeline leading in a south-western direction – was completed by 1956. The second section was then constructed in the form of the Jordan Canal: a 17 kilometre (11 miles) open canal flowing by gravity. Furthermore, the Israelis not only took as much water as they wanted, but drained Lake Hula and began pumping saline water and sludge into the system of the Jordan River south of Lake Tiberias.

To say the consequences were disastrous – for the environment and for the Jordanian economy – would be an understatement. Nominally, the capacity of the NWC was 320 million cubic metres, and thus well within the limits of the Unified Plan: however, the system included supplementary booster pumps that frequently doubled this capacity. Unsurprisingly, by 1963 – a full year before it was officially completed to the length of 134km – the NWC, the construction of which had gulped the then astronomic US$121 million (all financed by the USA), was diverting 60 percent of the river's total flow. Before long, the river was reduced to a stinking cesspool. In turn, the Dead Sea began rapidly shrinking, dropping at a rate of one metre (40 inches) per year.[11] Of course, for successive Israeli governments, this did not matter as much as their own economic development and additional immigration.[12]

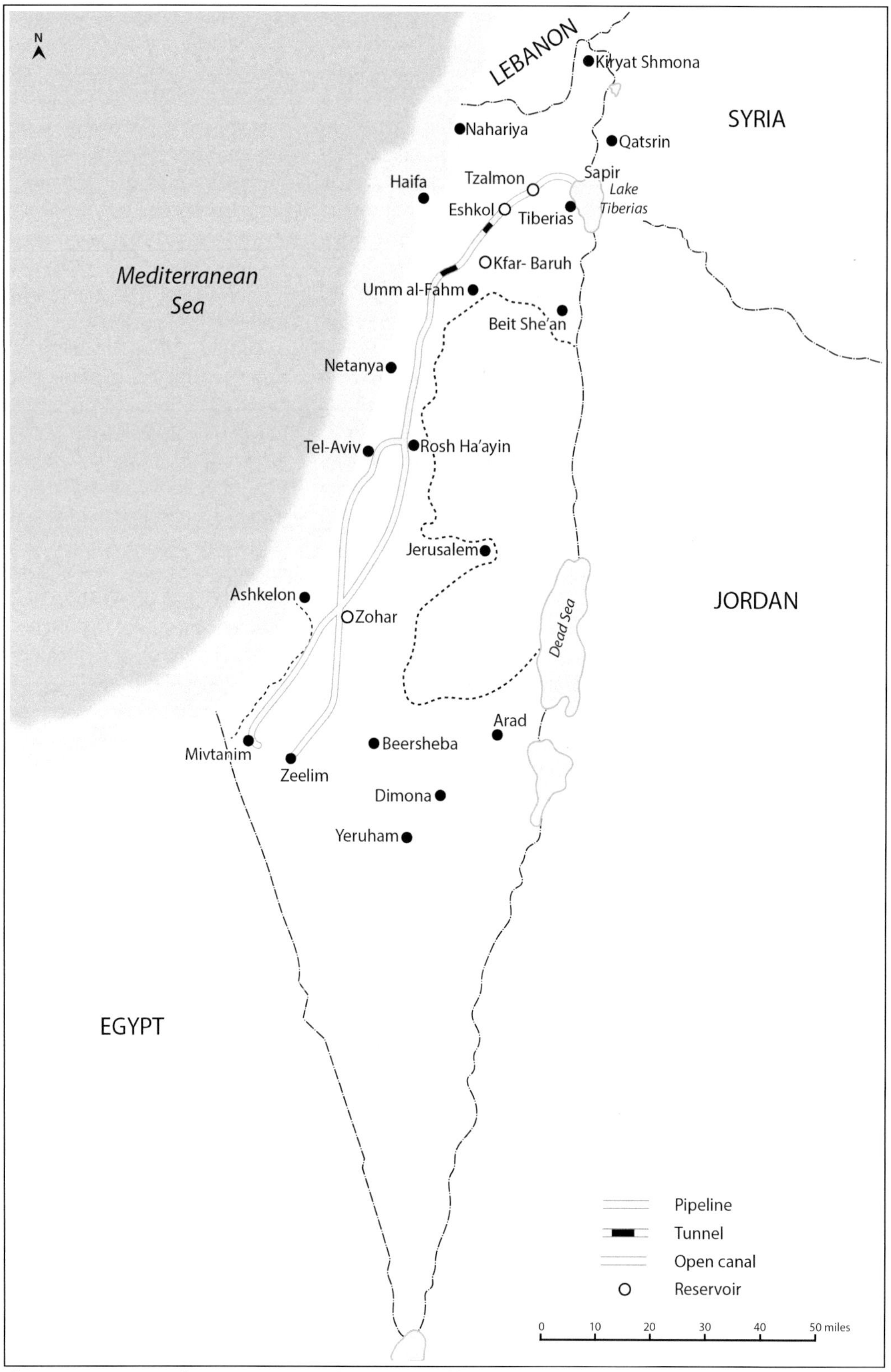

The NWC upon its completion in 1964. In total, this system of large pipes, tunnels, reservoirs and 34km of open canals was about 134km long and diverted at least 60 percent of the Jordan River's flow. Notably, its two southern prongs ended in Mivatahim and Zeelim, and thus already at the northern edge of the Negev Desert – imposing a huge question mark over the widely propagated myth according to which the purpose of the entire NWC was to provide water necessary to 'convert desert to arable land'. On the contrary, the system served the very purpose envisaged for such a project by related studies from the 1930s: enabling the settlement of millions of Jews in Palestine and the economic growth of the State of Israel, regardless the consequences for its neighbours. (Map by George Anderson)

SPOILED PEACE NEGOTIATIONS

The reason why the Arab League failed to react to the unilateral Israeli action was not only the fact that it 'accepted, sort of, the technical details of the Unified Plan', or that Jordan followed in fashion – and then, with help of US funding, launched its own project (the East Ghor Canal, nowadays known as the King Abdullah Canal) – but, and foremost, the fact that through 1954–1956, the Arab world was distracted by a series of dramatic developments in Egypt. Following years-long negotiations, in 1954 Cairo finally managed to convince the British to vacate all of their military bases in Egypt within the next two years. While announcing this achievement in a public speech in Alexandria on 26 October 1954, Colonel Gamal Abdel Nasser – a veteran of the first war with Israel and member of the junta that established itself in power in Cairo after toppling the Egyptian monarchy – narrowly survived an assassination attempt by the Muslim Brotherhood (an extremist Islamist sect from Egypt, roughly similar in its ideology to the Wahhabists). As panic broke out, he not only maintained his poise, but delivered a speech that promptly earned him the status of the national hero. In the matter of a few days, Nasser exploited the opportunity to purge the government, the armed forces, and the media of any opposition and then assumed power.

President Gamal Abdel Nasser waving to a crowed in el-Mansoura of 1960. (Bibliottheca Alexandrina)

A son of a postal employee who worked around the country, Nasser was vividly aware of the poverty facing most of his countrymen, especially in the rural areas: unsurprisingly, this fed his radical nationalist and anti-colonialist beliefs.[13] Once in power, he initiated a series of economic reforms, the centrepiece of which was water-related: the construction of a High Nile Dam near Aswan (better known as the Aswan Dam). Right since the beginning of its history, Egypt was dependent on the flow of the Nile River, the level of which rose and fell with the seasons. The dam was expected not only to help control flooding, but to increase water storage for irrigation and – crucial for Nasser's plan to industrialise the country – to generate hydroelectricity. However, this was a massive project, expected to take about 10 years to realise and cost several hundreds of millions of $US, at the time entirely unaffordable for Egypt. Correspondingly, the USA and the United Kingdom both offered to help finance it – on conditions such as Nasser's leadership in resolving the Arab-Israeli conflict and Egypt joining one of the Western-dominated military alliances. Insisting on Egypt's neutrality, Nasser refused to join any of the pacts. Nevertheless, he did try to negotiate: tragically, his secret peace-talks with Tel Aviv in 1954 were spoiled by a series of Israeli state-sponsored terrorist attacks on US interests in Egypt, best known as the 'Lavon Affair'. Moreover, through 1955 and early 1956, the Israelis launched a series of raids against Egyptian forces in the Gaza Strip, causing hundreds of casualties.

SUEZ WAR OF 1956

Repeated Israeli attacks put Nasser's newly-achieved status as the leader of Egypt under a big question mark: he had to find a way to defend his country against Israeli aggression, and that at the same time he was at odds with militant Islamists of the Muslim Brotherhood and had to secure the financing for the Aswan Dam. Therefore, in addition to seeking a dependable creditor, he began searching for modern armament too. London flatly refused, while Washington – obviously completely lacking understanding of the Egyptian position – demanded basing rights for US armed forces in Egypt. With Nasser only recently concluding negotiations to end the British military presence in the country, there was no way for him to accept such conditions. Ultimately, the strongman in Cairo was left without choice: he turned to the USSR instead.

Moscow proved keen to provide both arms and funding for the dam, and at very favourable terms, but its leaders were warry about provoking the Western superpowers. In an attempt to avoid an escalation, the Egyptians and the Soviets then masqueraded their agreement as one between Egypt and the Czechoslovak Republic: after all, at that time the latter was known as one of the major arms suppliers to Israel. The resulting 'Czechoslovak Arms Deal' of 1955 was run via Prague. In vain, and in the best fashion of the times, Washington misinterpreted the deal as a 'Communist penetration of the Middle East', while London and Paris were already setting their sights on Nasser because his politics threatened their domination of the Arab and Muslim world, and of Africa.

If all of this was not 'provoking enough', Nasser then added the proverbial 'drop that over-spilled the barrel': on 26 July 1956, he nationalised the Suez Canal with the aim of using the income from it to finance the construction of the Aswan Dam. The fact that Cairo dutifully paid the value of the Suez Canal Company to its owners and proved perfectly capable of operating the Canal was ignored: London and Paris reacted by promptly launching preparations for a military intervention that aimed both to topple Nasser and secure their control over the strategic waterway. Of course, just invading Egypt would have been a gross violation of the UN Charter, which defined such acts as a war of aggression. Correspondingly, Great Britain and France reached a secret agreement with Israel, aimed at 'providing a legal pretext' for an invasion of Egypt. On 29 October 1956, the IDF opened the war with a paratrooper raid deep into central Sinai, while attacking the Gaza Strip with ground forces. After three days of chaotic fighting the Israelis were actually on the way to achieving nothing, or even losing the war, but London and Paris thus had an excuse to invade: 'a threat to international shipping in the Suez Canal'. While a military success, their aggression proved a diplomatic and political disaster: it was condemned not only by the growing block of neutral nations and, predictably, the USSR and its allies, but, and more importantly, by the USA, whose economic pressure eventually forced London and Paris into a humiliating withdrawal.[14]

Faithful to aims already laid down in March 1948, Israel was not the least keen to withdraw from the Sinai. Indeed, this necessitated massive pressure from President Eisenhower – who not only threatened, but (again) stopped all the economic aid to the country: thus, the IDF completed its withdrawal only on 11 March 1957. Meanwhile, the situation remained tense enough to prompt the UN to establish the United Nations Emergency Force (UNEF), of some 9,000 'observers' deployed along the armistice lines between Egypt and Israel. Their presence helped reduce tensions along the armistice lines, foremost through preventing a repeat of the Israeli raids of 1954–1956. Beyond them, Egypt maintained a garrison of about 30,000 troops and airmen within the Sinai Peninsula.[15]

STRAITS OF TIRAN

Under a 'good faith agreement' brokered by UN Secretary-General Dag Hammerskjold and Canadian Premier Lester Pearson, Egypt agreed it would not alter the UNEF mandate without discussing the matter with the United Nations. In addition to controlling the armistice lines – and thus the future border between Egypt and Israel – the UNEF established a presence at Sharm al-Sheikh, then a small fishing village on a promontory overlooking the Straits of Tiran, a narrow body of water seven nautical miles wide, at the mouth of the Gulf of Aqaba, whose Arabic name is Ras Nasrani.

The Gulf of Aqaba was vital to Israel because of its port of Eilat – at the time still a minor town, through which most of the country's oil was imported under a covert agreement with Iran. So much so that, in an attempt to prevent any future blockade, and this becoming a cause for war under the UN Charter's self-defence clause, the contemporary US Secretary of State, John F. Dulles, pledged to Israel that any renewed blockade of the Straits of Tiran by Egypt would be considered 'an act of war', and the USA would aid Israeli efforts to break it.

Ironically, this is what Israel then used as an excuse in June 1967, although this pledge was provided without Eisenhower's or Nasser's knowledge, and was actually little but a 'verbal agreement' for which the American film producer Samuel Goldwyn famously observed '...was not worth the paper it was written on'. Unsurprisingly, it mattered very little in Cairo: not only was Nasser not informed about Dulles' pledge, but the Gulf of Aqaba was excluded from the 1958 Geneva Convention guaranteeing it international status because neither the United Arab Republic nor Egypt ever signed that agreement. Foremost, although maintaining the complete diplomatic and economic isolation of Egypt, Nasser decided not only *not* to blockade the straits but turned a blind eye to Israeli maritime traffic all through the late 1950s and 1960s, while – and rather unsurprisingly considering both the Lavon Affair of 1954 and the Tripartite Aggression of 1956 – keeping the Suez Canal firmly closed for Israeli shipping.[16]

Field Marshal Abdel Hakim Amer, while giving a speech during celebrations commemorating the Revolution of 1952, in July 1959. (Jens Heidel collection)

THE NASSER-AMER DUO

Although a qualified military officer and – in his capacity as President of Egypt – the Commander-in-Chief of the Armed Forces, and still frequently wearing his military uniform in public, before 1956 Gamal Abdel Nasser foremost considered himself a 'politician, playing a game of chess'. Correspondingly, and contrary to what is still frequently reported in the West, he hardly ever meddled into the issues related to the armed forces. Instead, this was the task of Nasser's best friend and close confidant, Major General Abdel Hakim Amer (colloquially addressed with the British equivalent rank of 'Field Marshal', despite 'Arabisation' of Egyptian military ranks introduced in 1958).

Appointed as the Minister of War and Chief-of-Staff Armed Forces in 1952 – mainly due to his close relationship with Nasser and the crucial role he played during the coup against the monarchy in the same year – Amer was an officer who distinguished himself during the First Arab-Israeli War but received no further military education after a staff course in 1950. Nominally at least, this mattered little, for his primary task was making sure the armed forces would remain loyal to Nasser.

The situation changed dramatically during the Suez War of 1956. Twice during the first two days of that conflict, Amer disobeyed Nasser's orders to withdraw Egyptian Army units from the Sinai Peninsula. Moreover, when disappointed by the performance of his service, Amer then sacked one of the president's favourites, the Chief-of-Staff Egyptian Air Force, Major General Mahmoud Sidqi Mahmoud. No doubt, Amer skilfully ran the army, and the Israelis failed to breach into the depth of Sinai. Indeed, it can be said that through ordering the air force to operate over the Sinai Peninsula in big formations, he was about to wrestle air superiority in Egypt's favour, too. However, when Nasser realised what Amer was doing, his reaction was one of rage: on the evening of 31 October 1956, he ordered Amer to reinstate Sidqi Mahmoud, and not only to withdraw the army from the Sinai, but also to ground the air force instead of letting it resist the Franco-British aerial offensive.

To say this was a disgrace for the Field Marshal would be an understatement. Indeed, feeling confirmed by subsequent developments and bitterly complaining about heavy losses and the destruction of military and civilian facilities caused by Nasser's decisions, he resigned. However, Nasser refused to accept his resignation and reinstated Amer to his position. Still, the result was a deep rift and a dead end. The rift was to grow massively over the following years and to a degree where Nasser suspected Amer of plotting a coup against him, and thus began appointing him to ever more political titles and positions in order to secure loyalty. In turn, Amer knew that he had nothing of Nasser's popularity and support with the public, and thus decided that in the future he would follow his orders to the last dot and comma. Primarily, each of the two became convinced that the success of decision-making by a single man justified them remaining in power, and surrounding himself with personal favourites.[17]

PAN-ARABISM AND POPULISM

For everyday Arabs, the 'sole hero' of the Suez War was Gamal Abdel Nasser, whom his own propaganda machinery declared as the man that defeated a joint invasion by Israel and two imperial powers. Unsurprisingly, he was confirmed in office by the new parliament elected in 1957, and subsequently re-worked the constitution so as to grant him the power to appoint and dismiss ministers, and to ignore any kind of parliamentary votes against his policy. Arguably, over the following two years his reforms began showing their effects: abolition of the feudal structure, land reform, and granting the right of women to vote, made him immensely popular; expanded education with school enrolment doubled literacy rates in a matter of a few years, while – although burdened by massive costs for the construction of the High Nile Dam (eventually completed only in 1970) – his rapid industrialisation resulted in solid economic development. However, Nasser was a populist who owed much of his popularity to the fact that he was in control of all the media in Egypt, and thus free to propagate his 'anti-imperialist credentials'. Combined with his (political) 'success' during the Suez War, and his excellent skills as an orator in which he expertly blended colloquial and classical Arabic, this rapidly made him a 'super star' of the Arab world: a person adored by millions and widely perceived as the leader of all Arabs. The result of his tirades about abuse of power by Western-supported Arab monarchies was a wave of pan-Arabism that swept over all of the Middle East and north Africa, prompting widespread unrest, popular uprisings, and coup attempts from Algeria to Iraq. Undoubtedly, his ego played a role, too, for Nasser felt confirmed as a 'great strategist' during the Tripartite Aggression of 1956: however, in turn he discussed his policy ever less often, and began dictating it instead. This was a gross mistake for an idealist and ideologist that lacked administrative skills, as commented by Akram al-Hawrani, one of the leaders of the Ba'ath Party in Syria: 'He knows how to start things, fine, but: he doesn't know how to finish'.[18]

This became obvious through 1958 when widespread unrest in Lebanon and Jordan was overpowered by US and British military interventions, and Egypt lacked the capability to counter in fashion. Therefore, Nasser requested a Soviet counter-intervention, but Moscow refused to heed the call. The result was a sort of 'Soviet-Egyptian Cold War' that was to last for years. Moreover, when, in July 1958, a military coup d'état toppled a British-imposed monarchy in Iraq, but the new strongman, Abd al-Karim Qasim, then did not create a union with Egypt as demanded and expected by many (including Nasser), the consequence was an 'Arab Cold War' – this time between Baghdad and Cairo.[19]

THE (DIS-)UNITED ARAB REPUBLIC

Ironically, it was in Syria that Nasser and Amer enjoyed the greatest popularity. The country's pluralist political culture was shattered by constant military meddling and by early 1958, the situation was on the verge of a civil war. Eventually, the government in Damascus found itself without option but to request that Nasser effect a union. Initially reluctant, the strongman in Cairo accepted when the Syrian political leadership agreed to a one-party state. On 22 February 1958, the two countries merged into the United Arab Republic (UAR).[20]

At that point in time, Nasser arrived at what was perhaps his worst political decision ever: he appointed Amer as administrator of Syria, now termed the 'Eastern Province'. Exactly as feared by opponents of the union, Amer began treating the 'province' as a second-class partner, and then an outright colony: he appointed his cronies to control all the important institutions, causing growing resentment through their patronising and overbearing attitude, and growing corruption. Moreover, he granted the Syrians only a third of the seats in the united National Assembly, imposed land reform, and flooded the country with cheap, Egyptian-made textiles, while undermining the domestic industry and removing major factories and much of its air force to Egypt.[21]

If it was Amer who caused widespread anti-UAR sentiments in Damascus, Aleppo and Homs, it was Nasser who placed the final straw on the back of the Syrians. When the UAR was created his views on a future society were fluid: however, by the early 1960s they drifted towards central authority, centralised planning and public ownership, which, de facto, meant control through the 'Egyptian wing' of the Armed Forces of the UAR. In August 1961, he decided to extend these philosophies to the Eastern Province by the means of replacing the regional authorities and moving the capital: Cairo was to serve as such for eight months, and Damascus for four months. Ultimately, the mix of Nasser's centralism and Amer's corruption prompted the 'Syrian wing' of the Armed Forces to stage a coup on 28 September 1961. This saw Amer arrested in his pyjamas and ignominiously bundled onto a flight to Cairo. A company of paratroopers sent to help loyalists proved 'too little, too late'. Egyptian paratroopers were arrested and disarmed, and then returned to Alexandria together with other Egyptian military personnel on board several ships over the following weeks – making it obvious that the Syrian support for the UAR had collapsed. Even then, the coup leaders in Damascus were still willing to retain the UAR on terms of greater equality: Nasser flatly refused, and the alliance was dissolved. It was a disgrace from which the 'leader of the Arab world' was never to recover.[22]

TEWFIK WAR/ROTEM AFFAIR

In addition to the Suez War of 1956 and the short-lived UAR, another crucial experience that was to influence the behaviour and decision-making of Nasser and Amer during the June 1967 War was a little-known episode related to the National Water Carrier of Israel.

In October 1959, the IDF – once again – violated the ceasefire agreement from 1949 by entering the central DMZ *vis-à-vis* the 'Eastern Province', and to 'cultivate the land' with *armoured* tractors. Having a standing order not to react to such provocations, the UAR Army did not open fire, but the affair was discussed at the meeting of the joint cabinet in Cairo, where the representatives from

The ignominious return of Egyptian paratroopers, by ship, in October 1961. (Albert Grandolini collection)

A typical armoured tractor of the IDF as used to 'cultivate land' inside the DMZs along the ceasefire lines with Syria in the early 1950s. (Tom Cooper collection)

Damascus demanded either military action to stop the Israelis, or political pressure through restoring the blockade of the Straits of Tiran. Keen to avoid a war with Israel, Nasser opted for neither: instead, he granted permission for the Union to launch its own project to divert the waters of the Yarmouk River, from a point south of the village of Lower Tewfik, three kilometres away from the DMZ.

Of course, the construction work in question took time to organise. Inpatient, the Israelis thus launched another series of provocations and, on 31 January 1960, the Armed forces of the UAR opened fire, killing an Israeli border policeman and wounding two others. Israel's Prime Minister and minister of defence, David Ben-Gurion, ordered a retaliation in the form of a nocturnal raid against civilian construction workers. Undertaken by a task force of the 1st 'Golani' Infantry Brigade of the IDF, the following night, this resulted in complete demolition of the village of Lower Tewfik, the construction equipment and related housing. Rather unsurprisingly considering the severity of this outrage and numerous civilian casualties, the UAR Army 'retaliated' – by shelling the kibbutz of Tel Katzirs – before a UN-mediated truce brought the fighting to a halt. Nevertheless, the following morning, interceptors of the IDF/AF and those of the United Arab Republic Air Force (UARAF) clashed in several air combats, and MiG-17 pilots of the latter claimed two Israelis as shot down, while the Israelis claimed one MiG as damaged.[23]

Certainly enough, the UAR Army in the Eastern Province then did put two of its brigades and an artillery regiment on alert, but in an attempt to prevent an escalation it sent only one tank company closer to the armistice line. Indeed, emboldened by the lack of 'Syrian' reaction, the IDF deployed paratroopers of the 50th and 890th Regiments into another raid: during the night from 1–2 February 1960, they completely demolished the village of Upper Tewfik after expulsing its population. When the reports about this attack reached Cairo, together with intelligence obtained by the Main Directorate of Military Intelligence (DM1) – which reported that the IDF was reinforcing its troops along the armistice lines with the Eastern Province – it caused serious concerns. However, Nasser remained disinterested in an escalation, and thus ordered Amer not to put the armed forces on alert. With there being no fighting, no matter how much desired by the 'hawks' in Tel Aviv, the Israelis eventually withdrew from the DMZ and the crisis appeared to be over.[24]

Then, on 12 February 1960, another incident took place on the armistice line between the Eastern Province and Israel, in which two IDF troops were killed in what the Israelis assessed as a 'clear Syrian provocation'. A stern warning from Tel Aviv proved counterproductive: Cairo remained calm until 15–16 February, when the DM1 received intelligence – most of it completely false – about Israeli preparations for another attack on the Eastern Province, to be carried out on 22 February, the anniversary of the creation of the UAR. Correspondingly, on 16 February 1960, during their visit to Damascus, Nasser and Amer ordered a 'silent' mobilisation of the armed forces and the deployment of the 2nd Infantry and 4th Armoured divisions of the UAR Army on the Sinai Peninsula. Over the following two days, the units took positions in the area between Umm Katef, Abu Ageila and el-Arish, and were then followed by additional reinforcements: by 27 February 1960, the UAR Army had six of its 10 infantry brigades, and all three of its armoured brigades – including a total of about 500 tanks – in positions 5–15km from the armistice lines with Israel.

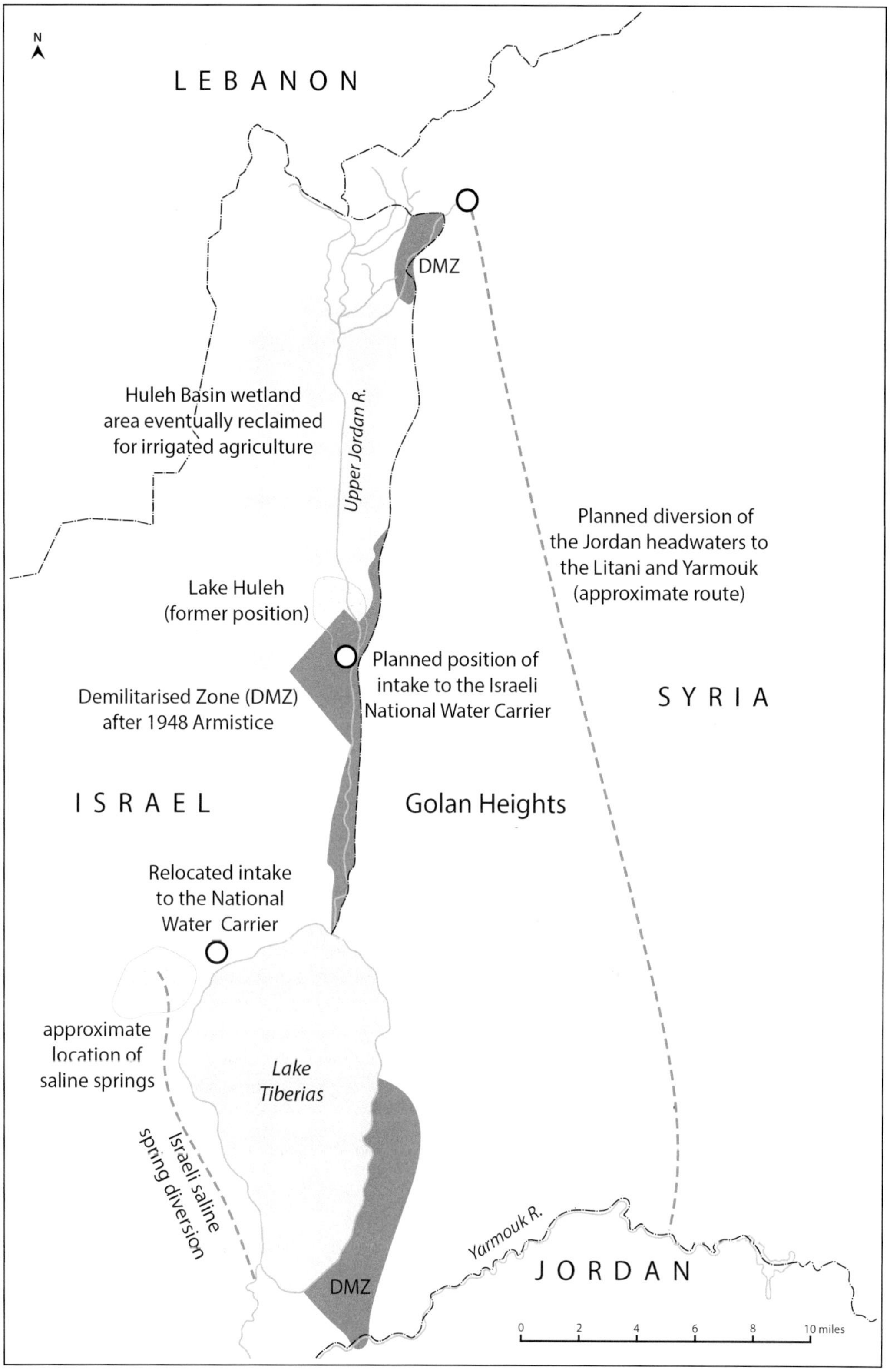

A map of the area in which the little-known Tewfik War (known as the 'Rotem Affair' in Israel) was carried out, in January and February 1960. (Map by George Anderson)

Contrary to the myth according to which the Israelis completely failed to detect this deployment, the Israeli military intelligence actually reported it to the government in Tel Aviv on the same day it began: it 'just' failed to stress its importance. Thus, it was only on 24 February, when an Israeli reconnaissance aircraft violated UAR airspace over the Sinai Peninsula and brought back photographs of large troop concentrations close to Israel, that the government in Tel Aviv realised the seriousness of the situation. In attempt to keep a low profile, Ben-Gurion only put the regular units of the IDF on alert, and – acting not only as prime minister but the minister of defence too – deployed them in defensive positions both in the north and the south of the country. Instead of escalating, he opted for a 'diplomatic offensive', making the mobilisation of the UAR Army public, and – via Washington – warning Nasser that he would mobilise should the troops not be withdrawn. This was enough for the strongman in Cairo: he was satisfied that his politics of calming the tension and preventing the war by 'mere flexing of muscles' was working, and that Israel ceased exercising pressure upon the Eastern Province. By the time the brigades of the UAR Army began their withdrawal to base on 9 March 1960, the crisis was all but over. At least from his point of view – and certainly in related communiques of Radio Cairo – Nasser thus won a major propaganda victory *vis-à-vis* both Israel and the rival government in Baghdad, and that without any help from Moscow.[25] Considering this experience, it is actually unsurprising that, seven years later, he went on to attempt *repeating exactly the same exercise* – even if on a much larger scale and in a far more public fashion.

FATAL ERROR

If the formation of the UAR in 1958 was the high point in the political career of Gamal Abdel Nasser, the Syrian counter-coup and dissolution of the union in 1961 marked the beginning of his decline. By that time, he had been diagnosed with diabetes and the strain of leadership took its toll. Moreover, not only did his disputes with Moscow carry on, but so did those with the leadership in Baghdad, and the governments of Syria, Jordan, Saudi Arabia, and Yemen. While still at odds with Moscow, despite repeated orders for Soviet arms (see below for details), the President of the United Arab Republic – a title Egypt retained as its official designation until 1972 – reacted by gradually improving relations with the USA, where the new president, John F. Kennedy, offered an attractive economic aid package, including provision of wheat and other basic commodities for free. By the end of 1962, up to 10 percent of the Egyptian population was receiving US food. This was just in time, because Nasser – determined to create new allies if he could not win anybody to his side – embroiled the UAR into its most ruinous adventure.

On 19 September 1962, Imam Ahmad, the monarch of the Imamate of Yemen, died. With the Imamate of Yemen being the most underdeveloped and most isolated of Arab countries, Nasser had largely ignored it at earlier times. However, Yemen's short, quasi-membership in the UAR, lasting from 1958 until 1960, had left its traces: fuelled by pan-Arab ideals, by 1962 the dissent within the armed forces reached a point where no fewer than four groups of officers were plotting a coup against the Imam – at least two of these with the support of the UAR. Eventually, the clique around the Egyptian-trained Brigadier General Abdullah as-Sallal was the quickest: on 20 September 1962, only a day after Imam Ahmad died, it deposed his successor, Prince Muhammad al-Badr, and declared the Yemen Arab Republic. After visiting Sana'a to meet Sallal, Nasser's aide Anwar el-Sadat delivered an enthusiastic report in Cairo, and demanded that the nascent republic be supported against a possible military intervention of the US-supported Kingdom of Saudi Arabia. On 30 October 1962, Nasser gave his order for an Egyptian military intervention and assigned overall command over this enterprise to no nobody less than Amer.[26]

The intervention came just in time, for although declared as dead, Prince Badr survived the coup and fled to Saudi Arabia. Moreover, the British – always keen for 'payback for 1956' – then convinced the Saudi royals to support Badr financially, and thus enable *them* to provide for recruitment of a group of British and French military veterans that would train an insurgency. Certainly enough, London was perfectly aware of the fact that the resulting guerrilla conflict paid for by Saudi gold never enjoyed widespread popular support and had no chance of removing Sallal from power. However, London got precisely what it wanted: despite the overwhelming success of early counterinsurgency efforts conducted by Amer, the overall result was an endless, costly, and shameful war for which Nasser never found a political solution, and which added much to the ruin of his reputation in the Arab world.

UNREST IN BAGHDAD AND DAMASCUS

While the Egyptians became preoccupied with Yemen, both the Iraqis and Syrians remained preoccupied with their internal dispute. On 8 February 1963, a group of civilians from the Arab Socialist Ba'ath Party, in cooperation with pan-Arabist officers, staged a coup d'état in Baghdad, ending the five-year-long dictatorship of General Abd al-Karim Qasim. In his place a regime presided over by Major General Abd as-Salim Arif established itself in power. Emboldened by this 'success' of its Iraqi brethren, on 8 March 1963, the Military Committee of the Syrian Regional Branch of the Ba'ath Party launched a coup in Damascus. Ending the two 'happy years' – a period of significant economic recovery – the plot established the Ba'ath-dominated government of Salah ad-Din al-Bitar in power, but the actual strongman in the country became Lieutenant Colonel Salah Jadid. Both coups resulted not only in hundreds of deaths but also in widespread purges of the armed forces and indeed the effective end of civilian influence in political life. In Iraq, the new government ended nearly all relations with the USSR, while the armed militia of the Ba'ath Party mercilessly persecuted the well-organised Iraqi Communist Party – including its members within the armed forces. In Syria, Jadid's control over the government was secured by his aides – Colonel Muhammad Umran and Captain

A T-54 main battle tank of the 20th Brigade of the Iraqi Army on the streets of Baghdad during the coup of 8 February 1963. (Albert Grandolini collection)

A T-34/85 medium tank of the Syrian Arab Army on the streets of Damascus during the coup of 8 March 1963. (Albert Grandolini collection)

Salim Hatum. On the international level, both juntas copied Nasser's extensive use of propaganda to position themselves as 'fiercely anti-Israel'. However, while President Arif initially favoured a federation with Egypt, he found Nasser frustrated by 'disappointments' in Syria and Yemen. Moreover, in July 1963, Jadid's regime narrowly survived a counter-coup by Nasserist officers within the Syrian armed forces: from that point onwards, his propaganda machinery began fiercely criticising President Nasser and the UAR.

ARAB LEAGUE SUMMITS

Through 1963, the DM1 obtained intelligence that the Israelis were about to conclude the construction of the NWC. With the new US president, Lyndon B Johnson, remaining as unsuccessful in securing agreements on the basis of the Unified Plan as Eisenhower and Kennedy before him, Israel significantly increased the amount of water it diverted from Lake Tiberias to more than the 490 million cubic metres allotted in agreement from 1955 and threatened military action against anybody trying to disturb the remaining construction works. The situation created a dilemma for Nasser: he recognised that to prevent the Israelis from fulfilling their plan, he might be forced to go to war in support of both Syria and Jordan and at a time when he had a major military commitment in Yemen and his armed forces were not yet ready for a major showdown.

In attempt to quieten the discord, negotiate a ceasefire in Yemen, and focus everybody's attention upon the dispute with Israel, the President of the UAR called for the first summit of the Arab League, in Cairo, between 13 and 17 January 1964. During the conference, Nasser found himself exposed to fierce accusations from the Syrian representatives about Egyptian 'reluctance for military confrontation with Zionists', and inactivity regarding the NWC in particular, while the Saudis and Jordanians complained about his support for Sallal's Republicans in Yemen. In reaction, the strongman in Cairo changed his strategy: he negotiated a formal recognition of the Palestinian entity; he decided to de-escalate the war in Yemen through the policy of peaceful coexistence with the Arab monarchies; he proposed the establishment of a unified military command for defence against Israel; and he negotiated for Lebanon, Jordan, and Syria to initiate their own projects for the diversion of water to prevent it from reaching Israel.[27]

WATER WAR, TAKE TWO

The latter decision of the Arab League was expanded during its Second Summit, in September 1964: because this included a plan to reroute two out of the three principal sources of the Jordan River, this became known as the Headwater Diversion Plan. In Syria, the project was to include a diversion of the Hasbani River, high on the Golan Heights, a few kilometres away from the northern tip of the armistice lines with Israel. In Jordan, the project aimed to construct the East- and West Ghor Canals, which were to supply fresh water from Hasbani, Banias and Yarmouk to the West Bank.

Israeli reactions were fierce: Tel Aviv declared these projects to be an infringement of its sovereignty. However, the new Prime Minister of Israel, Levi Eshkol was far more restrained in pursuing Ben-Gurion's aggressive foreign policy. Instead of him, over the following years, it was the General Staff of the IDF that began taking things into its own hands and acting at its own discretion. The body was led by Lieutenant General Yitzhak Rabin, who – together

The heads of the Arab states during the Arab League Summit in Cairo in 1964. Visible sitting at the table are (clockwise), Ahmed Shukairi (Chairman of the Palestine Liberation Organization), Ahmed Ben Bella (President of Algeria), Habib Bourghiba (President of Tunisia), Ibrahim Abboud (President of Sudan), Amin Hafiz (President of Syria), Abdul Salam Arif (President of Iraq), Gamal Abdel Nasser (President of the United Arab Republic/Egypt), King Saud of Saudi Arabia, King Hussein of Jordan, Emir Abdullah al-Sabah of Kuwait (behind King Hussein), and Crown Prince Ali Hassan of Libya. (Bibliotheca Alexandrina)

The construction of an open canal section of the NWC, seen in the early 1960s. (Albert Grandolini collection)

Nevertheless, all though the 1950s, Israel bitterly complained about consistent 'terrorist attacks' on its territory: unsurprisingly, this myth is deeply ingrained not only in the country's conscience, but also in that of the Western public. However, as stressed by several Israeli historians since, the majority of such 'cross-border activities' were related to Palestinian refugees: civilians who either fled or had been ethnically cleansed from their villages in 1947–1949, attempting to access their land. Nevertheless, Israel always insisted on indiscriminately designating all of them as terrorists, regardless of the fact that the vast majority were never armed. Correspondingly, any such activities – armed or not, and regardless of whether resulting in attacks on Israeli citizens or their possessions – were reported as 'terrorist attacks', and the IDF and the government of Prime Minister Ben-Gurion described them as having been launched by or with support of the Egyptian, Jordanian, Lebanese or Syrian armed forces, while publishing wildly exaggerated figures about the 'damage' they had caused. Inevitably, this created the impression of Israel being under 'near-constant' and 'murderous' attacks.[31]

with the commander of the IDF Northern Command, Brigadier David Elazar – had particular loathing for the Syrians: indeed, both were convinced that violence was the only way of dealing with them. Together, Rabin and Elazar devised two plans. One was for a campaign against the Syrian diversion project, and carried out in the form of provocations, in which 'peaceful Jewish settlers' were 'working their farmland' with armoured bulldozers inside the DMZs. This was initiated in June 1963, causing several minor clashes. The second was Operation Hatchet, which envisaged a two-division push into the Golan Heights, followed by an advance all the way to Damascus – to be completed in a matter of 80 hours: obviously, this was shelved for some time in the future.[28]

Eventually, both Amman and Damascus initiated the work on their diversion schemes in 1964. The IDF reacted against only the Syrian plan: in October 1964, hoping the Syrians might open fire and deliver a pretext for an attack on their construction equipment 'in retaliation', Elazar ordered armoured vehicles to move along a disputed road. The Syrians did open fire, but both Syrian and Israeli tanks failed to hit anything of importance. A renewed attempt 10 days later hit Syrian tanks but not their artillery, which 'retaliated' by shelling civilian settlements – in 'retaliation' for which Elazar ordered the IDF/AF into action.

Additional tit-for-tat incidents followed into the summer of 1965 and while Israeli armour gradually improved its precision, the Syrians again turned to their gunners who were engaging targets 20 kilometres inside Israel. Tel Aviv again turned to its airmen and in July 1965 air attacks upon earthmoving equipment forced the Syrians to excavate further eastwards. Eventually, by early 1967, as Rabin later confirmed, Damascus had effectively abandoned its attempts to divert the headwaters of the Jordan.[29]

THE PALESTINIAN FACTOR[30]

Perhaps the most ironic aspect of the entire Arab-Israeli conflict is that although Israel signed separate ceasefire agreements with all of her neighbours in 1949, it never did so with any representatives of the Palestinians – whether those still around on the territory that now became Israel, or those that were ethnically cleansed. On the contrary, the latter were de facto declared to be 'un-people': immigrants foreign to their own country and the neighbourhood, and thus somebody else's problem. As described above, except for Jordan and Syria, most of the Arab countries followed in fashion.

In reality, and as confirmed by dozens of contemporary accounts, and by a host of documents released by Israeli historians since, all neighbouring Arab governments followed the policy of strictly curbing any activities by Palestinian militants and any crossings into Israel by Palestinian civilians: not only because they opposed a non-negotiated return of Palestinians, but because they were keen to prevent another war. In Jordan in 1949, the Arab Legion took care to disarm all the members of both the Arab Salvation Army (formed and armed by the Arab League in 1948), and the Army of Holy War, and all irregulars, and to disband their units. Similarly, in Egypt, both the Palestinian irregulars and Egyptian volunteers of the Muslim Brotherhood were disarmed, and their radio station in Gaza was dismantled. The principal problem of subsequent control of former combatants was the length of the armistice lines and the lack of troops necessary to control the hundreds of thousands of people ethnically cleansed from Palestine. Especially in the case of Egypt, such problems were further aggravated by the terms of the armistice agreements of 1949, which strictly limited the number of the Egyptian Army troops and police officers deployed in the Gaza Strip.[32]

Through the 1950s, most Arab governments were insistent on the idea that, 'Arab unity is the road to the liberation of Palestine'. Taking a contrary view, different Palestinian activists began realising that the liberation of Palestine was a more important and an immediate goal, and that 'Arab unity' could follow only once that task was accomplished. Obviously, autonomous action was not in Nasser's interest and in December 1952 – a few months after Palestinian students in Cairo organised their own union – the Egyptian government created the Palestinian Border Police (PBP): armed with British-made weapons and commanded by Egyptian officers, this was almost exclusively tasked with *restraining* cross-border activities.

Table 1: PLA units under Egyptian Control, June 1967

Divisions	Brigades	Sub-Units	Notes
20th Division			
	19th Brigade		nominally 'Palestinian National Guard Brigade'
	107th Brigade	319th, 320th, and 321st Battalions	nominally 'Palestinian Border Guard Brigade'
	109th Brigade	322nd, 323rd, and 324th Battalions	

Although eventually expanded into a battalion, the PBP proved hopelessly insufficient, even more so because the Muslim Brotherhood of Egypt had returned to Sinai and then the Gaza Strip, and – from 1953 – began organising (genuinely) armed infiltrations. When Israel then reacted with 'retaliation' attacks on PBP and Egyptian Army units in the Gaza strip, Cairo did not even consider strikes against the enemy proper: instead, it reorganised and expanded the Palestinian Border Police into the Palestinian Border Guard (PBG) – a three-battalion force tasked exclusively with curbing cross-border activities by Palestinians. The mass of the 4,000-strong PGB was captured by the IDF during the Suez War of 1956: between 900 and 1,200 were summarily executed before the Israelis withdrew.[33]

During this conflict, the Palestinian Students Union organised its own 'commando battalion' to help the Egyptian war effort, but this saw no action and was deployed to help with de-mining in 1957. Meanwhile, Nasser and Amer decided to return to the policy of establishing and maintaining Palestinian armed formations that were under *their* control. In 1957, two new units staffed by Palestinians came into being: the 107th Brigade and the 141st PBP Battalion. However, both were based in the Cairo area. A new impetus to the creation of armed Palestinian formations was provided only by Qasim's regime in Iraq in 1960, when the Palestine Liberation Regiment came into being. Certainly enough, this was disestablished as soon as Qasim was overthrown, in February 1963, but its existence did prompt Nasser and Amr to order the redeployment of Palestinian formations to the Gaza Strip and their further expansion. Still, the situation experienced a fundamental change only during the First and Second Summit of the Arab League in 1964, when two Palestinian organisations came into being: the Palestine Liberation Organization (PLO), as an umbrella for at least 11 different political factions that was to act as a government in exile, and the Palestine Liberation Army (PLA).

Soon, both the PLO and the PLA were ripped apart due to the divergent interests of different Arab dictators. The PLO was initially led by Ahmad al-Shukeiri, a Palestinian lawyer and Nasser's protegee, who had served as a member of the Syrian, and then the Saudi, delegations to the UN. On Nasser's insistence, it was headquartered in Jordan, because Nasser – even without knowing about secret negotiations between Amman and Tel Aviv – wanted to embarrass King Hussein through allowing his country to be used as a base for guerrilla raids into Israel. Moreover, the organisation was dominated by the Palestinian National Liberation Movement (Fatah, which also stood for 'Conquest'), led by Yasser Arafat, who – thanks to financing primarily provided by Kuwait – had managed to keep his wing a semi-sovereign political entity, and was insistent on launching an insurgency inside Israel. However, because the strongman in Cairo rejected all demands of Arafat, Algeria and Syria for guerrilla operations, the Arab League was left without choice but to establish the PLA as a regular, conventional armed force of the PLO, staffed by Palestinian refugees that would be drafted in several host countries, instead of serving in the local armed forces.

Planned to be based in Egypt, the PLA was to consist of five infantry brigades and six commando battalions, with a total of 16,100 troops, and capable of training up to 56,000 reservists a year. However, Nasser and Amer permitted the recruitment of only about 3,500 in the Gaza Strip and never put the PLA under the control of the PLO's Military Department. Furthermore, nearly all officers and NCOs remained Egyptians, and Amer took care to prevent it from receiving 44 T-34/85 medium tanks and 12 D-30 122mm howitzers purchased from Moscow, and 45 mortars and other armament purchased from Beijing. Instead, the PLA received just 10 M4A4 Sherman tanks (all modified through the installation of the FL-10 turret of the French AMX-13 light tank, with 75mm gun), and 10 old, British-made 25-pounder (88mm) guns. While eventually expanded to about 11,500 men by 1966 – organised as shown in Table 1 – the force remained subordinated to the Egyptian Army, which used it as its 20th 'Palestine' Division and was meanwhile experiencing significant recruitment shortfalls.

Rather unsurprisingly considering their mutual rivalries, other Arab regimes rushed to establish 'their own' Palestinian formations, most of which were declared to be elements of the PLA for propaganda purposes. For example, Damascus organised the 12,000-strong Hittin Brigade, consisting of eight battalions, while the Syrian Ba'ath Party established the Vanguard of the Liberation War (abbreviated with SAIQA, which also means 'Thunderbolt'): a commando force trained for guerrilla attacks into Israel. Similarly, Iraq established the Qadisiyyah Brigade. That said, the only Palestinian units to see any kind of action prior to the June 1967 War remained very limited in size and numbers.

UNITED ARAB COMMAND

Another result of the First, Second, and Third summits of the Arab League (in Alexandria in September 1964) was the creation of the United Arab Command (UAC). Established on Nasser's proposal and provided with a sizeable budget of US$345 million (later expanded to US$600 million) for the first 10 years, the UAC was to audit all the Arab armies in respect of their organisation and equipment and then standardise their strategy, tactics, and weaponry, coordinate their planning, and – in the event of war – their operations. In theory, this promised to offer sound solutions for many of the problems marring the underfunded armed forces of Lebanon, Syria, and Jordan in particular. It was also a solution strongly irritating Israel. However, in practice, this effort misfired – and then for entirely unrelated reasons.

Lieutenant General Ali Ali Amer was appointed the commander of the United Arab Command, with Major General Abd el-Moneim Riyadh as the chief-of-staff, while Brigadier General Shalaby el-Hinnawy was appointed the Head of the Air Defence Department UAC. Taking their duties seriously, Amer, Riyadh, and Hinnawy not only worked fast, and appointed numerous, carefully selected Syrian and Iraqi officers to crucial position in their new command, but by early 1965 developed a plan for a joint air defence strategy for all of Israel's neighbours. Problems arose when they recognised significant weaknesses in the Jordanian and Syrian air defences, and recommended deployment of UARAF units equipped with MiG-17s and MiG-21s to these countries. Rather unsurprisingly considering mutual animosities between Amman, Cairo and Damascus, the Jordanian and Syrian governments flatly refused any such ideas. From that point onwards, the UAC was rendered, '...a rigid, crippled and ineffectual body.[34]

2

DIVERGENT DOCTRINES

Rabin and Elazar's planning for operations against Syria in 1964 appear surprising considering the usual mythology about Israel's military inferiority (and all the other possible military vulnerabilities), especially in comparison to the 'unified' armies of the neighbouring Arab states, as widely published in Israel and the West since 1948. Indeed, there is little doubt that Israel and the West took the issue of a possible Arab union seriously enough for this to become an important reason for their continuous political and military interventions all over the Middle East, including those in Lebanon and Jordan in 1958, and – via Saudi Arabia – in Yemen in 1962. A union of Arab Muslim countries controlling the area from the Atlantic Ocean to the western borders of Iran, with a population (as of the late 1950s) of well over 100 million, held together by common religion and rich in natural resources like oil and gas – was certainly not in the interests of any foreign powers. In similar fashion, any major arms acquisition by one or another Arab state was promptly declared to be another 'mortal threat' to Israel and a 'Soviet penetration' – even though the leaders in Amman, Baghdad, Beirut, Cairo, Damascus, Rabat, Riyadh, and other Arab capitals were all openly anti-Communist, and constantly at odds with each other to the degree where their mutual enmities frequently outmatched their declared animosity towards Israel (even more so considering several of them were running clandestine negotiations with the 'Zionist Entity').

However, public perceptions of the military balance between Israel and her neighbours were fundamentally different to that of professional military intelligence analysts. Indeed, ever since the First Arab-Israeli War, all the professional military intelligence estimates – whether prepared in Israel, USA, Great Britain, or France, just for example – came to the same conclusion: Israel was in possession of military superiority compared to all of her neighbours, unified or not, and was always expected to defeat them, all together, or one-on-one, with various degrees of ease. For example, a report by the US Joint Chiefs of Staff from May 1967 observed:

'Israel will be militarily unchallengeable by any combination of Arab states at least during the next five years. As presently trained and equipped, the armed forces of Israel are greatly superior in effectiveness and firepower to those of their potential opponents individually and collectively.' There was an entire host of reasons for this.[1]

DOCTRINAL FAILURES OF ARAB DICTATORSHIPS[2]

In the dictatorships of the major Arab countries of the 1950s and 1960s – whether that in Egypt, dominated by the relationship between Nasser and Amer, or that of Arif in Iraq, or Jadid in Syria – there was no place for 'thinkers': for officers developing new doctrines, strategies and tactics, and even less so for those demonstrating any kind of initiative. The principal reason was that the primary task of these armed forces – and that since the times most of them were established under the British and French tutelage of the early twentieth century – was protection from 'internal enemies'. This task dictated their indoctrination following ideologies pursued by the dictators in Amman, Baghdad, Cairo, and Damascus. In that atmosphere, there was no place for great strategists or master tacticians: dictators do not like smart, and even less so independent-minded military officers. Indeed, there was not even place for any remembrance of highly successful Arab officers of the Ottoman armed forces from the early twentieth century, like the Baghdad-born Mahmoud Shevket Pasha, author of two tactical manuals coauthored in cooperation with German General Colmar Freiherr von der Goltz, and the basic textbook that guided Mustafa Kemal Atatürk into forming the Turkish Republic along the ideals of a 'nation at arms'; or the Damascus-born Yusuf al-Azma who distinguished himself during the Gallipoli campaign, before being appointed the minister of defence and attempting to repeat Atatürk's success through establishing the armed forces of the short-lived Arab Kingdom of Syria, in 1919–1920.

Abd el-Moneim Riyadh in an official photograph while serving as Chief-of-Staff of the Egyptian Armed Forces, 1967–1970. (Bibliotheca Alexandrina)

This should not mean that there were no thinkers. Preoccupied with politics and thus lacking time to undergo advanced military education on their own, in 1958 Nasser and Amer sent several of their ranking officers for higher military education abroad. One of them was Brigadier General Abd el-Moneim Riyadh – already considered the most professional and best-educated Egyptian officer of the time: a year later, he graduated from the prestigious Military Academy of the General Staff of the Armed Forces of the Soviet Union with the Golden General award. Riyadh returned deeply impressed by the Soviet military thinking of the times. Oversimplified, this insisted on theories that high-flying strategic bombers armed with nuclear weapons represented the ultimate weapon, and assigned absolute priority to the means of countering that threat. Correspondingly, the Soviet armed forces of the late 1950s and early 1960s, were rapidly developing an integrated air defence system (IADS) covering the entire Soviet territory: this depended on a dense network of radar stations, manned interceptors, and SAMs capable of early detection, interception and destruction of bombers operating at high altitudes. Appointed Adviser for Air Defence to the High Command of the UAR Armed Forces, Riyadh

Mohammad Assad Moukiiad (Assistant Chief-of-Staff, SyAAF, 1967–1970, visible in the front row, third from left), with Salah Jadid (to the left from Moukiiad), and a group of Egyptian officers from the UAC, seen in 1966. (Mohammad Assad Moukiiad collection)

persistently demanded the development of a similar IADS covering the UAR. This is what resulted in large Egyptian orders for MiG-21s and S-75s from 1961, and what led to Egyptian MiG-21 pilots being trained according to contemporary Soviet tactical manuals (which emphasised operations at high speeds and high altitudes). However, Riyadh wanted to go a step further and develop such a system for all Arab air forces neighbouring Israel. Although Nasser and Amer were in full agreement with this idea, the UAR could not realise them at the pace demanded by their general. Ultimately, this led to a rift that, in 1964, resulted in Amer being more than happy to get rid of the 'maverick' by appointing him to the UAC.

Similar was true for the second most prominent 'thinker' amongst Egyptian generals of the time: Major General Madkoor Abu al-Ezz. Succeeding Hosni Mubarak as the commander of the Air Force Academy at Bilbeis, Ezz trained several generations of UARAF cadets before being sent on a tour of duty in Yemen in 1963–1964. There, he played a role in devising tactics in which selected insurgent strongholds were first subjected to air strikes, and then to heliborne assault by commando units – which later became famous through the 'Fire Force' in Rhodesia during the 1970s. On the basis of these experiences, Ezz became a vocal proponent of the combined arms doctrine and insistent on the UARAF learning to conduct all aspects of air power, mainly through close cooperation with the ground forces. In Egypt of the time, and especially with Amer in charge of the armed forces, this was anathema: thanks to his preference for micromanagement of all administrative and operational issues for the sake of the security and loyalty of the armed forces to Nasser's regime, each branch of the armed forces was indoctrinated to operate on its own. Unsurprisingly, the Field Marshal was more than happy to get rid of such a 'troublemaker' as Ezz – by convincing him to resign his commission and appointing him the governor of the Aswan Province.

A sort of anti-example was that of Hafez al-Assad in Syria. Upon graduating from the Military Academy in Homs of 1954, he requested reassignment to the SyAAF, and then earned his 'wings' flying Chipmunks, Texans, Fiat G.46 and G.55 fighters in 1955. As one of the top cadets of his class, he was selected for a Meteor operational conversion course in Great Britain and, in 1956–1957, requalified to fly MiG-17s. However, his military career de facto ended during the times of the UAR, when – while serving with the MiG-17PF-equipped No. 31 Squadron deployed in Egypt – he did not undergo any kind of staff courses but busied himself with creating a secret circle including several pro-Ba'ath officers of Syrian origin. Discharged from the UARAF and arrested after the Syrian coup of September 1961, he returned to civilian life in Syria: as an activist of the Ba'ath Party, during the coup of March 1963 he persuaded the commander of Dmeyr AB, Colonel Heitham Muhaini to disobey the orders of Qudsi's government, thus significantly contributing to the success of the plot. As a new 'star' of the Ba'ath, he was reinstated into the SyAAF with the rank of lieutenant colonel and was appointed as the commander of Dmeyr AB. During the Nasserist coup attempt of July 1963, Assad remained loyal to the party and played a similar role again. On the basis of this experience, Jadid then ordered the entire SyAAF to be reorganised along similar lines as Assad has organised Dmeyr AB: henceforth, all flying- and ground-based units on one base were subordinated to the local base commander, who was always hand-picked for his loyalty to the regime. This reorganisation was not prompted by military necessities or because Hafez al-Assad was a grand strategist and a military genius, but because of his proven loyalty – to Jadid and to the Ba'ath Party – and because experience had shown that when officers loyal to the 'party' were in control, any kind of coup attempts against its rule were doomed to fail.

The same factors contributed to Assad's appointment as the Chief-of-Staff SyAAF in October 1965. This is how he was able to prove his loyalty again during disputes between Jadid and Muhammad Umran, his minister of defence, in February 1966. As a reward, the strongman in Damascus then appointed Assad the new minister of defence, atop of his function as the Chief-of-Staff Air Force. Ironically, Assad thus became so deeply involved in the politics that he was forced to appoint an Assistant Chief-of-Staff – in the form of Brigadier General Mohammad Assad Moukiiad – to run the Air Force's everyday operations. While there is no doubt that Moukiiad was an excellent technical officer and administrator, he was neither a strategist nor tactician by profession. Unsurprisingly, both Assad and Moukiiad's influence upon the capabilities and planning of the Syrian Arab Air Force remained extremely limited – primarily in retaining the air force as a 'force in being', regardless the

Munthir al-Windawy, a Hunter pilot of the Iraqi Air Force who played a crucial role in both coups in Baghdad in 1963. (Nour Bardai collection)

circumstances, and that for the purpose of serving as a powerbase for the former.

Something similar was true for all the top Iraqi air force officers of the 1950s and 1960s, the best examples for which were Arif Abd ar-Razzaq and Munthir al-Windawy. Between 1948 and 1966, British-trained Razzaq served with distinction as a pilot of the Avro Anson and Hawker Fury during the First Arab-Israeli War; was the first commander of the first IrAF units equipped with de Havilland Vampires and Venoms, and then with Hawker Hunters; then served as the wing commander of Habbaniya Air Base, Chief-of-Staff IrAF, minister in several governments, and then as a prime minister – in addition to playing a crucial role in several military coups and coup attempts. While thus becoming more than versed in strategy and tactics, he left behind no related publications. Windawy's career was even shorter: trained in Great Britain to fly Hunters, and in the USSR to fly MiG-21s, and under Razzaq's tutelage, he played the crucial role in both coups in Baghdad in 1963, and in the establishment and build-up of the National Guard, an armed militia of the Ba'ath Party in Iraq, thus providing a precedent for Hafez al-Assad's establishment of a similar militia (led by his brother Rifat) in Syria. However, Windawy was forced to flee to Syria after the coup attempt in November 1963, and never returned to Iraq and nor did he leave behind any kind of writings about his experiences

AN ILL-FATED EXPERIMENT IN ARAB UNITY: THE ARABA SQUADRON

Ever since the shockwaves of pan-Arabism swept over the Middle East in the 1950s, there was no end of reports about close cooperation between different Arab armed forces. Actually, instances of serious cooperation could be counted on the fingers of one hand, and even the creation of the UAC changed very little in this regard. Indeed, the most notable result of the UAC's establishment was little more than a token gesture: the application of lots of red paint on the noses, fins, rudders or wing and fin tips of most of Iraqi, Jordanian, Lebanese and Syrian fighter-bombers in the mid-1960s.

That said, Arab states did attempt to establish joint military units. The first known effort was initiated in January 1957, when four or five pilots each from Algeria (then officially still a part of metropolitan France, but already fighting for independence), Egypt, Jordan, and Syria (including Hafez al-Assad) received an order to gather at Nayrab Airport, then the base of the Syrian Air Force College. Their joint training, planned to result in the establishment of a 'pan-Arab squadron', was interrupted in April of the same year, when pan-Arabist General Ali Abu Nowar launched a failed coup attempt against King Hussein of Jordan, and all the Jordanian pilots were sent home.

Others continued their joint training until the creation of the UAR in February 1958, when the entire SyAAF was assimilated into the emerging UARAF, and most of its aircraft and ground equipment transferred to Egypt. For example, MiG-17PFs acquired by Syria (though never by Egypt), were reorganised into No. 31 'CrowBat' Squadron which until 1961 was always commanded by an officer from the Eastern Province.

A new 'pan-Arab' squadron came into being rather by accident than design. In 1962, when – in reaction to the UAR military intervention in Yemen – King Hussein of Jordan ordered a deployment of his air force to Saudi Arabia, not only the commander of the Royal Jordanian Air Force (RJAF), Colonel Sahel Hamzeh, but also six of his pilots defected to Egypt, flying a De Havilland Dove VIP transport and four Hunter F.Mk 6s. Although King Hussein offered an amnesty to the defectors, and Nasser eventually ordered the return of all five aircraft to

A night-time photograph of a MiG-17PF from No. 31 Squadron taking off. Notable is the CrowBat insignia applied on the forward fuselage: the unit remained operational – and its aircraft continued wearing the same crest – through the June 1967 War. (Dr David Nicolle collection)

in regards of military sciences. In both cases, meddling in politics not only ruined highly promising military careers, but left no trace whatsoever in the 'Arab' military thinking, strategy and tactics of the 1960s, or since.

On the contrary, the combination of ideologies like a strong military-controlled state, nationalism and pan-Arabism, and also spreading corruption, favouritism, and nepotism of the mid-1960s, resulted in the leading Arab regimes learning only one lesson: if they acquired specific types of combat aircraft and then taught their pilots for a specific number of hours in navigation, aerial gunnery, and ground attack, these would achieve the same level of proficiency as the Royal Air Force (RAF of Great Britain) – which was still the service after which all the Arab air forces of the time were patterned. Ironically, because their top brass lacked advanced military education and understanding of modern firepower and speed of weapons systems, they also completely ignored the mass of operational experience from different 'air policing' operations – whether in combat in Yemen, or against the Kurds of Iraq, or from different coups and coup attempts. Indeed: in an entirely unsubstantiated conclusion, they felt confirmed by these.

In similar fashion, all the experience from fighting Israel in 1948 and 1956 was disregarded as was the fact that adaptation of Soviet technology and military thinking to British traditions resulted in anything but the 'automatic' growth of their capabilities. Finally, neither Nasser and Amer, nor Jadid, King Hussein, or Arif in Iraq could ever permit the serious growth of air power. This was not so much for the lack of funding, as in the case of Jordan, but foremost because air power operating independently, or with greater autonomy than could be imagined by the ground-warfare officers that dominated the top brass of their armed forces (as demanded by Riyadh), and air power operating in close cooperation with ground and naval forces (as demanded by al-Ezz), were 'too dangerous' for their own positions.

The unavoidable result of this mix of factors was a continuous decline in readiness rates, quality of training, and the overall combat effectiveness of all the Arab air forces. Indeed, it can be said that especially those in Egypt in the mid-1960s had plummeted below all acceptable levels.

THE MEN WHO MADE THE IDF

While much lauded for its performance during the Suez War in public, internally, the IDF was anything but pleased by its performance. Moreover, the constant growth of the Egyptian and Syrian armed forces caused concern that their improvement might erode Israeli superiority. Finally, the General Staff IDF remained insistent on its ideas about the expansion of Israel, regardless of

Amman, the Jordanians decided to continue their careers with the UARAF. Tahsin Fuad Hussein Saima and Harib Arif Sandoukah were assigned as pilots to the MiG-19-equipped No. 20 Squadron, while Saqid ash-Shra served as a ground control officer that gained some fame for his call-sign: Jordan.

In 1964, No. 20 Squadron's depleted MiG-19S fleet was reinforced through a donation of aircraft of the same type from Iraq. Thus came into being the 'al-Araba Squadron'. This became famous for decorating its jets with the names of major Arab cities (known examples are *Baghdad*, *Beirut*, *Casablanca*, *Damascus*, *Khartoum*, *Mecca*, *Mosul* and *Riyadh*) applied in large white Arabic script in white, for regular participations in parades, and for escorting airliners carrying Nasser or other foreign dignitaries around the UAR.

Pilots of No. 20 'al-Araba' Squadron discussing their next training sortie in front of one of their mounts. The jet in the rear clearly carries the name of a major Arab city in white on the fuselage below the cockpit but, sadly, this remains unreadable because of the poor resolution of this photograph. (Albert Grandolini collection)

No. 20 'al-Araba' Squadron was not only a ceremonial unit, but very much retained its combat capability: pilots and jets from this unit were involved in numerous engagements with Israeli jets over Sinai between 1963 and 1966. Moreover, in 1966, the squadron was forward deployed to Yemen to escort UARAF Il-28 bombers in strikes on Royalist insurgents: reportedly, it also saw at last one engagement with Hunters of the Royal Saudi Air Force piloted by foreigners.

A Mirage IIICJ serial number 09 (the 'prefix' 4 was added to confuse foreign observers) seen early during its career with No. 101 Squadron, IDF/AF. (IDF)

what orders it received from the politicians. Successive Israeli governments provided ever less input, resulting in a situation where the General Staff and the Planning Department enjoyed almost complete autonomy in developing strategy, aims, and the resulting planning – and, just like the Imperial General Staff of the First World War in Gerfmany, they tended to focus upon military affairs in complete disregard of geopolitical and economic factors. The only politician actually in the picture about their activities was the minister of defence; however, both Ben-Gurion and Eshkol acted as their own defence ministers, and both tended to rubber-stamp nearly all IDF decisions. The ultimate result was that Israel became a heavily militarised country, with a population indoctrinated with the constant fear of looming annihilation, in which the politicians lost control over the armed forces: instead of being dictated by politicians, the objectives of the June 1967 War rose from the bottom up, from the IDF to the governmental level.[3]

While planning its 'expansion of Israel's borders', in the late 1950s the General Staff and the Planning Department began searching for new ideas and solutions. Because of the local climate and terrain – usually including good, clear weather, and lack of vegetation, which meant that air power could easily find and attack ground forces, and thus dominate the battlefield – they began focusing on obtaining the ability to knock out the enemy air power at the start of any future conflict, and then on obtaining the capability to drive their ground forces deep and fast into the rear of enemy ground formations. Initially, the principal problem for any such operation was the doctrinal differences between Moshe Dayan and his successor as Chief-of-Staff, Lieutenant General Haim Laskov. During the Suez War of 1956, Dayan insisted on splitting armoured units into small formations tasked with supporting infantry. On the contrary, highly educated and experienced Laskov (who not only distinguished himself during the First Arab-Israeli War, while commanding both the IDF/AF and the Armoured Corps of the IDF, but also while presiding over a committee responsible for the definition of Israeli military strategy) proved not only versed in supply and maintenance-related issues, but also insistent on concentrating tanks into a mobile strike force.[4]

Moreover, Laskov became a staunch proponent of the German-developed concept of *Auftragstaktik*: 'mission command', in which senior officers assign the overall mission to their subordinates, but let them use their own initiative, ideas, and planning to execute the mission. As a result of Laskov's decision to adapt this concept, higher Israeli commanders began only outlining objectives: field commanders were to draw up plans which were then constantly revised – often in great haste – to face new circumstances. To support this method of operations, Major General Matityahu 'Matti' Peled then persuaded the General Staff IDF to adopt the then new US logistic system of 'pushing' supplies forward from major depots to the front-line units, rather than pausing and letting combat units 'pull' supplies through requests. Ironically – perhaps even typically – Laskov, sometimes described as the 'most professional and most civilised Chief-of-Staff the IDF ever had' – ended his career much too early and under farcical circumstances: in 1959, he was blamed for causing a public panic throughout the country by using a 'wrongly formulated' codeword, and fired, together with director of the AMAN.[5]

Major General Yitzhak Rabin, Chief-of-Staff IDF, with Brigadier General Chaim Bar Lev (left) and Brigadier General Ezer Weizman, Chief-of-Staff IDF/AF and then Chief of Operations. (Albert Grandolini collection)

To the great luck of the IDF, Laskov's successor, Tzvi Tzur, went to great extents to implement his reforms and the new doctrine. A 'nuts and bolts' type of character (so colourless that several histories of the IDF fail to mention him even once), Tzur added the practice of careful selection and retention of officers (primarily with the help of incentives like the provision of French-made cars), and was far-sighted enough to play a crucial role both in the acquisitions of Mirage III interceptors, US-made M48 Patton main battle tanks, and MIM-23 HAWK SAMs, regardless of their immense costs. Tzur was highly influential upon his much-respected, soft-spoken and shy deputy, Rabin, who had already shaped most of the IDF's training doctrine before being appointed Operations Director in 1959, and who maintained excellent relations with Levi Eshkol.[6]

On assuming the post of the Chief-of-Staff in 1964, Rabin first took care for the IDF to absorb all the new and complex weapons systems, before upgrading support services through introduction of computer-supported management technology. Next, he strengthened the IDF/AF and the Armoured Corps through assigning the most-ambitious officers to them. It was his influence that converted all the paratrooper units into de facto special forces assets, and it was his decision to assign all the infantry-related training to the Northern Command's 1st Infantry Brigade, thus greatly increasing the quality of that branch, too. Finally, in attempt to improve the quality of reservist units – the mass of which was staffed by troops with low educational standards – Rabin also began appointing top officers (many of them paratroopers) to their command, even if this led to a dilution of the latter.[7]

EXPLOSIVE DEVELOPMENT OF ISRAELI MILITARY STRATEGY

After Laskov, Tzur, and Rabin, the fourth figure to become instrumental in planning the coming war was Ezer Weizman. Related to Dayan via his wife (she was the sister of Dayan's wife), Weizman was a colourful officer who had served with the British Army during the campaigns in Egypt and Libya during the Second World War, before joining the Royal Air Force and serving in Rhodesia, Egypt, and India. In 1948, he joined the IDF/AF, and commanded a squadron of light aircraft before converting to Czechoslovak-made Avia S.199s. In 1951, he attended the RAF Staff College in Andover, and was then appointed commander of Ramat David Air Base (AB). Having experienced the Suez War first hand, Weizman was fully aware that the IDF/AF's biggest problems were related to planning, command and communications. During the Suez War of 1956 and for years after, the radar network proved woefully insufficient, while available radio communications were so poor that it required the deployment of two C-47 transports as radio relays to communicate with pilots and the ground troops involved in operations in Sinai. Through relocating the HQ of the IDF/AF to The Kiryah, the Ministry of Defence's compound in Tel Aviv, and through training and equipping forward air controllers that travelled with the ground and naval forces, Weizman improved coordination with other services; while, through using radars made by the French company Thompson-CSF and advanced communications equipment acquired in the USA, he sought to improve the existing radar network through its strict centralisation. The result was the creation of the main military air traffic control centre – Unit 333 – at Mount Meron – the highest point in Israel. By 1967, two additional ground control stations were constructed and in operation, and they began sharing their tasks: Mount Meron, supported by a US-made General Electric AN/FPS-89 system, assumed responsibility for IDF/AF operations over northern Israel, Jerusalem for the centre, while the Mitzpe Ramon centre in the south was supported by a Bendix AN/FPS-100 radar with a range of around 400 kilometres, constructed at Mount Aricha.

Weizman proved crucial not only in improving the recruitment of better-educated cadets, but also in their retention: with the help of several public-relations campaigns, he managed to convince a growing number of air and ground crews about their vital role, while attractive contracts convinced conscripts to continue serving as professionals. He fostered an aggressive spirit within the force through intensive training and frequent competitions, and the encouragement of unit commanders to lead by example, take the initiative, and motivate their subordinates to think creatively. Starting in July 1959, the IDF/AF began honing skills of its ground

Major General Hod in front of a Mirage IIICJ (decorated with a kill marking) immediately after the June 1967 War. (Bill Norton collection)

crews in rapid refuelling and re-arming of aircraft, thus significantly shortening their turnaround times and massively increasing the maximum number of sorties each unit could launch per day. From 1963, Weizman not only ordered the construction of hardened aircraft facilities and sun shelters for combat aircraft on all bases but sought to involve his service in a growing number of engagements with Syria. Finally, he began preparing the IDF/AF for the kind of operations in which it was to excel in June 1967: sustained and massive air strikes on enemy air bases which aimed to knock out the enemy air power right at the start of any conflict. Preparations in this regard went as far as to construct a target airfield in the Negev Desert, on which air-to-ground gunnery and bomb attacks were regularly trained, until pilots learned to hit with every bomb and a minimum of shells. The pilots of fighter-bombers were taught to approach the target at relatively slow speeds for better accuracy, and to ignore ground fire. Moreover, the service ran extensive simulations and war-games examining the problems of the desired 'knockout blow': this included testing different types of ordnance which – amongst others – revealed that even relatively light bombs of 70kg were sufficient to create a 'carpet' of craters making any runway unusable.

Weizman also improved the training at the Flying School – which moved from overcrowded Tel Nov to newly-constructed Hatzerim AB, in April–October 1966 – through modernising the curriculum and methods of instruction, while replacing all foreign instructors with Israelis. Although the training became more demanding, the introduction to service of the Fouga CM.170 Magister jet trainer in July 1960 enabled not only improvements in regards of elementary and advanced training of future pilots, but bolstered the combat strength of the entire force because the school established its own attack squadron, equipped with this type.

Arguably, shortages of ammunition made the early version of the resulting plan for an onslaught on enemy air bases – Operation Anvil, developed by summer of 1965 – unrealistic. However, after Prime Minister Eshkol made sure that the deficiencies were rectified, in early 1967 a new plan came into being: Operation Focus. By then, the IDF/AF was commanded by Major General Mordechai 'Moti' Hod, who continued honing the air force to a fine edge for its airbase-attack operations, and then led it during the June 1967 War.[8]

Overall, following almost a decade of intense planning, acquisition, and training – for which there was not even a trace of an equivalent on the Arab side – the IDF felt supremely confident. The sole problem was that at the time due to Arab disunity and the continued Egyptian commitment in Yemen, the General Staff IDF did not expect an opportunity for its realisation in the same year.

Israeli air force and intelligence officers gathering around the Yak-11 flown by Captain Mohammad Abbas Helmy to Israel in 1964. (Albert Grandolini collection)

INTELLIGENCE SERVICES

Riding the wave of pan-Arabism of the late 1950s and early 1960s, and amid fierce competition for public approval between Amman, Baghdad, Cairo, and Damascus, various Arab statesmen and the public were extremely proud of their armed forces. Any military success – regardless how diminutive or unsubstantiated – was widely publicised, as were almost all details about equipment and deployments of different units. On the contrary, the aspect of internal security was greatly neglected. At the same time, next to no one busied themselves with studying the Israeli armed forces and their equipment. Indeed, this was even prohibited, as experienced by at least two UARAF pilots, both of whom were fired in 1963 for discussing the capabilities of Israeli-operated combat aircraft with their colleagues. This kind of practice resulted in one of the most important differences between 'Arab' armed forces and those of Israel as of 1967: the quality in the work of their intelligence services, and their influence upon political and military decisionmakers. Precisely this – often overlooked – aspect was to prove crucial for Israel's overwhelming success in June 1967.

In Israel at that time there were two agencies collecting 'military-grade' intelligence. The Institute for Intelligence and Special Operations – colloquially 'Mossad' – was the national intelligence agency. Its director (equivalent in rank to that of a Major General of the IDF) was directly subordinated to the Prime Minister and updated him on all major developments relevant to the security of the country on daily basis. As such, Mossad was highly influential for all political and military decisions. This is particularly interesting considering the agency's missions, objectives, purposes, and powers – indeed: even its budget – were never defined by any laws.

Officially established in 1949, and organised into divisions, during the 1960s the agency earned itself a widely-famed reputation – especially through its activities related to the Arab air forces. Arguably, its early attempts to lure British and then Egyptian pilots to defect to Israel along with their aircraft, were all fruitless: all British pilots contacted in the late 1940s turned down any offers, while a Mossad network of five of informers was arrested in Egypt in January 1961 and three of them sentenced to death a year later. However, Mossad remained persistent and in 1964 was successful in bribing Captain Mohammad Abbas Helmy of the UARAF to defect to Israel flying a Yakovlev Yak-11 trainer.

This success emboldened the Israelis, who were already on the trail of a group of 15 officers of the Iraqi Air Force (IrAF) undergoing a staff course at Randolph Air Force Base, in Lackland, Texas, USA. Undertaken in the USA in early 1964, the first attempt failed when 1st Lieutenant Hamid Dhahee turned down the offer by Mossad's 'honey trap': an attractive young woman, who assassinated him in a bar during a 'power outage'. The second ended almost in similar fashion: because of Dhahee's murder, the Iraqis withdrew their officers from training in the USA, but three of these returned to Baghdad followed by attractive 'lovers'. Eventually Captain Shaker Mahmoud Yusuf turned down the offer he received in an apartment in Baghdad, and was shot to death on 6 July 1965. The third IrAF officer approached by Mossad, Captain Mohammad Raglob, survived only half a year longer: he was thrown out of a high-speed train on 11 February 1966 during a trip to Germany. Finally, Captain Munir Ruefa (also 'Redfa') – freshly appointed the commander of MiG-21F-13-equipped No. 11 Squadron, IrAF, in June 1966 – was confronted with the 'silver or lead' offer: he accepted on condition of the Israelis taking care of his entire family of 17. Once his wife, two children, their parents and eight brothers were all evacuated to Iran, Ruefa flew a MiG-21 jet of his unit to Israel on 13 August 1966, delivering a major intelligence and propaganda coup for Mossad.[9]

Another notable Mossad operation of this period included infiltrating Wolfang Lotz from West Germany to Egypt where he collected a list of German rocket scientists working for Cairo and sent letter bombs to several of them. Moreover, Lotz's activities enabled Mossad to hire Otto Skorzeny – an Austrian, and a former officer of the Waffen-SS, who became famous during the Second World War for his involvement in the 'liberation' of the arrested Italian dictator Benito Mussolini – to assassinate Heinz Krug, the chief of a Munich company involved in the Egyptian missile industry, and to send a bomb that exploded in a factory in Helwan, killing five Egyptian workers. However, Mossad's biggest coup was the infiltration of the highest echelons of the Syrian government by Eli Cohen. Before being discovered by the Syrian and Soviet intelligence, tried and publicly executed in 1965, Cohen provided a complete plan of the Syrian defences on the Golan Heights, the Syrian Arab Army order of battle, and a complete list of its weapons inventory.

The second most important service of this kind in Israel was the Israeli Military Intelligence (abbreviated as AMAN in Hebrew). Created in 1950, this was an independent, yet overarching branch of the IDF responsible for developing the intelligence doctrine and directing the work of all intelligence services, the collection and evaluation of intelligence for security policy and military planning, the collection of military technology intelligence, mapping, and

Ex-Iraqi MiG-21F-13 flown by Munir Ruefa to Israel in August 1966, as seen a few years later, partially repainted in with highly-attractive bright red and with (PR-effective) serial '007'. (Albert Grandolini collection)

for military censorship. Although not as successful as Mossad in external operations – for example during the 'Lavon Affair', the entire group of 10 of its agents involved in an attempt to bomb US interests in Egypt was caught and sentenced (two of them to death) in 1955 – AMAN was quite successful in other fields, including operations to tap telephone cables in nearly all of Israel's neighbours.

As early as of 1954, the Syrian Arab Army caught a team of five soldiers of the 1st Infantry Brigade IDF while they were moving near an unspecified Syrian post on the Golan Heights. Given that even official Israeli military reports confirm that the task of this team was to, 'replace the batteries that powered a tap on a telephone cable used by the Syrian army', it is clear that the tap in question had already been in service for some time.[10]

This was not an exception but a rule, which is why the IDF/AF's involvement in the Suez War of 1956 began with its North American P-51 Mustang piston-engined fighter-bombers sweeping low over Sinai to cut telephone cables connecting various Egyptian air bases. Indeed, additional tapping operations were continued by AMAN and special forces of the IDF in Sinai in the 1960s. Known examples include Operation Pioneer (August 1963), and Bee-eater (March 1964), both of which were motivated by experience from the Tewfik War/Rottem Affair of 1960. However, the largest enterprise of this kind was Operation Kachal (1–2 December 1965), when three Sikorsky S-58 helicopters led by Major Eliezer Cohen deployed three parties of Sayeret Matkal – a long-range reconnaissance/special forces unit subjected directly to the General Staff IDF – deep into Sinai.[11]

The last known undertaking of tapping Egyptian telephone cables before June 1967 was Operation Yargezi (20–21 February 1967), when Aerospatiale SA.321 Super Frelon helicopters introduced to service with the IDF/AF barely a year earlier, inserted another Sayeret Matkal team. Although none of the available reports specifically mention tapping Egyptian telephone cables, they did state that all of the involved helicopters carried 'special equipment' in addition to the special forces operators. A classic type of contemporary 'special equipment' likely to be deployed on such opportunities were sealed containers of various size, containing tapping devices, recording and transmitting equipment and a power supply. Considering the level of praise and decorations the involved Israeli soldiers received from their superiors after the June 1967 War, as well as a number of specific reports from high-level Arab sources about the use of open telephone lines – and the repercussions of such actions – it is almost certain that most of these Israeli operations were related to the planting of listening devices on various Egyptian, Iraqi, Jordanian and Syrian communication cables. As numerous accounts of the involved Egyptian officers to follow will show, it is obvious that during the days before the war – and especially so on the morning of 5 June – not only numerous Arab military commanders, but also top statesmen made extensive use of public telephone communications, conferring on various issues at length. Tapping of telephone cables were thus the only logical source for the extremely

Israel acquired four French-made SA.321 Super Frelon helicopters in 1966, and they were promptly rushed into clandestine operations well inside Egypt and other Arab countries – so also those related to tapping of telephone cables. (Bill Norton collection)

precise intelligence the AMAN continued collecting throughout the morning of 5 June 1967, and its – and thus the IDF/AF's – intimate knowledge about the dispositions, capabilities and intentions of Arab air and ground forces.[12]

As well as telephone tapping operations, Israeli intelligence was heavily reliant on aerial reconnaissance: correspondingly, the IDF/AF regularly flew photo-reconnaissance operations over all of the neighbouring countries, collecting huge amounts of excellent intelligence on all air bases, airfields, major military bases, and other installations of interest. During the 1950s, this task was primarily assigned to old Boeing B-17G bombers and De Havilland Mosquitoes. For example, one B-17 overflew Jordan to reach western Iraq and take photographs of the airfield near the H-3 pumping station on the pipeline connecting Kirkuk with Haifa: a site that was to play its role during the war in June 1967. Such operations were subsequently relegated to Meteor FR.Mk 9, and then to Vautour IIBs: on 23 January 1962, a single Vautour overflew the breadth of Egypt to the border with Libya and then back, evading numerous interception attempts by the UARAF. Starting in 1964, the task of photo-reconnaissance was assumed by modified Mirage IIICJs and then by custom-equipped Mirage IIIRJs: over the following years, these flew dozens of high- and low-altitude penetration operations over Lebanon, Syria, Jordan, Iraq, and Egypt, enabling both the AMAN and the Intelligence Department of the IDF/AF to ready extremely precise files on every single enemy air base. Meanwhile, two Vautour IIBs were modified for electronic warfare reconnaissance: they proved crucial not only for the IDF/AF's capability to monitor the work of enemy radar stations but even the slow build-up of the Air Defence Command (ADC) of the UAR: indeed, thanks to their work, the Israelis obtained the capability to develop electronic countermeasures that could severely disrupt the work of both enemy early warning radars and ADC's Soviet-made S-75 surface-to-air missiles (SAMs; ASCC/NATO reporting name for S-75s was 'SA-2 Guideline').

KINDERGARTEN[13]

In comparison to AMAN, Mossad, and the Intelligence Department of the IDF/AF, the functionality and effectiveness of nearly all national and military intelligence services of the Arab countries in the mid-1960s can only be described as a 'kindergarten': their principal task was securing the loyalty of all top civilian authorities and military officers – and thus controlling them, *instead* of espionage against the Israelis. A confirmation of this was provided by Air Vice Marshal Abdul Hamid Abdul Salem Daghedi, General Officer Commanding the Eastern Air Command, UARAF, who during the investigations into the reasons for the catastrophic defeat of June 1967, bitterly complained:

> The intelligence service in my command station… was spying on me, not for me. Their information was often contradictory because they were fighting for power. I discharged the entire intelligence services only days before the war broke out. I therefore depended on my own men, but one of them betrayed me and did not perform his patrol sortie at the designated time. He had left the command office and gone home. Hours later, the air strike took place.

However, not only a cross-examination of information provided by a host of other sources – whether in Egypt or in Israel – but also simple logic reveals this statement as a cheap excuse. Not only was there no way the good Air Marshal could change anything at all if depending on information from a single 'patrol sortie', but because the problem was systemic and – as usually in cases of this kind – starting from the head: no matter what kind, all Arab intelligence services were primarily tasked with securing the survival of the regimes they served. There is no better example for this than of the Air Force Intelligence Directorate in Syria, which Hafez al-Assad converted into his very own, private security service, primarily tasked with ascertaining his survival and that of Jadid's regime, and suppressing any kind of opposition.[14]

A possible exception was the DM1 in Egypt. However, in that case, the question is what kind, and how much intelligence was collected by this service, and what of that ever reached Nasser, Amer, or any military commanders to whom it was relevant? Was it put to any use, and did it influence their decision-making in any way?

While the answer might appear to be 'obvious' at first glance, it is anything other than certain upon a closer examination. According to the memoirs of DM1's contemporary director, General Mohammed Sadek, the service did its duty, but the top Egyptian political and military leadership ignored the provided intelligence and warnings. A closer study reveals quite a colourful set of answers. Perhaps the best example is that after the catastrophe of the June 1967 War, Sadek complained that the UARAF flew only two reconnaissance sorties over Israel during the 1950s and 1960s. This is now known to be incorrect: Ilyushin Il-28R reconnaissance bombers of UARAF are known to have flown at least five such sorties between April 1958 and September 1961 alone. Moreover, these subsonic jets – considered 'hopelessly obsolete' ever since Israel pressed into service supersonic Mirage IIIC interceptors in 1963 – are known to have also flown at least two reconnaissance sorties along the armistice lines with Israel in May 1967. Finally, nobody is known to have prohibited Sadek from requesting the UARAF to send its Il-28Rs on additional reconnaissance sorties during the second half of May and early June 1967. On the contrary, and as explained below, MiG-21F-13 pilots from No. 45 Squadron, forward deployed at Meliz AB, in Sinai, flew a series of 'joy rides' around and over Israel during the same period of time, but none was equipped for reconnaissance purposes, and thus they collected exactly zero intelligence in that fashion. The truth was that lacking a better and less vulnerable reconnaissance platform than the Il-28R, the DM1 and UARAF practically gave up their attempts to track developments in Israel by the means of aerial reconnaissance; and that it was only after 18 May that Nasser and Amer began basing their decisions on intelligence provided by the DM1 – instead of upon Soviet sources.[15]

Ultimately, this combination of their regimes' obsession with internal security, massive underestimation of the Israelis, and professional incompetence at the top, rendered all of the 'Arab' intelligence services near-useless. While Mossad, AMAN, and the Intelligence Directorate of the IDF/AF were providing excellent and detailed information directly to top political and military decision makers, services like the DM1 were providing too little and much too unreliable information, and rarely exercised serious influence in any kind of decision-making.

3

ESCALATION

With hindsight, the conclusion can be drawn that not only were all the ingredients for the next Arab-Israeli War in place as early as 1964, but that the outcome of such a conflict was near certain around the same time. The governments in Amman, Cairo and

Damascus knew they were ill-positioned to fight a war with Israel, but continued running fierce propaganda campaigns against each other, while in Israel Rabin and Weizman began exercising pressure upon Eshkol's government to start deploying air power against the construction site of the Syrian irrigation project.

THE DAN INCIDENT

Ironically, Israeli pressure upon Syria was playing straight into the hands of Jadid's regime. Deeply unpopular at home, the regime needed a suitable distraction and concluded that Israel's NWC was the perfect target. Therefore, when – on 7 October 1964 – the IDF moved its armoured bulldozers into the southern DMZ again, the Syrian Arab Army promptly opened fire. The Israelis withdrew – only to return in force. On 3 November, the IDF resumed construction work on a 'patrol track' inside Syria, made to prevent the Syrians from gaining control over the River Dan's underground rivulets. This had the desired effect: with the Syrian Arab Army units usually deployed on the Golan Heights being largely staffed by Arabs and Druze ethnically cleansed from northern Palestine, it did not take them long to retaliate with an artillery barrage against Kibbutz Dan, the nearest Israeli settlement. The IDF/AF 'retaliated' with the deployment of more than 80 fighter-bombers, covered by a similar number of sorties by interceptors. These hit not only the 'provoking' Syrian artillery positions, but completely demolished the construction site outside the ruined village of Tewfik, killing at least a dozen civilian workers.[1]

The Syrian Arab Air Force did not react. Only a day later, when a SNCASO SO.450 Vautour IIBR reconnaissance fighter of the IDF/AF attempted to take post-strike reconnaissance photographs, two MiG-21F-13s were scrambled from Dmeyr AB. When the jets approached the Golan Heights at high altitude, they were attacked by a pair of Mirage IIICJs, and one was damaged by cannon fire. The Syrian wingman turned around and fired both of his R-3S infrared homing, short-range, air-to-air missiles (ASCC/NATO reporting name 'AA-2 Atoll'), but these appear to have missed. Eventually, all five jets returned safely to their bases.[2]

GOADING INTO A WAR

Ironically, the party most fiercely complaining about what became known as the 'Dan Incident' – was Israel. Tel Aviv announced that Israel's survival depended on 'adequate' supply of water, and that any attempts to prevent it from taking its 'fair share' of the River Jordan would be considered an attack on its sovereignty. Damascus was shocked by the ferocity of the Israeli strikes, but ignored the warning and ordered the resumption of the construction work.[3]

The next clash followed only a month later but, rather unexpectedly, occurred over the West Bank and then in the wake of a series of violations of Jordanian airspace by the IDF/AF. On 21 December 1964, four Mirage IIICJs attacked a pair of Hunters scrambled to inspect an airspace violation in the Hebron area. Reinforced by another pair of their jets, the Jordanians turned

A still from a gun camera film taken by George Matta from No. 1 Squadron, RJAF, during air combat with Israeli Mirages on 21 December 1964. The IDF/AF denied losing any of its interceptors: only decades later it became known that one of its jets supposedly ran out of fuel while returning to base. (RJAF via Patricia Salti)

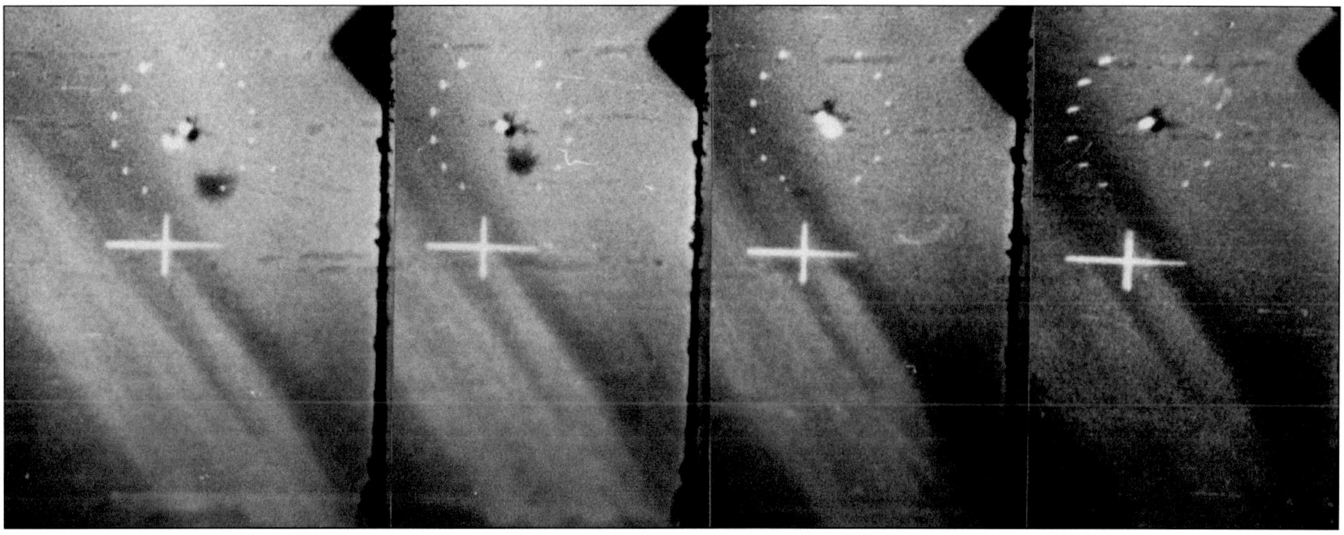

A sequence of stills from the gun camera of the Israeli Mirage IIICJ that damaged a SyAAF MiG-21 on 14 November 1964. Despite considerable damage caused by at least two 30mm hits, the Syrian pilot managed to land his aircraft safely. (IDF, via Albert Grandolini)

into the threat and outmanoeuvred all of their opponents, in turn claiming one as shot down and the other three as damaged. The Israelis denied suffering any losses in combat, but later admitted that one of the Mirages crashed because it ran out of fuel.

At this point in time, Fatah became involved: on 31 December 1964, a squad from its al-Asifa military wing, entered Israel from Lebanon with the aim of destroying one of the pumping stations for the NWC and thus provoking an Israeli counterattack which they expected would then ignite a 'pan-Arab offensive to destroy the Zionist Entity'. However, their explosive charges failed to detonate and the entire group was arrested after returning to Lebanon. Indeed, keen to avoid fighting a war with Israel, Nasser reacted by ordering a 'quiet' arrest of all Fatah activists in Egypt and Gaza. Moreover, when leaders of the PLO called for the replacement of the Hashemite monarchy in Jordan, King Hussein was not amused: this organisation's office in Amman was closed and 200 'subversives' arrested, prompting its redeployment to the healthier climate of the Gaza Strip. Of course, the Syrians promptly exploited the situation to condemn both Egypt and Jordan for not doing enough to support the Palestinians: eventually the three governments were goading each other into 'striking Israel', while doing their utmost to avoid getting directly involved.[4]

WATER WAR, TAKE 3

By March 1965, a stretch of 15 kilometres of the Syrian diversion project was ready when an IDF patrol entered Syrian territory along the 'patrol track' – and came under Syrian fire. Having an entire armoured brigade deployed nearby, the IDF reacted with withering fire: as well as demolishing the position from which the Syrians had fired, the Israelis also hit the construction site. Undaunted, Damascus shipped new equipment and also issued a strict order that its officers were to avoid firing in reaction to the Israeli provocations. Therefore, it was left to the Israelis to provoke again: on 13 May 1965, Israeli tanks entered Syria, drove to the construction site, and opened fire at the machinery and workers: instead of another 'retaliation', the Ba'ath-regime in Damascus reacted with bitter complaints about Cairo and the Arab League.[5]

With his armed forces committed to Yemen, Nasser remained keen to avoid an escalation: during several of his public appearances through 1965 and 1966, he warned of a confrontation with Israel, stressing this would put the Arab world against the might of the USA and other Western powers, and that it was unrealistic to expect the Soviets to provide support. Several times, he attempted to convince Syria to stop or at least postpone their diversion works, even threatening them that if Israel attacked Syria, the UAR would not come to their rescue. Aside of this, in mid-1966, he sent his head of unconventional weapons projects, General Azm ad-Din Mahmud Khalil to Paris, for a meeting with Meir Amit, director of Mossad. Sadly, the talks proved inconclusive.[6]

This time, it was Moscow that came in between. On 25 March 1966, the Soviet Foreign Ministry informed the Israeli ambassador that it 'knew' the IDF was massing on Syria's borders and was ready to invade. The Israelis took the accusations very seriously: the ambassador denied vehemently, and Eshkol did the same to the Soviet ambassador to Tel Aviv, adding assurances for Syrian territorial integrity. Satisfied that its 'warning' was enough, and also 'proof of the Soviet solidarity with the Arab nation', Moscow left it at that. However, in August 1966, Tel Aviv returned to the practice of provoking. After accusing the Syrians of 'attacking Israeli night fishermen and stealing from them', on 14 August 1966 an IDF landing vessel patrolling Lake Tiberias opened fire at a Syrian fishing boat and then beached on the lake's eastern shore in violation of the ceasefire agreement of 1949. The following morning, nearby Syrian army units took it under fire, injuring several crewmembers: in turn, these were hit by a series of Israeli air strikes. Rather slowly, the SyAAF reacted by sending a pair of MiG-17Fs escorted by four MiG-21F-13s to counterattack: however, the two fighter-bombers missed with their unguided 57mm rockets and one was shot down by Israeli 20mm cannons and crashed, killing the pilot. When two additional MiG-21F-13s scrambled to provide cover for the withdrawing formation appeared on the scene, they were ambushed and one jet shot down, together with its pilot.[7]

Concerned by renewed tensions, in September 1966 Nasser sent Major General Sa'adi Najib Ali and Brigadier General el-Hinnawy of the UAC to Damascus with an offer of help. However, neither Jadid, nor Assad would even meet them. Instead, Major General Suweidani, Chief-of-Staff of the Syrian Arab Army, explained to them that his country lacked the facilities necessary for the deployment of Egyptian combat aircraft and ground troops. Certainly enough, this was a blatant lie, but perhaps one that was understandable: during the same month, Major Salim Hatum – apparently supported by the

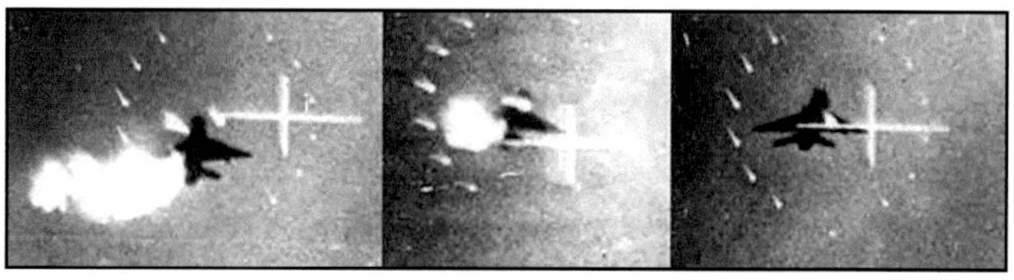

A sequence of stills from a gun camera film taken by the Mirage IIICJ piloted by Yehuda Koran on 14 August 1966, recording the first confirmed victory for this type in the form of a Syrian MiG-21F-13. (IDF)

A quartet of Mirage IIIs (led by a Mirage IIIBJ single-seater) from No. 119 Squadron IDF/AF, the unit based at Ramat David Air Base, and thus most often involved in clashes with the Syrian Arab Air Force of the mid-1960s. (IDF)

The right wing of Lieutenant Ghazy Abdul Kader el-Wazwazi's MiG-17F after it was recovered from Lake Tiberias, together with the body of the pilot, about two weeks after the clashes of 14–15 August 1966. (IDF)

Jordanian Secret Service and the Central Intelligence Agency (CIA) of the USA – attempted a coup in Damascus: this was only averted by the quick reaction of Assad's militia, and his threat to deploy the SyAAF in an all-out attack on Hatum's birthplace Suweida: eventually, the mutineer and his surviving aides fled to Jordan. Unsurprisingly, Jadid and his aides were not interested in letting any foreign troops into the country.

SAMU RAID

In an attempt to bolster the standing of Damascus, in October 1966 Moscow again accused Israel of massing troops near the armistice line with Syria. This time, the warning appeared to work because for a while afterwards the Israelis proved reluctant to resume their provocations and redirected their 'retaliations' against Jordan. Nevertheless, during the visit of a senior RAF officer in mid-October 1966, both Rabin and Weizman openly talked about a plan for a major operation to occupy the Golan Heights.[8]

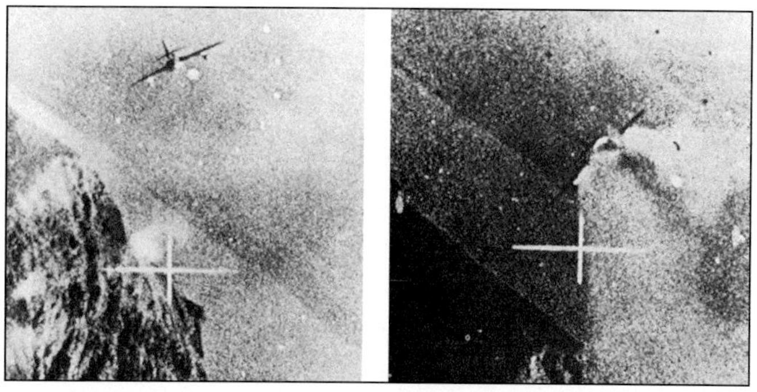

Two stills from the gun camera film taken by the Mirage IIICJ piloted by Ran Ronen showing the moment the Hunter F.Mk 6 piloted by Jordanian Muwaffaq Salti was hit and began streaming fuel while banking to the left. (IDF)

Concerned about rising tensions but keen to avoid a war, Nasser then officially recognised Fatah while entering a mutual defence pact with Syria, signed on 4 November 1966. This stipulated that Damascus was to restrain from actions that might provoke Israel, and that in the event of war it would put its armed forces under the control of the UAC. Surprisingly enough, this act achieved at least one objective, even if temporary: it deterred Israel from launching additional attacks on Syria. Instead, when on 11 November 1966 an Israeli border patrol vehicle hit a mine placed by Fatah, killing three and wounding six, the IDF turned its attention to Jordan – the government of which was not only abstaining from supporting attacks on Israel, but was meanwhile secretly negotiating peace. Alleging that the attack had originated from Jordan, and aiming to destroy three villages south of Hebron, early on 13 November, a brigade-sized force of the IDF crossed the armistice lines into the West Bank and entered Samu, Kirbet el-Markas and Kirbet Jimba: most of the civilians were cleared out of their houses and these then blown up. The 48th Battalion of the Jordanian Army attempted to intervene, but was ambushed and suffered heavy losses. The Israelis then withdrew leaving behind three Jordanian civilians and 15 soldiers killed, and 41 wounded. A pair of RJAF Hunters scrambled from Mafraq AB found themselves under attack from at least eight

Flight Lieutenant Farouq Abdeen in the cockpit of the Hunter F.Mk 6 serial number 706/G he flew on 13 November 1966, proudly showing a kill marking for an Israeli Mirage he claimed shot down during the air battle of Samu. (Farouq Abdeen collection)

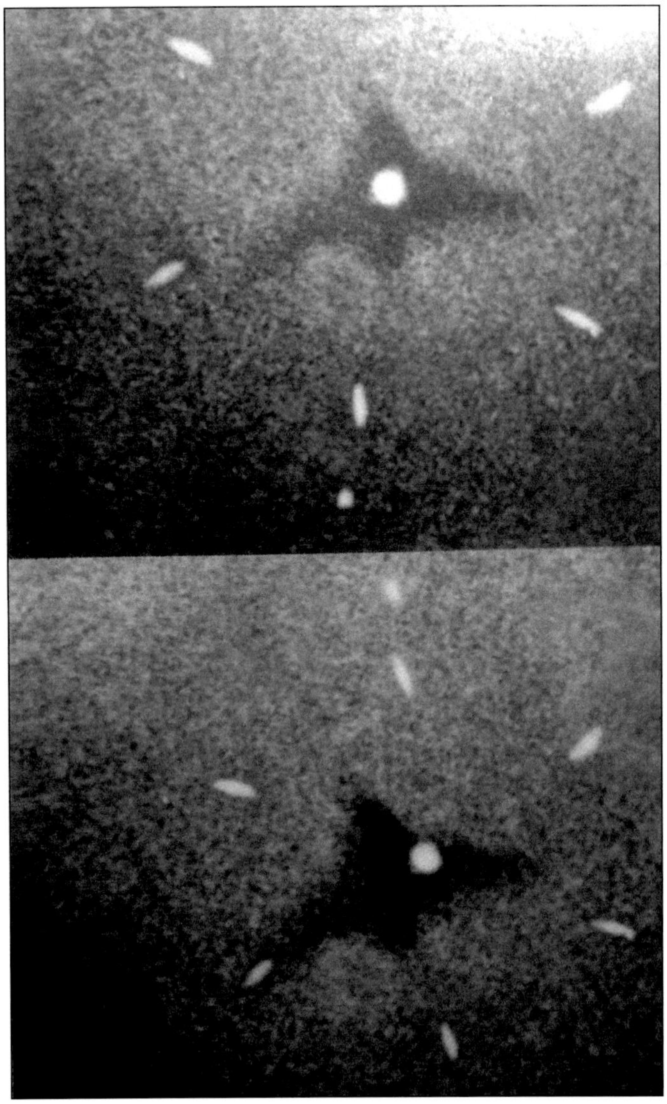

Two gun-camera stills from the film shot by Flight Lieutenant Farouk Abdeen on 13 November 1966, showing his pipper right on one of two Israeli Mirages at which he fired that day. Abdeen was credited with a confirmed kill, while the Israelis denied any losses. (Farouk Abdeen collection)

Mirages, and were forced to evade by manoeuvring at low altitude. Despite the intervention by two additional Hunters, the Israelis then shot down one Jordanian fighter, killing its pilot. In turn, one of the Jordanians claimed to have hit a Mirage with a burst into the left wing: UN personnel underway inside Israel reported this aircraft making a forced landing near Acre, and thus the RJAF pilot was credited with an aerial victory.[9]

What became known as the 'Samu Incident' or the 'Battle of Samu' was another unprovoked and disproportionate Israeli attack that was disapproved of even by Washington yet had no consequences for Israel. It completely ruined its relations with Jordan and threatened even the position of King Hussein, who found himself facing not only an aggression but also a near mutiny from within his armed forces that felt humiliated. However, suspecting that the Israeli provocation was designed to set off a Jordanian retaliation that could be used as a pretext for an Israeli invasion of the West Bank, he decided not to react.[10] Instead, King Hussein accused Nasser of not doing enough to defend Palestinians and 'hiding behind the skirts' of the UNEF contingent in the Sinai Peninsula. This was a blow that was well-remembered by Nasser – and by Ameer: henceforth, they became eager to get rid of the UN forces.

That Israel was undeterred by international reaction to its attack on Jordan became obvious on 29 November 1966, when a

A sequence of stills from a gun camera film taken from the Mirage IIICJ piloted by Michael Haber showing the MiG-19S flown by Lieutenant Khalid el-Daly in the process of being hit by fire from 30mm guns. El-Daly ejected safely: his wingman, Lieutenant Mohammed Abdel Moneim, was killed by an R.530F air-to-air missile fired by Haber about a minute earlier. (IDF via Albert Grandolini)

Piper light observation aircraft of the IDF/AF was intentionally sent into the UAR airspace over Sinai. Two MiG-19S from No. 20 Squadron UARAF were scrambled from Kabrit AB to investigate. As they approached the area in question at medium altitude, they were ambushed by a pair of Mirage IIICJs that approached from low altitude before each fired one Matra R.530F air-to-air missile. One missed, but the other destroyed the MiG-19 of the Egyptian wingman, killing its pilot. The leader attempted to engage but was hit by cannon fire and forced to eject.[11]

AIR BATTLES OF 7 APRIL 1967[12]

In February 1967, Cairo accused Tel Aviv – and Tel Aviv accused Damascus – of troop build-ups along the ceasefire line with Syria. Before long, officials from both sides were involved in the detailed description of threatening moves made by the other side. Interestingly, UNTSO observers could not confirm anything of that kind: but nobody asked them. Meanwhile, Fatah conducted several attacks from Lebanon into northern Israel, some of which began reflecting improvements in training and equipment. On 31 March 1967, Fatah guerrillas blew up an irrigation pump and a railway running alongside the River Jordan, inside Israel. Reacting according to pre-established practice, the following day the IDF drove its armoured tractors into the southern DMZ with Syria, provoking machine gun and anti-tank fire from the Syrian Arab Army's positions next to the ruins of Tewfik. Concerned, but having prepared its forces to sufficient degree, the General Staff IDF began demanding that Eshkol and his government authorise a major operation with the aim of not only conquering the Golan Heights but also toppling the government in Damascus. Fearing a Soviet military intervention, Eshkol continued searching for diplomatic solutions: even Moscow – concerned about the possibility of the conflict in the Middle East causing a showdown with the USA – began cautioning Damascus to cool its rhetoric. However, Eshkol's efforts were thwarted by Rabin and the top brass of the IDF at every opportunity. On 7 April, two armoured tractors moved into the southern DMZ, but both were hit by Syrian anti-tank guns: the IDF responded with tank fire, against which the Syrians retaliated with artillery. When stray shells fell on Kibbutz el Katzir, the IDF/AF was ordered into action.

By the time Israeli fighter-bombers appeared on the scene, the fighting was actually over, nevertheless, they heavily bombed the

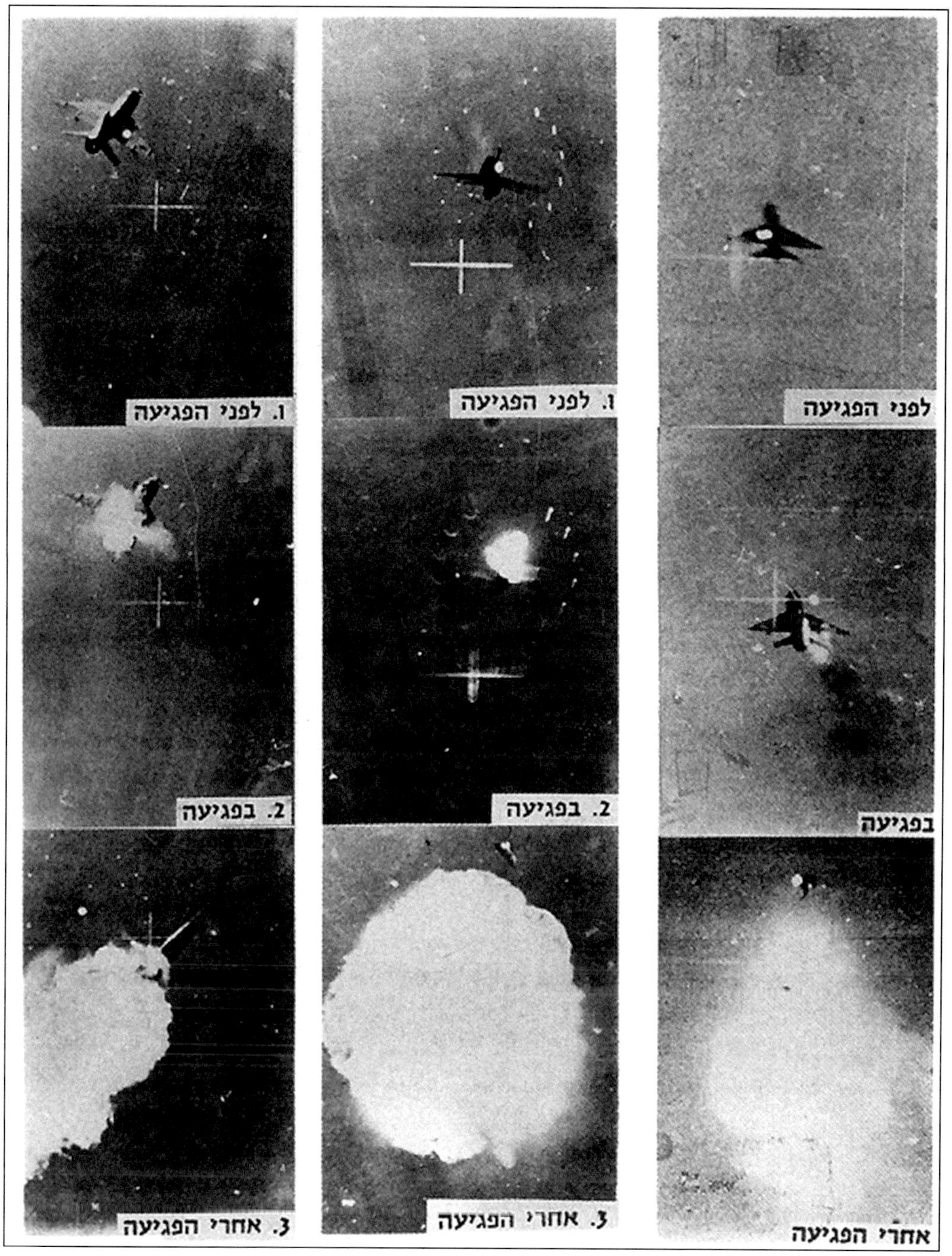

Gun camera stills taken by three different Israeli Mirages during air combats with Syrian MiG-21F-13s on 7 April 1967, showing the demise of three out of six jets claimed by IDF/AF as shot down that day. While the Syrian claim for five Israeli Mirages in return appears exaggerated, the officially admitted loss of four MiG-21s is confirmed both by official British accounts and the recollections of Syrian eyewitnesses. (IDF via Albert Grandolini)

village of Sigufiya, destroying 40 homes and killing 14 civilians. At 14.50hrs a pair of SyAAF MiG-21s attempted to catch one of the Israeli formations, when ambushed by Mirages that approached them from within Lebanese airspace: the two Syrians were forced to beat a hasty retreat. Around 15.25hrs, Syrian artillery opened fire at Kibbutz Gadot, causing heavy damage, and the IDF/AF was scrambled into a new attack: this time the villages of Amrat Azzedine, Nasarieh, and Jalabina were heavily hit by dozens of bombs. Around 15.50hrs, four MiG-17s hit back at Kibbutz Ein Gev, before the escorting pair of MiG-21s came under attack from two Mirages, but all six Syrian pilots escaped into the clouds before any was hit. At that point in time, Weizman escalated the situation beyond what he was authorised to do and upgraded a 'local border incident' into a move of strategic significance: he ordered two formations of Mirages into Syrian airspace. One of these clashed with a pair of MiG-21s and after missing with Shafrir Mk 1 infrared homing air-to-air missiles, re-attacked with guns: one of the Syrian jets was shot down and its pilot killed. Emboldened, the IDF/AF continued sending interceptors into the enemy airspace and around 17.10hrs four MiG-21s were scrambled from Dmeyr AB. They engaged six or eight Israeli jets southeast of Damascus – with grave consequences: three MiGs were shot down. All three pilots ejected safely and descended under their parachutes south of the Jordanian border, where they were arrested at gunpoint. Ultimately, the Israelis claimed to have shot down six Syrian fighter jets for no loss of their own. Damascus acknowledged the loss of four aircraft but claimed five Israelis as shot down in return.

Once again, and despite heavy Syrian losses in civilians and MiG-21s, Nasser did everything in his power to prevent a further escalation. On 10 April 1967, he sent Air Marshal (Major General) Sidqi Mahmoud and Field Marshal (Major General) Muhammad Fawzy to Damascus, to investigate reports about an Israeli military build-up along the armistice line, plea for the Syrians to end support for Fatah, and to abstain from provoking Israel. However, there was little the Syrians could do, because they were the party that had been systematically provoked by the Israelis. Unsurprisingly, Jadid refused to end his support for Fatah. More surprising was that he rejected an offer for deployment of UARAF interceptors in Syria. Ironically, Sidqi and Fawzy then made a 'U-turn' and agreed that, in the event of war, the UARAF would operate according to Operation Rashid, developed by the UAC, with the aim of pinning down the bulk of the IDF/AF, and thus enabling the Syrian Arab Army to drive across Galilee to Haifa.[13]

LIGHTING THE FUSE

Unknown to everybody involved, over the following two weeks, the situation had reached the point of no return. Not only had Eshkol and Rabin publicly threatened Syria: on 12 May 1967, the United Press International published a story based on information from a 'high Israeli source', according to which the IDF was poised to take military action to topple the government in Damascus if they failed

BREZHNEV'S FATEFUL MISCALCULATION

General Secretary of the Communist Party of the Soviet Union and Chairman of the Presidium of the Supreme Soviet (head of state), Leonid Brezhnev – the man who lit the fuse to the crisis that led to the June 1967 Arab-Israeli War, while attempting to steer the developments in the Middle East 'by remote control'. (Albert Grandolini collection)

For decades after the June 1967 Arab-Israeli War, there was intense debate between politicians and historians alike about the reason for Moscow providing false information to Egypt. Most of the decision makers involved were 'sure' that the USSR had provided fake intelligence about Israeli intentions towards Syria to Nasser. However, there was no firm evidence for this, and the question was why did Moscow do it?

Contemporary director of the DM1, General Sadek, suspected the Soviets were eager to provoke a confrontation between Damascus and Tel Aviv to prompt the Israelis into an invasion that would topple Jadid's regime and thus open the way for the Syrian Communist Party to assume power from the Ba'ath. Others argued that the USSR instigated the war in order to increase the Arab dependence upon itself, even though it had no desire to bring about the destruction of either Israel or Syria. Yet others contended that the Soviet leadership was divided over its Middle East policy as a result of a power struggle between members of the top political leadership, with the 'adventurous' group – led by the Secretary of the Communist Party of the Soviet Union (CPSU), Leonid Brezhnev – being prepared to go to war and instigating a conspiracy to precipitate an armed conflict, while the other wing was sceptical about the Arabs being prepared for a war and therefore advocated a cautious policy. A fourth version contended that Moscow had no desire to encourage a war against Israel and only attempted to avert the danger of an Israeli attack on Syria. According to this version, Nasser then misinterpreted these intentions and blocked the Gulf of Aqaba without Moscow's knowledge.

In 2002, Israeli historian Uri Bar-Noi obtained Brezhnev's secret report issued at a plenary session of the Central Committee of the CPSU on 20 June 1967 from the Polish archives. His conclusions were published within the frame of the Cold War International History Project, as e-Dossier No. 8, by the Woodrow Wilson International Center for Scholars.[17]

According to Brezhnev's report, Moscow had no intention of inciting an armed conflict, but the June 1967 Arab-Israeli War was the result of grave miscalculations by the top leaders of the Central Committee of the CPSU concerning their ability to control leading Arab statesmen, particularly Nasser. The paper confirmed that there was no Soviet conspiracy to destroy Israel but that Moscow suspected that the country was planning an act of aggression against Syria. Determined to rescue the government in Damascus, the Soviets informed Egypt about the (supposed) Israeli mobilisation, hoping to manipulate Nasser into assisting Syria through concentrating Egyptian armed forces on the border with Israel. While relatively apologetic in tone, the document in question did not shed light on the controversial information regarding the supposed concentration of Israeli troops on the Syrian border, as conveyed to the Egyptians by the Soviet government in mid-May 1967. Interestingly, it did not even link that action with the outbreak of hostilities. Furthermore, the same document showed that Moscow mistakenly estimated that Israel was militarily weak and could not cope with a war on two fronts, and therefore Moscow consented to Nasser's decision to eject the UNEF contingents from Sinai.

However, from that point onwards, Moscow lost control of the crisis. The Soviets were taken aback by Nasser's blockade of the Gulf of Aqaba without having first consulted them, and then by Israel launching a swift attack that resulted in a victory within only six days. Even so, Moscow was not inclined to take any military action against Israel. It was only when the occupation of Damascus by the Israel Defense Forces (IDF) seemed imminent that the Kremlin sharply increased pressure upon Israel and even resorted to military threats. This forced the US President Lyndon B. Johnson to intervene and persuade the Israeli government to stop the fighting.

to restrain the Palestinians. The source turned out to be nobody less than Brigadier General Aharon Yariv, Director of AMAN.[14]

It was against this backdrop that on 13 May the Soviet leadership made one of its most fateful decisions: during a short visit by Sadat to Moscow, it 'informed' him that Israel was setting up an invasion of Syria for 16–22 May, with a total of 10 or 12 brigades.[15]

The moment Sadat landed in Cairo, shortly after midnight of 14 May, he rushed to Nasser's home to find the President and Amer discussing the news. By that time, several messages had arrived from Suweidani, 'confirming' the Soviet reports. Because they thought they were critically short on time – Amer's calculations were that the UAR Army would need 72 hours to deploy to Sinai, while the Soviets had announced an Israeli invasion of Syria by 16 May – the resulting conference lasted into the morning hours. It was dominated by the – meanwhile – very deep rift between Nasser and Amer: indeed, the former was still reluctant to embroil the UAR in another war. Moreover, he doubted the accuracy of the Soviet intelligence and was concerned that a war with Israel would also involve the USA. However, ultimately, Amer prevailed because he had the entire armed forces at his back, and Nasser nothing similar: on the contrary, considering the experienced from the Tewfik War of 1960 he expected to bolster his popularity with the public through countering accusations about inactivity regarding Israel. Therefore, this time the mobilisation was announced to the public.[16]

4

EGYPTIAN AIR FORCE

On 25 May 1950, Great Britain, France, and the USA issued the Tripartite Declaration: aiming to help stabilise the situation in the Middle East, this guaranteed the territorial status quo as determined by armistice agreements between Israel and her neighbours, outlined the parties' commitment to peace and stability in the area, and their *opposition to use even the threat of force.*[1] Moreover, the Tripartite Declaration reiterated the three great power's opposition to the emergence of an arms race between the Arab states and Israel. While acknowledging that both sides needed to maintain a certain level of armed forces for the purposes of legitimate self-defence, the three powers agreed to consider all applications for arms or war materials by the countries of the Middle East in the light of these principles. To strengthen the Tripartite Declaration as a proper instrument of ensuring neutrality in the Arab-Israeli feud of the West in general, and of the USA in particular, the parties set up the Near East Arms Coordinating Committee (NEACC) in June 1952. This body was tasked with coordinating arms sales to all parties in the conflict.[2]

It is entirely unsurprising that the sheer existence of the Tripartite Declaration and the NEACC are nowadays entirely forgotten, for both proved an entirely pointless exercise even before coming into being. The administration of US President Harry S. Truman realised the severity of mistakes in its Middle East policies only days after officially recognising Israel, and subsequently attempted to treat the Arabs and Israelis more even-handedly. This is why it became instrumental in the creation of the Tripartite Declaration and why the subsequent administration of President Eisenhower remained faithful to the pledge and continued to refuse any major arms deliveries to the Middle East. However, it was already too late: not only were all subsequent US actions viewed with deep suspicion by leading Arab politicians, but the governments of Great Britain and France acted in an entirely different fashion. Considering how many major arms deals were negotiated and concluded between Cairo and London between 1950 and 1954 and then cancelled, one might think that the United Kingdom respected the Tripartite Declaration. France, however, followed by several other European countries, could not care less. In 1951 it signed the first of several major contracts for arms deliveries with Israel. Together with additional agreements in 1954, the French actions rendered both the Tripartite Declaration and the NEACC completely futile: a major arms race was now on – and nowhere was this more obvious than in regards of the growth of the air forces through the 1950s and the 1960s, presented in this and the following chapters, and in alphabetic order.

NEVER-ENDING SEARCH FOR EQUIPMENT

Originally established in 1932 and converted into an independent branch of the armed forces in 1937, the Egyptian air force experienced decades of British dominance early during its existence: essentially, it received only the equipment London was ready to deliver; rarely what the government in Cairo wanted or was able to afford. Always mistrusted by the British, it was held back and saw little involvement in the Second World War, although dozens of its pilots served with RAF units responsible for transfer of aircraft over western Africa to different frontlines. Although lacking modern equipment and pilots with significant combat experience, it distinguished itself during the First Arab-Israeli War and flew combat sorties over the emerging Israel until the final day of that conflict.[3]

Egypt became the first country in the Middle East to place an order for jet-powered aircraft, when – in August 1948 – it issued an order for eight Gloster Meteor F.Mk 4s and six refurbished T.Mk 7 two-seat conversion trainers in Great Britain. London delayed the delivery to October 1949. Ten additional examples followed by early 1950, but by then the Egyptians had become severely frustrated with British delays. For example, an order for 50 De Havilland Vampire FB.Mk 52s and their licence production was cancelled after delivery of just 20 (and one FB.Mk 5). This is why during the First Arab-Israeli War, in the summer of 1948, Egypt had little choice but to purchase a total of some 19 Fiat G.55As and two G.55B two-seat conversion trainers from Italy, followed by 62 Macchi C.205Vs, deliveries of which lasted into 1951.

Because of chronic shortages of training aircraft, both types were relegated to training duties as soon as London permitted the delivery of 19 Spitfire F.Mk 22s and one T.Mk 9 in 1950. Two years later, London finally granted permission for deliveries of Meteor F.Mk 8s to Egypt, but only four arrived before another embargo was imposed and, to add salt to the injury, four of the remaining eight examples from this order were sold to Israel instead. The other four followed only in 1955, when London also agreed to sell six Meteor NF.Mk 13 night interceptors equipped with the massive AI.10 radar set installed in a stretched nose. While these reached Egypt in early 1956, due to the lack of support in regards of technical documentation and instruction only two are known to have actually entered service. Rather unsurprisingly, in 1954–1955, Cairo contracted Rome for the delivery of 58 refurbished Vampires manufactured by Aermacchi.

The Egyptian search for a modern advanced trainer to replace about 20 North American T-6 Texan/Harvards left over from the Second World War, proved at least as problematic: in 1953, London embargoed an order for 15 Canadian-built examples, and Cairo was only able to acquire 22 De Havilland Canada DHC-1 Chipmunks from Canada instead.

CZECHOSLOVAK ARMS DEAL

In addition to the Israeli raids of 1954–1955, the on-off nature of Egypto-British relations of the time led to the Czechoslovak Arms Deal. This resulted in deliveries of 80 MiG-15bis and six MiG-15UTIs, 45 Ilyushin Il-28 light bombers, four Il-28U conversion trainers, 20 Ilyushin Il-14 transports, and 25 Yakovlev Yak-11 training aircraft to Egypt. A series of additional contracts with Moscow secured, amongst others, the delivery of 24 more powerful MiG-17Fs and 26 Czechoslovak-made Mraz Sokol basic trainers in 1956.

The first MiG-15s reached Egypt in August 1955 and they formed the backbone of the Egyptian air force during the Suez War of 1956, by when MiG-17s were also in service. Contrary to most Western reports, thanks to the hard work of the Czechoslovak advisers, the Egyptians had enough pilots to man all of their new jets: indeed, by October of that year, the Egyptian air force possessed a rudimentary radar network, which was to prove its worth early during the conflict when MiGs were wrestling with Israeli jets for control of the airspace over the Sinai Peninsula, and then – together with Meteor NF.Mk 13s – became involved in attempts to intercept some high-flying British bombers.

Pilot posing with a MiG-17F (serial number 269?) of the Fighter Training Unit (FTU) of the UARAF in 1959. Notable in the right corner is the antenna of the Kremniy-2 'identification friend or foe' (IFF) system, installed atop the centre fuselage. Frequently ignored by pilots of this period, IFF systems became highly important once both Israel and Egypt introduced SAM systems to service in 1965–1966. (Dr David Nicolle collection)

A rare air-to-air view of a MiG-15UTI – the principal training jet of the UARAF in the early 1960s. In addition to the unit insignia applied on the forward fuselage, clearly visible are the traditional identification stripes around the wingtips (three) and the rear fuselage (two), always applied in black. (Dr David Nicolle collection)

Prompted by the Israeli acquisition of Boeing B-17 Flying Fortress four-engined heavy bombers during the First Arab-Israeli War, the Egyptian air force sought to acquire its own bomber component. In 1949–1950, London granted permission for the export of nine Avro Lancaster B.Mk 1s and nine Handley Page Halifax A.Mk 1s to Egypt, but curbed the provision of spares and training for them. While still including three aircraft of each type, as of 1955, all of these were grounded and Egypt's bomber fleet effectively ceased to exist.

The Egyptians did not suffer such massive losses in training before the Suez War of 1956, nor in combat during that conflict as usually claimed by the British, French, and the Israelis, but: there is no doubt that their air force was significantly degraded. Only 32 MiG-15bis and six MiG-17Fs, together with at least 20, possibly up to 37 Il-28s, were still operational as of mid-November of that year. However, the training and transport fleets were almost completely obliterated. Correspondingly, in February 1957, when Cairo and Prague concluded their third arms deal – which aimed to replace attrition losses – this included orders for 30 MiG-15bis and six MiG-15UTIs, 30 Il-28s and two Il-28Us, 40 Yak-11s, 50 Zlin Z.226Ts, 10 Aero L-60 Brigadyrs, and five Ilyushin Il-14s, while 77 MiG-17Fs were acquired to expand the fleet. Moreover, 20 surviving MiG-15bis originally purchased by Syria – delivered to Egypt in early 1956, because their crews were to be trained there (the other 21 Syrian MiG-15bis were destroyed during the Suez War) – were donated by Damascus.

ALL-OUT ACQUISITION

Despite the above-mentioned cooling in relations between Cairo and Moscow, starting in 1957 a practice was introduced where a new major arms deal would be negotiated – and the related contracts signed – every second year. As well as the above-listed aircraft, in 1957, Egypt ordered the construction of a factory capable of overhauling all the Czechoslovak- and Soviet-made aircraft in the country. Moreover, in 1958, the Egyptian and Syrian air forces were integrated into the United Arab Republic Air Force (UARAF): as a result, all the Chipmunks, MiG-17PFs and Il-28s acquired by Damascus were transferred to Egypt, while only two squadrons of MiG-17Fs were deployed to the Eastern Province.

In 1959, in the aftermath of a series of clashes with Israel in 1958–1959, the UARAF was forced to conclude that the brand-new Dassault Super Mystère B.2s (SMB.2s) of the IDF/AF were superior to its MiG-17s and MiG-17PFs. Moreover, Moscow had already supplied supersonic MiG-19S interceptors to Baghdad. Correspondingly, Cairo placed an order for 56 jets of the same type. Due to the ongoing disagreements with Nasser, and because the series production of that type was now over, the Soviets were slow to deliver, and what arrived in Egypt were only superficially overhauled aircraft from surplus stocks of their air force. Unsurprisingly,

Symbolic of the two principal new combat aircraft types of the UARAF in the early 1960s, this photograph shows a row of three MiG-21F-13s (the one to the left wears serial 5819) while overflown by three Tu-16 medium bombers. (Jens Heidel collection)

A Tu-16 (left, with serial number 4012, the 'last two' of which were repeated on the nose), and MiG-21F-13 in flight over Cairo during an annual military parade. (Jens Heidel collection)

the attrition of the MiG-19S was heavy: by 1962, the number of operational airframes was reduced to just 20: the type remained in service in 1967 only because in 1964 Baghdad donated its remaining MiG-19S fleet to the UARAF.

Intensive industrialisation of the United Arab Republics in the late 1950s, and a massive drought in its 'Eastern Province' (Syria) during 1959–1960, left the country severely indebted. This meant that Cairo was short of the money necessary for the next major deal expected in 1961. However, Moscow was meanwhile concerned about losing any semblance of influence and more than keen to continue delivering at ever more favourable terms. When in June of that year Nasser demanded deliveries of 30 SA-2 SAM systems, 150 MiG-21s, 24 Tupolev Tu-16 medium bombers, and 24 Antonov An-12 transports, the Soviets rushed to please and promised almost everything except for the interceptors in question: by that time the production of the initial operational variant – MiG-21F-13 – was nearing its end, while new variants were not yet ready. Therefore, this contract stipulated deliveries of 'only' 48 such aircraft. Moreover, SA-2s – famed for the downing of the CIA's Lockheed U-2 reconnaissance jet piloted by Francis Garry Powers over Sverdlovsk, on 1 May 1960 – were in such demand at home, that their production and deliveries to Egypt were stretched over several years.

For reasons that are going to be explained in the next chapter, the next major arms deal with Moscow, eventually signed in June 1963, provoked major differences between the leadership in Cairo, and ended with the effective exile of several Egyptian generals. At this point in time, it is important to bear in mind that as the DM1 obtained better intelligence on the Israeli order for Mirage IIICJs, the conclusion was that the 48 MiG-21F-13s ordered two years earlier would not suffice. Although Egyptian industry was developing its own supersonic jet (see the box on the ill-fated Helwan HA-300), this project lacked the support of the UARAF's commander, who actually wanted to acquire Sukhoi Su-9 interceptors. Eventually, the Soviets turned down all the related requests: instead, they agreed to

Table 2: UARAF Order of Battle, 5 June 1967

C-in-C UARAF: Air Marshall Mahmoud Sidki Mahmoud
Deputy CO UARAF: Air Marshall Abdul Amin Hafiz
Chief-of-Staff UARAF: Air Vice Marshall Ismail Labib
Chief of Operations: Air Vice Marshall Muhammad Sadid al-Jawahiri
CO UARAF in Yemen: Air Vice Marshall Fuad Afifi Ahmad

Eastern Air Command UARAF, HQ Ismailia
CO: Air Vice Marshall Abdul Hamid Abdul Salem Daghedi
Deputy CO: Lieutenant General Fawzi Desuki
Chief-of-Staff: Lieutenant General Gallal Ibrahim Zaid

Unit	Base	Equipment	Remarks
Air Group 1	Fayid (AB.233)		Base CO: Brigadier General Salah el-Manawy Air Group 1 CO: Brigadier General Tahsin Zaki
No. 1 Squadron	Cairo West	13 Su-7BMK (1)	Unit not active, all 13 aircraft in the process of assembly but all pilots reassigned to No. 31 Squadron on mobilisation
No. 55 Squadron	Fayid	17 Su-7BMK	CO: Major Abd el-Moneim el-Shennawy; 19 pilots present
AAA Regiment ??	Fayid	4 ZPU-4 and 16 S-60	CO unknown
Air Group 2	Kabrit (AB.228)		Base CO: Brigadier General Nabih al-Masry Air Group 2 CO: Lieutenant Colonel Mamdouh Ahmad Taliba Air Group 2 Chief-of-Staff: Lieutenant Colonel Firky el-Gahramy
No. 18 Squadron	el-Arish (AB.259)	6 MiG-17F 6 MiG-15bis	CO unknown; 5 MiG-15bis evacuated to Cairo West on 4 June; 8 pilots present
No. 24 Squadron	el-Sur (AB.248) Cairo West	6 MiG-15bis 9 MiG-15bis	CO unknown; nine pilots present
No. 25 Squadron	Bir Thamada (AB.260)	8 MiG-17F	CO unknown; unit previously assigned to Air Group 12; reassigned to Air Group 2 as of 26 May 1967; 9 pilots present
AAA Regiment 72	el-Arish	4 ZPU-4 and 16 S-60	CO unknown; only one battery deployed at el-Arish; others reassigned to various Army units
AAA Regiment 81	Bir Thamada	4 ZPU-4 and 16 S-60	CO unknown; originally deployed at Kabrit; redeployed to Bir Thamada; ZPU-4s ordered to redeploy back to Kabrit on 5 June
Air Group 7	Abu Suweir (AB.229)		Base CO: Brigadier General Saad Rifat Air Group 7 CO: Brigadier General Fuad Kamal Air Group 7 Deputy CO: Farouk el-Ghazzawy
No. 26 Squadron	Abu Suweir	18 MiG-21PFM (2)	CO: Maj Abd el-Hamid Helmi, 18 pilots present
No. 45 Squadron	Meliz (AB.244)	14 MiG-21F-13	CO: Maj Abdel Kafi Subhi; 18 pilots present
No. 47 Squadron	Fayid	16 MiG-21F-13 (3)	CO: Maj Amosis Azer; unit officially assigned to Air Group 7 but operating under the command of Air Group 1
Air Group 15	Hurghada (4) (AB.286)		Base CO: Brigadier General Abd al-Aziz Badr Air Group CO: Lieutenant Colonel Alaa Barakat
No. 20 Squadron ('el-Araba' Squadron)	Hurghada Fayid	12 MiG-19 8 MiG-19	CO: Maj Sayd Shalash; 15 pilots present CO: Maj Alaa Barakat; 8 pilots present
No. 40 Squadron	Hurghada	6 MiG-21FL	CO Maj Zine el-Abidine; 8 pilots present
AAA Regiment 77	Hurghada	4 ZPU-4 and 16 S-60	CO unknown; originally deployed at Inchas
Air Group 61	Abu Suweir (AB.229)		Base CO: Brigadier General Saad Rifat Air Group 61 CO unknown
No. 8 Squadron	Abu Suweir	8 Il-28	CO: Major Hanafy Mahgoub
No. 9 Squadron	Abu Suweir	7 Il-28	CO unknown
?? Squadron	Abu Suweir	8 Il-28R	CO unknown (5)
Yemen Flight	al-Rawda AB Sana'a (Yemen)	8 Il-28	CO unknown Unit forward deployed in Yemen
AAA Regiment ??	Abu Suweir	4 ZPU-4 and 16 S-60	

(Continued opposite)

Central Air Command UARAF, HQ Cairo West
CO: Air Marshall Gamal al-Din Afifi
Deputy CO: Lieutenant General Qala'awi
Chief-of-Staff: Lieutenant Colonel Abd al-Ra'uf Abd al-Hamid

Air Group 9	Inchas		Base CO: Brigadier General Abd al-Hamid Helmy Air Group 9 CO: Brigadier General Sami Fuad
No. 43 Squadron	Inchas	20 MiG-21FL	CO: Major Samir Abdullah; 16 pilots present
No. 49 Squadron	Inchas	16 MiG-21F-13	CO: Major Adil Nassr; 10 pilots present
2 AAA Batteries	Inchas	8 M1939	
Air Group 12	Cairo West (AB.310)		Base CO unknown Air Group 12 CO: Lieutenant Colonel Mohammad Nabil al-Masry
No. 5 Squadron	Cairo West	13 MiG-17F (6)	CO: Major Hassan Abd al-Qadir; unit reassigned from Air Group 1 to Air Group 12 during May 1967; 4 instructors and 17 student pilots present
FTU (OCU)	Cairo West	8 MiG-21F-13/FL	CO unknown; unit equipped with various marks of MiG-21 used for conversion purposes
AAA Regiment ??	Cairo West	4 ZPU-4 and 8 M1939	CO unknown; all four batteries of S-60s redeployed elsewhere
No. 31 Squadron	el-Arish, then Kabrit	17 MiG-17F and PF 5 MiG-15UTI	CO Major el-Derayni; including pilots qualified on Su-7s and slated to reestablish No. 1 Squadron; 14 pilots present
2 AAA batteries	Kabrit	8 ZPU-4	Newly established on 3–4 June
3 AAA batteries	location unknown	12 ZPU-4	Scheduled for redeployment to Kabrit on 5 June
Air Group 32			CO unknown
No. 11 Squadron	Bilbeis	6 Il-14	CO unknown
No. 14 Squadron	Almaza	42 Il-14	CO unknown; 22 crews available, at least 1 aircraft at el-Arish and 2 at Meliz
No. 16 Squadron	Cairo International	22 An-12BP	CO unknown; at least 2 aircraft at Cairo IAP
Air Group 65	Cairo West		CO: Lieutenant Colonel Hossni Mubarak; 17 complete Tu-16 crews present
No. 34 Squadron	Bani Suweif	8 Tu-16	CO: Lieutenant Colonel Hossni Mubarak
No. 36 Squadron	Bani Suweif	9 Tu-16	CO: Major Kamal Darwish
No. 95 Squadron	Cairo West	6 Tu-16KS	CO unknown
AAA Regiment ??	Bani Suweif	4 ZPU-4 and 16 S-60	CO unknown
Air Group?			CO unknown
No. 7 Squadron	Almaza Bir Thamada	8 Mi-6 4 Mi-6	CO unknown
No. 12 Squadron (7)	Almaza	6 Mi-1 6 Mi-4	CO unknown Subordinated to the 'Rescue Command'
No. 42 Squadron	el-Dikhelia	15 Mi-4	CO unknown; subordinated to the Navy
AAA Regiment ??	Almaza	4 ZPU-4 and 16 S-60	

(1) Okasha in *Conflict in the Sky*, Chapter 3, variously citied the presence of 16 or 17 aircraft and 19 pilots with No. 55 Squadron on the morning of 5 June 1967; at least one Su-7 was non-operational.
(2) Okasha, cited the presence of 19 MiG-21s at Abu Suweir as of the morning of 5 June 1967.
(3) Okasha, citied the presence of only 12 MiG-21s and 18 pilots at Fayid as of the morning of 5 June 1967.
(4) Note that the deployment of the Air Group 15's units to Hurghada was not related to any kind of Israeli intelligence operations, as usually reported, but took place for two reasons: the return of MiG-19s of No. 20 Squadron from Yemen, and the necessity to provide support for the above-mentioned operation against Eilat.
(5) All three Il-28 units based at Abu Suweir as of the morning of 5 June 1967 had a total of 24 fully qualified crews.
(6) Okasha in *Conflict in the Sky*, Chapter 3, citied the presence of no fewer than 26 MiG-15s and MiG-17s at Cairo West on the morning of 5 June 1967, but mentioned no MiG-21s of the FTU.
(7) Some of these helicopters were permanently assigned to the so-called Rescue Command. Before the June 1967 War, the sole task of this unit was search and rescue after an accident, and it received no training to undertake such operations under combat conditions, or beyond enemy lines. Note that although medical facilities within the Egyptian Armed Forces were generally quite good, and all the UARAF air bases of the time had small, very well-equipped hospitals capable of dealing with minor injuries and/or sickness, any serious casualties had to be sent to the Central Military Hospital in Cairo.

An Il-14 (serial number 1146) of No. 14 Squadron UARAF seen in the mid-1960s. (John Fricker collection via Simon Watson)

deliver 48 radar-equipped MiG-21FLs, and promised deliveries of Sukhoi Su-7BMK fighter-bombers.[4]

Shipments of new MiG-21F-13s, MiG-21FLs, and SA-2s were still incomplete by the time the Egyptian MiG-21s scored their first kill – which proved ruinous for relations between Cairo and Washington. On 23 December 1964, a Fairchild C-84 Packet owned by John Mechan, a millionaire from Texas and a close friend of US President Lyndon B Johnson, violated UAR airspace over the Sinai. The aircraft was intercepted by two MiG-21F-13s, the pilots of which misidentified it as an Israeli Noratlas: it first acted as if it was to follow their instructions and land at Cairo International, but then retracted the landing gear and turned away in the direction of Alexandria, and was shot down by three bursts of 30mm gunfire into one of its engines, and crashed, killing everybody on board. Mechan's death caused massive displeasure in the White House, where President Johnson made continuing provision of US economic aid to Egypt conditional upon Cairo's effort to end the war in Yemen and withdraw. Nasser reacted with several inflammatory speeches that bit the hand that fed him, prompting Johnson to abandon the traditional US policy of neutrality in the Middle East and order a halt of wheat supplies to the UAR. All of a sudden, Cairo was facing an economic collapse. Alarmed, Nasser sent the president of the parliament, Anwar el-Sadat, to Moscow, with a request for help. To Egyptian's big surprise, Moscow promptly grabbed the opportunity to rebuild its standing in Cairo – and not only supplied the necessary wheat, but also wrote off 50 percent of Egyptian debts, reduced the scheduled annual payments of some and delayed payments of others until 1971–1974. Ironically, this also resulted in the next major arms deal, which stipulated the substitution of the still incomplete MiG-21FL deliveries with the more advanced MiG-21PFM, and the expansion of the original contract for MiG-21F-13s through an additional batch. Finally, the Soviets promised to start delivering the Su-7BMKs ordered in 1963, and to help complete the work on the build-up of the Air Defence Command. However, because the series production of that type began only in 1965, and it experienced numerous technical problems immediately after, it was only in early 1967 that the first Su-7s reached Egypt.[5]

The 'fantastic news' Sadat brought back from Moscow in the summer of 1966 actually brought no respite to the armed forces of the UAR. Certainly enough, Cairo was suddenly free of its debt burden, and deliveries of additional Soviet arms reopened the prospect of a further, rapid build-up – in turn opening many opportunities for advancement in rank for Nasser and Amer's favourites. However, additional Soviet arms also caused a massive rise in defence expenditure, which the economy of the UAR was unable to sustain. Left without choice, in late 1966, the government in Cairo severely curtailed the activity of its armed forces. For example, while UARAF pilots used to fly at least 200–240, often 300 and more hours a year at earlier times, most had just 20–40 hours through the first half of 1967: barely enough to remain current on their types. To cover up the crisis, and mid-way through the conversion process of half a dozen UARAF units to their new MiG-21PFMs and Su-7BMKs, Amer officially granted lengthy leave to the mass of officers and pilots. While this certainly made the Field Marshal even more popular amongst 'his' officers, it only served the purpose of further weakening the combat capabilities of the armed forces just short of the next major international crisis.

Overall, as of 4 June 1967, the UARAF thus had a total of 382 aircraft, of which 322 were serviceable and based in Egypt. Its fighter units boasted a strength of 257 aircraft, of which 189 were serviceable, including:

- 100 MiG-21F-13/FL/PFMs (89 serviceable)
- 34 Su-7BMKs (only 17 serviceable; 13 were at Cairo West but lacked pilots, while four awaited assembly)
- 27 MiG-19s (19 serviceable; remainder awaiting assembly at Hurghada)
- 70 MiG-17F/PFs (41 of these were in Egypt and serviceable; 12 in Yemen and the remainder in storage)
- 26 MiG-15bis/UTIs (21 serviceable).[6]

Two Air Groups could draw upon 23 Tu-16 medium bombers (all serviceable) and 34 Il-28 light bombers (31 serviceable). Finally, the transport units had a total of 68 transport aircraft (of which 59 were serviceable), and 39 helicopters (20 were serviceable) at their disposal. Ten additional Il-28s, as well as a similar number of MiG-15s and MiG-17s, were forward deployed at Sana'a and Hodeida air bases in Yemen.

Where crews for all these aircraft were concerned, the usual Israeli and Western mythology stresses an 'acute shortage of pilots': indeed, that the Egyptians never had enough crews to man all the aircraft and helicopters they had acquired. The reality was fundamentally different: as of 5 June, the UARAF had a total of 127

As of 1967, all MiG-15bis and MiG-17Fs of the UARAF (and SyAAF) were left in their original livery. This consisted of two layers of clear lacquer mixed with 10 percent and 5 percent aluminium powder, respectively, and was named 'silver grey' by both pilots and ground crews. Applied on Egyptian combat aircraft for the first time during the First Arab-Israeli War of 1948–1949, black identification stripes remained a norm over the following 20 years: two were always applied around the rear fuselage and three around the wingtips, where the middle stripe was three times as thick as the two outer ones. Depending on their origin, MiG-15bis of the UARAF either wore three-digit serials in the range 901–999 (ex-Syrian examples donated to Egypt in 1956), or four-digit serials in the ranges 1901–1999 or 2601–2799. (Artwork by Tom Cooper)

MiG-15bis serial number 2648, a reconstruction of which is shown here, was one of at least two jets of No. 24 Squadron UARAF still at Jebel Libni when that base came under attack from Mirage IIICJs from No. 117 Squadron. While Egyptian ground crews managed to start repairing 2648, one MiG-15bis – probably serial number 2664 (based on pilot log-books) – was completely destroyed by multiple 30mm hits and the resulting fire. Notably, during overhauls at Helwan in the mid-1960s, these jets were modified to carry MiG-17-type drop tanks and received a pair of double launchers for Sakr unguided rockets under each wingtip but never received rear-view mirrors atop their cockpit transparencies. (Artwork by Tom Cooper)

In 1958, the UARAF established an aerobatic team including six, and later nine, MiG-17s. All the jets were decorated with chequerboards on their rudders, mostly applied in red: at least two had these (and their wingtips) painted in blue instead. The MiG-17Fs flown by the team retained this livery when they received two launch rails for Sakr unguided missiles under each wingtip, and were then temporarily deployed to Yemen in 1963–1966, and after their overhauls at Helwan in 1966. The result was the appearance illustrated in this example – serial number 2235 – which was destroyed on the ground in el-Arish by two successive flights of Ouragans that attacked this base on the morning of 5 June 1967. (Artwork by Tom Cooper)

Originally acquired by Syria in 1957 (though never by Egypt), radar-equipped MiG-17PFs were integrated into the UARAF and served with No. 31 Squadron a year later. During the short-lived union of Egypt and Syria, this unit was always commanded by an officer of Syrian origin. After the dissolution of the UAR, No. 31 Squadron continued serving with the UARAF until most of its jets were destroyed on the ground in the course of five successive strikes on Fayid AB by SMB.2s of No. 105 Squadron IDF/AF. The jet reconstructed here – serial number 2803 – was one of the few that managed to take-off: it was claimed as shot down (and officially credited to an Israeli pilot). In actuality, Mustafa Hafez managed to land it safely, despite severe damage to the fin and one wing. (Artwork by Tom Cooper)

MiG-19Ss acquired by Egypt and Iraq in 1959–1961 were all painted in satin 'air superiority grey' colour overall, and wore the national insignia in the usual positions (including six roundels and fin flashes). The 56 jets originally delivered to Egypt are known to have worn serials in the range 3001 to 3099. In 1964, when No. 20 'Araba' Squadron was created through re-grouping all of the surviving Egyptian MiG-19S and aircraft donated by Iraq, many of its aircraft received the names of major Arab cities applied in white below the cockpit. Recently discovered photographs indicate that the ex-Iraqi examples also received four-digit serial numbers applied in black on the forward fuselage: most likely, these were in the range 3101–3199. This is a reconstruction of an Egyptian example with identification stripes and the name 'Qahira' (Cairo). (Artwork by Tom Cooper)

The most important fighter-bomber of the UARAF in June 1967 was the MiG-21F-13: the service had received nearly 60 by this time, of which 46 were assigned to three operational units (Nos. 45, 47 and 49 Squadrons), and eight served with the Fighter Training Unit. All wore the same 'silver grey' overall livery, together with the standard set of national insignia and identification stripes. Relatively small serial numbers in the range 5001–5299 were applied in black on the forward fuselage. Their primary armament consisted of a single 30mm gun installed internally, and a pair of R-3S air-to-air missiles, as illustrated in this example that was probably assigned to No. 45 Squadron and destroyed in the first minutes of the June 1967 Arab-Israeli War. (Artwork by Tom Cooper)

Except for their cockpit and fin, MiG-21PFMs of the UARAF differed very little from earlier MiG-21F-13s and MiG-21FLs: they were still delivered in silver grey overall, and wore the usual set of roundels in six positions, and fin flashes. Two black identification stripes were applied around the rear fuselage, and three around the wingtips. Serials were relatively small, and in the range 5401–5499. This jet – serial number 5440 – was operated by No. 26 Squadron from Abu Suweir AB: the UARAF unit that managed to scramble the highest number of its interceptors in reaction to the Israeli onslaught. Two of these, flown by Asim Ghazi and Awad Hamdi, caused the loss of two SMB.2s of No. 105 Squadron as these were returning from the opening strike on Kabrit AB. (Artwork by Tom Cooper)

Acquired as a replacement for MiG-17s, the Su-7BMK initially proved nothing but trouble. They were extremely sensitive to foreign object damage and short-ranged. The S-3K unguided rockets – illustrated in this example from No. 55 Squadron installed on their original seven-round launchers on hardpoints under the fuselage and the wing – proved entirely useless. Out of 36 Su-7BMKs delivered between August 1966 and May 1967, 34 were still around, but four of these were awaiting assembly, while 13 were stored at Cairo West in expectation of their pilots completing their conversion training. As of 5 June 1967, conversion of pilots for No. 1 Squadron was months behind schedule, and most of the pilots of No. 55 Squadron flew fewer than 20 hours in the first half of 1967. All Su-7BMKs were left in 'silver grey' livery, but had an 'anti-glare panel' applied in light grey in front of the cockpit, and none ever received the usual identification stripes seen on other models. (Artwork by Tom Cooper)

Between 1962 and 1966, the UARAF received a total of 24 second-hand Tu-16 bombers. Six were Tu-16KS, equipped with KSR-1 radar-guided anti-ship missiles; 23 were still available as of 5 June 1967. The fleet was operated by three units of Air Group 65 home-based at Cairo West. All were left in silver grey overall and wore the usual set of national markings. Bombers (like the example shown inset) had serial numbers in the range 4000–4099, the last two of which were usually based on their Soviet bort numbers, left in place as applied by their former owners. Missile-carrying Tu-16KS, as shown in the main artwork, received serials in the range 4101–4199. KSR-1 missiles were usually painted in light admiralty grey overall (BS381C/697). All but six bombers were destroyed by Mirages in the first minutes of Operation Focus on 5 June 1967. (Artworks by Tom Cooper)

One of the least-known, but most important air strikes during the first wave of Operation Focus included four flights of No. 147 Squadron's CM.170 Magisters tasked with striking Egyptian radar stations in Sinai. Armed with 68mm and 80mm unguided rockets installed underwing and internally installed 7.62mm machine guns, they knocked out P-8 radar stations in el-Arish, Bir Lahfan, and Jebel Hof without losses in return. However, this jet – piloted by Arnon Livnat, leader of one of the flights – was felled by Egyptian air defences in the Jiradi area, while on the way back to Israel. The majority of CM.170s of the IDF/AF were painted in brown (RAL8008) and blue (RAL5008) on upper surfaces and sides, and undersurface grey (RAL7044) on undersurfaces. Their orange self-adhesive stripes usually applied on the nose, wingtip fuel tanks, and butterfly fins were all removed shortly before the war. (Artwork by Tom Cooper)

Nominally, the first flight of Ouragans from No. 113 Squadron to reach their target was the one led by Ran Alon, tasked with striking Meliz AB (better known as 'Bir Gifgafa') in north-eastern Sinai. After achieving complete surprise and successfully cratering the runway with bombs, the four jets turned to attack four MiG-21F-13s from No. 45 Squadron which attempted to scramble. Two MiGs were destroyed by gunfire before they could lift-off, but the other two managed to get airborne: one was shot down immediately after, while the other either flew away (according to the Israeli version) or engaged the Ouragans in an air combat (according to the Egyptian version). The Number 3 of No. 113 Squadron's flight was the Ouragan serial number 86 piloted by David Yariv with: according to the Israelis, this jet crashed either into an Egyptian jet that was trying to take-off, or into an enemy air defence position. (Artwork by Tom Cooper)

Another MD.450 Ouragan from the same formation of No. 113 Squadron that attacked Meliz AB was the aircraft with the serial number 74, piloted by Mordechai Lavon as the Number 2. His jet was badly damaged, forcing Lavon to eject over the Mediterranean Sea, from where he was recovered by Egyptian fishermen to become a prisoner of war. Notable on these two Ouragans are their – apparently – 'completely different' camouflage patterns. Actually, all fighter-bombers of the IDF/AF wore one of four different versions of exactly the same pattern, of which there was a 'standard' and its 'reverse', and then a 'mirror' and 'reverse mirror' variants. In all cases, the colours brown (RAL8008 or FS30215) and blue (RAL5008) were used on top surfaces, and underfuselage grey (RAL7044) on undersurfaces. (Artwork by Tom Cooper)

Between 1962 and 1967, Israel received a total of 76 Mirage IIICJ interceptors, two Mirage IIIRJ reconnaissance fighters, and three (out of four that were on order) Mirage IIIBJ two-seat conversion trainers with combat capability. Initially, the type's service in Israel was marred by technical problems related to its Cyrano radar, weapons system, and engine, and the Mirage's effectiveness was low. Moreover, pilots found themselves ill-prepared to counter slower but more manoeuvrable types like MiG-15s, MiG-17s and Hunters. This is a reconstruction of the first Mirage IIICJ considered an operational loss: serial number 27 from No. 101 Squadron. On 21 December 1964, while returning from a clash with Hunters of the Royal Jordanian Air Force, it ran out of fuel while on finals to Hatzor AB, forcing the pilot Michael Barazam to eject. (Artwork by Tom Cooper)

Pending delivery of two custom-tailored Mirage IIIRJs in 1964, the IDF/AF modified several IIICJs for reconnaissance purposes: essentially, the aircraft received locally-manufactured noses containing Zeiss RMK-A cameras with 152mm focal lens (interchangeable with the standard nose containing the Cyrano Ibis radar). The first operational sortie of such a jet is known to have been flown on 26 May 1963. On 11 November 1963, one of the modified jets – serial number 53 – then suffered a failure of the Atar 9B engine's gearbox. The pilot, Ran Ronen, ejected safely, but the Mirage made a pilotless landing in a field near Hatzor AB, suffering only minimal damage in the process. The post-accident inspection enabled the IDF/AF to find out the reason for engine-related issues and greatly improve the technical reliability of the type. By 1967 modified Mirages, and the two dedicated IIIRJs, flew reconnaissance all over the Middle East, collecting immense volumes of precious intelligence. (Artwork by Tom Cooper)

By 1966, all 76 Mirage IIICJ interceptors had been delivered to Israel. The example illustrated here – serial number 84 – was one of the last to arrive. It was also one of fewer than a dozen equipped with the Thomson BZ radar warning receiver, the installation of which was recognisable by the antenna installed on the fin, directly above the rudder (the other Mirages known to have been equipped with the BZ were serial numbers 16, 18, 70, 71, 76, 77, 79, 80, 83, and 86). In February 1966, this jet was assigned to No. 119 Squadron, and thus received the red flash of that unit applied across the fin. On 13 November of the same year, during the Battle of Samu, it was piloted by Ran Ronen when he was credited with the downing of the Hawker Hunter F.Mk 6 flown by Muwaffaq Salti of the Royal Jordanian Air Force. (Artwork by Tom Cooper)

On 29 November 1966, the IDF/AF sent a slow-flying Piper Cub into Egyptian airspace over Sinai. When the UARAF reacted by scrambling a pair of MiG-19S from No. 20 Squadron, they were ambushed by a pair of Mirage IIICJs from No. 101 Squadron, which approached them from low altitude. While piloting this jet, serial number 34, the Israeli flight-leader Michael Haber then shot down the MiG-19 flown by Mohammed Abdel Moneim using one Matra R.530F air-to-air missile. About a minute later, Haber then manoeuvred behind the second MiG-19, flown by Khalid el-Daly, and shot it down with fire from 30mm DEFA guns, thus becoming the first Israeli Mirage pilot to score an aerial victory using air-to-air missiles, and the first to score two victories. The Mirage IIICJ serial number 34 went on to score three additional victories while in service with the IDF/AF. (Artwork by Tom Cooper)

As of 5 June 1967, 63 IIICJs and BJs, and both IIIRJs were available, and all but one operational. While 12 were held back for air defence purposes, the mass of the fleet was rushed into air strikes against the major air bases of the UARAF. This example – serial number 30 – was flown by the CO No. 117 Squadron, Amichai Shmueli, in the opening strike on Abu Suweir AB. The formation reached its target entirely unmolested and cratered the sole runway with a total of eight 250kg bombs. However, it did not return for the usual strafing attacks, but was tasked with flying a combat air patrol over central Sinai, where the IDF expected fierce resistance by MiG-21s from Meliz AB. Instead, this decision enabled the scrambling of multiple MiG-21s from Abu Suweir, which caused problems in the Canal Zone. (Artwork by Tom Cooper)

Another major Egyptian air base – Cairo West, housing the Tu-16 fleet of the UARAF – was subjected to no fewer than six successive air strikes by a total of 24 Mirage IIICJs. The first formation to reach it, at 08.45hrs, comprised three jets from No. 101 Squadron (the fourth aborted on take-off), led by Amos Lapidot, that unit's CO, in the IIICJ with the serial number 73. On the way to the target, Lapidot and his wingmen had to overtake a flight of slower Ouragans by flying underneath them. Over Cairo West, they encountered no opposition and cratered the runway in five positions (one bomb failed to detonate), before turning around to claim the destruction of more than a dozen Egyptian bombers with their 30mm guns. The jet is shown with its drop tanks removed to better display details of two 250kg bombs installed on the centreline pylon. (Artwork by Tom Cooper)

With 35 aircraft available, No. 105 or "Scorpion" Squadron was the largest IDF/AF unit as of 5 June 1967: all of its assets were hurled into action during the first wave, striking some of the most important targets. The fact that this was no easy task – but also what could have happened had Israeli air strikes been only a notch less effective – was proved by the drama that developed when a flight of four SMB.2s attacked Kabrit AB, around 08.45hrs. This illustration is a reconstruction of the leading jet in that formation, piloted by Alex Armon. His flight successfully bombed the runway and began strafing targets on the ground when a lonesome Il-14 transport appeared on the scene and Armon's Number 2 – Yacov Nevo, earlier CO of No. 105 Squadron, and about to assume command of Hatzor AB – drew away everybody's attention in that direction. (Artwork by Tom Cooper)

The Number 3 in Armon's flight was Zvi Umshweif, who flew the SMB.2 serial number 43. He finished off the already damaged Il-14, causing it to crash within the perimeter of Kabrit AB and his aircraft eventually received a kill marking. Moments after the Il-14 crashed, Nevo ordered the entire flight back to base before it had completed its planned fourth strafing pass. Before reaching the Suez Canal, the four SMB.2s then encountered another Il-14 in the Ismailia area – only to come under attack from two MiG-21PFMs, flown by Asim Ghazi and Awad Hamdi from No. 26 Squadron, scrambled from Abu Suweir AB. Nevo overruled his flight-leader and turned to engage, but it was too late. As the Israeli formation broke and spread, Ghazi fired an R-3S … (Artwork by Tom Cooper)

… although the R-3S missed, the jet targeted by it – the SMB.2 serial number 40, piloted by Amiram Manor and illustrated here – crashed while trying to evade. Meanwhile, Nevo completed the circle around the two MiG-21s and opened fire: however, both Egyptians were supersonic and the Israeli's final shells missed their target. Never looking back, Awad Hamdi continued his attack and fired both R-3S missiles: one of these hit the jet piloted by the Israeli flight-leader, causing it to crash, killing Alex Armon. While both Ghazi and Hamdi came away in their faster jets entirely unmolested, No. 105 Squadron thus began the war with a painful loss of two jets and two pilots: the unit went on to lose seven additional SMB.2s, together with five pilots, four of whom were killed and one became a POW. (Artwork by Tom Cooper)

Like the SMB.2s, Mystère IVAs of Nos. 109 and 116 Squadrons were heavily tasked with the opening strikes. The example shown here was piloted by Ronen Hagai from No. 109 Squadron: the leader of the third strike on Meliz AB. After cratering the runway with eight additional 250kg bombs, Hagai and his wingmen turned around for strafing runs. Their primary targets became two Mi-6s that were still intact, and four MiG-21s parked on the apron, one of which was already on fire. By knocking out the latter four, they had completed the destruction of No. 45 Squadron of the UARAF. By the time of their appearance over Meliz, the Egyptian air defences were fully alerted, and two Mystères suffered extensive AAA damage, which rendered at least one of them non-operational for several days. Notable on the jet with serial number 10 was the direction in which the squadron crest was applied on the fin. The kill marking was applied after the war. (Artwork by Tom Cooper)

A reconstruction of probably the most secretive aircraft of Operation Focus: originally manufactured as a Vautour IIN, the first jet in this series was equipped as a test-bed for the Cyrano Ibis radar before delivery to Israel. In service with the IDF/AF, it received the serial number 70. In May 1967, while still wearing the bare metal overall livery – but already decorated with a nick applied in red and black – it was slated for conversion to reconnaissance configuration. Before this could be applied, the May 1967 crisis erupted. On the morning of 5 June 1967, it was equipped with a pair of Thomson-CSF Calypso jamming pods (known as 'Yabelet' in Israel and shown below the main artwork), and – together with the similarly-equipped Vautour IIB serial number 65 – escorted by two Mirage IIICJs, flew a stand-off electronic support mission over the Mediterranean Sea, north of Port Said, disturbing the work of Egyptian early warning radars and SA-2 SAM sites. (Artwork by Tom Cooper)

Thanks to their long range, Israeli Vautours could reach targets beyond the reach of other types. Even then, most such missions had to be flown at high altitude to conserve fuel. Because of this requirement, their participation in the opening air strikes was limited to one strike against Beni Suweif AB: even that mission had to be launched from the slightly closer Tel Nov rather than from their home base at Ramat David, intended to be on target at 09.10hrs, local time, a full 20 minutes after H-Hour. This jet was assigned to the flight in question, but its pilot was forced to abort due to the failure of the canopy lock system: instead of attacking Beni Suweif, it returned to Ramat David where it was quickly repaired and back in action only two hours later. (Artwork by Tom Cooper)

This is a reconstruction of the Hunter F.Mk 6 serial number 706/G, as flown by Farouq Abdeen during the air combat at Samu on 13 November 1966. Painted in dark sea grey (BS381C/638, FS36173), and dark green (BS381C/241, FS34079) on top surfaces and sides (applied in the standard pattern), and left in high-speed silver finish on undersides, the jet had its nose and fin painted in red, according to the UAC order from 1964. Abdeen then applied a kill marking in the form of a small blue Star of David on a white field, outlined in blue, directly below the cockpit. The aircraft is shown in standard configuration for quick reaction alert of the time, including four 100-gallon drop tanks, and gun blast diffusers. Notably, the jet had the 'late', slightly longer version of No. 1 Squadron's insignia with 10 instead of eight red and white fields per line. (Artwork by Tom Cooper)

On the dissolution of the UAR, the reestablished SyAAF inherited about 40 MiG-17Fs, most of which were mounts of No. 101 Squadron. The jets included a mix of aircraft originally delivered to Syria before 1958 (serials in the range 901–999) and those delivered to Egypt (serials in the range 2201–2399). All were left in silver grey overall, and through the 1960s wore national markings in the form of red-white-black roundels and fin flashes with three green stars (the latter often applied rather crudely). By 1965, many of the MiG-17Fs of what was now Air Brigade 3 also had insignia below the cockpit. In the case of this jet (serial number 966), the insignia was a roaring wolf: it remains unclear if this was the pilot's personal insignia or a squadron crest. (Artwork by Tom Cooper)

While left in silver grey overall, starting in 1964, many Syrian MiG-21F-13s had large parts of their forward fuselage and rudders painted in red, according to the UAC order. Some seem to have also had wingtips painted in red. According to the practice introduced once they entered service in 1963–1964, they had no roundels at all: these were applied on top and bottom wing surfaces only. Clear photographic confirmation of their serials remain unavailable, but the latest reports from Syrian sources indicate that they were in the range 401–499. Standard armament was the same as that of Egyptian and Iraqi examples and included one 30mm gun and a pair of R-3S air-to-air missiles. (Artwork by Tom Cooper)

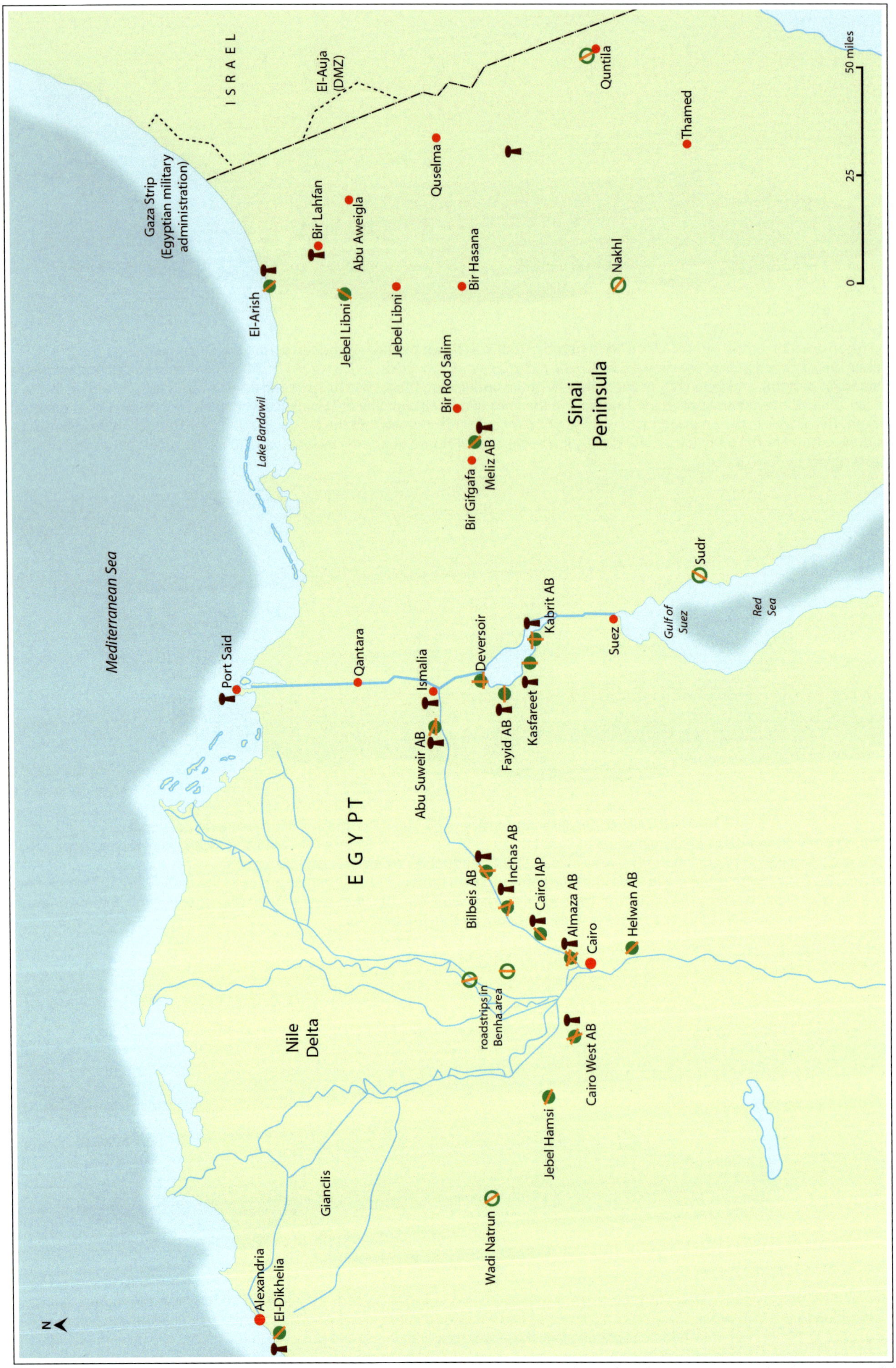

A map of major bases (green circles with yellow runways), secondary airstrips (green circles with yellow runways), and radar stations of the UARAF as of 5 June 1967. (Map by George Anderson)

An An-12BP of No. 16 Squadron, photographed around 1967. (Tom Cooper collection)

fully qualified MiG-17, MiG-19 and Su-7 pilots, as well as 97 pilots qualified to fly MiG-21s, and all of them 'all weather and night' qualified. No fewer than 81 pilots were qualified to fly Il-28s and Tu-16s, while 185 other pilots were qualified to fly various transports and helicopters. In summary, around 522 fully qualified pilots were available, while about 50 cadets who had recently graduated from the Air Force Academy were about to start their conversion training to combat types. Rather than numbers, the problem was that the mass of Egyptian pilots flew very little in the first months of 1967: even cadets graduating from the Air Force Academy had barely 35 hours on MiG-15UTIs, instead of the usual 85. Correspondingly, as of June 1967 the UARAF pilots were badly lacking in terms of recent flying experience, and even more so in regards of air combat and ground attack training.[7]

In contrast, the UARAF ground personnel had reached a high state of efficiency and provided their pilots with excellently maintained aircraft, despite the hot, dry, sandy and dusty climate that increased maintenance problems. Thanks to the aviation industry in Hewlan, even depot-level maintenance was undertaken in Egypt. The principal problem was that the standard, one-hour turnaround rate for combat aircraft between two sorties was to prove entirely inadequate during the subsequent conflict.

EGYPTIAN AIR DEFENCE COMMAND

In addition to intelligence, the lax approach of Nasser, Amer and their favourites regarding the safety of the UAR during the early 1960s is obvious from the story about the creation of the Air Defence Command – a factor almost entirely ignored even in Cairo in 1967 (not to mention almost all historians since): probably because this service was largely rendered useless by the decisions of Air Marshal Sidqi Mahmoud, and the developments of 5 June 1967.

As of 1955, Egypt had only about a dozen British-made radars, until it acquired a number of Soviet-made P-8s. With the help of Czechoslovak advisers, in October 1956 these were networked into an effective fighter control system which proved its worth during the Suez War. However, while some additional work on expansion of that system was then undertaken in 1957–1958, and despite the growing number of known deficiencies, the Egyptian radar network largely remained the same until 1961, when the decision was taken to order SA-2 SAMs from Moscow.

The production and deliveries of SA-2 related equipment for Egypt – all belonged to the SA-75 Dvina-A and/or Dvina-AK sub-variants – began in 1962 and were concluded during the following year. Eventually, a total of 27 systems ('battalions' or 'SAM sites', each including six launch rails and three reloads) was rolled out, including 18 in 1962 and 9 in 1963. Egypt received a total of 792 V-750VMV missiles, and 53 training rounds.[8]

Since neither the Egyptians nor the Soviets were in a hurry – or were preoccupied with developments in the Eastern Province/Syria, and then in Yemen – the training of the first crews for a total of 13 SAM sites, and for four radio-technical battalions, began only in late 1963. As the personnel completed their training in 1964, a total of 10 SAM battalions came into being, and Nasser and Amer then agreed with General Riyadh's demands to establish the ADC as an independent branch of the UAR armed forces. For this purpose, a sum of 165,000 Egyptian Pounds was budgeted for the next eight years. The aim was to have the ADC fully operational by 1972, covering the Suez Canal, the northern coast of Egypt, and Cairo. The personnel for the new command were drawn from both the air force and the army.[9]

Eventually, three major units of the future command – Air Defence Brigades 92, 93, and 94 – were operational by early 1965. Their typical sub-units were such as the 418th and 425th Air Defence Battalions: both officially established on 4 December 1964 from personnel trained by Soviet advisers in Egypt. As of June 1967, the 418th was responsible for protection of Cairo International Airport (IAP), while the 425th was responsible for the defence of Fayid AB, in the Canal Zone.[10]

Meanwhile, all three air defence brigades were put to the test in the course of an exercise in May 1965: this revealed that they had to be networked with all the available radar sites of the UARAF for their better function. Moreover, both the available early warning radars and new SAM units proved unable to detect and target MiG-21s and Tu-16s of the UARAF flying at altitudes below 500 metres. Correspondingly, in November 1965, Cairo placed an order for five Vozdukh-M1E automatic tactical management systems, each of which included a large computer that integrated all available data about up to 41 enemy aircraft, and calculated intercept vectors, eight PRV-11 height-finding radars, four to six P-15 early warning radars, and six P-30 Khrustal two-dimension surveillance radars working in the E/F-band and used for ground control of interceptor operations (ASCC/NATO reporting name 'Big Mesh').[11]

Moscow agreed with this request during Sadat's visit in August 1966: however, it was only in February 1967 that the first P-15s reached Egypt, and they arrived without any technical documentation and without operating manuals. These were brought by a group of

A MiG-21F-13 in the process of landing following a sortie during the exercise of May 1965, when the equipment and organisation of the ADC were put to test for the first time. (*Binaa al-Watan*)

Soviet instructors that arrived in April 1967. Consequently, it was only once the P-15s were pressed into service, in late May 1967, that the Egyptians discovered that – contrary to Soviet promises – their new radars did not meet requirements in regards of low-altitude detection. Moreover, at this time, not only all the Vozdukh-M1E systems, but also eight PRV-11 height finders and six P-30s were still in Odessa, waiting for their shipment to Alexandria [12]

If this was not enough, and despite gradually increasing tensions through 1965 and 1966, the ADC – which was still officially supervised by the air force – was not once put to any kind of further testing, nor ever conducted any additional exercises, either on its own or in cooperation with the UARAF. Unsurprisingly, the service was concluded to be ill-prepared to defend the country from a sudden air strike.[13]

What was worse, the high command of the UARAF ignored all the advice of the ADC officers despite them having undergone extensive advanced training in the USSR. On 20 May, a conference of the top officers of both services was held at the Institute of War Studies at Almaza, in the presence of Air Marshal Sidqi Mahmoud, during which officers of the ADC recommended that the UARAF:

1. camouflage all of its aircraft;
2. build hardened aircraft shelters;
3. allow the ADC to assume command of air defences (including manned interceptors);

SA-2 GUIDELINE

For the reasons described above, contrary to what might be expected – and to some disagreement amongst Egyptian veteran fighter pilots interviewed – the primary weapon of the ADC in October 1973 were not manned interceptors, but the Soviet-made SAM systems. The oldest of these was codenamed 'SA-2 Guideline' by the ASCC and NATO: originally designated the 'Volga' by the Soviets, it was developed for the strategic defence of major urban areas and military facilities against high-flying aircraft. First pressed into service in 1956, it was subjected to a series of upgrades and further development, which eventually resulted in the emergence of variants such as the Volkhov, Desna and Dvina. Very bulky (all of the components for just one SAM site together weighed well over 100 tonnes), the system was made mobile (even if at a relatively slow rate), and gradually adapted as a general-purpose air defence weapon, capable of engaging even tactical aircraft down to altitudes of around 300 metres (990ft). The centrepiece of each SA-2 SAM system – or a battalion – was the fire-control radar designated 'Fan Song' by the ASCC/NATO. Supported by three other radars, and controlled from the command post, this served the purpose of engaging one target at a time with up to six (though usually two or three) SAMs. Egypt had acquired its first Volga SAM system (widely known as 'SA-1' within the ADC and the EAF) – in 1962.

Table 3: Equipment of a typical SA-75 Dvina (SA-2 Guideline) SAM site of the ADC, June 1967

Equipment and Remarks	Number of Systems per SAM Site/ Battalion
UV fire-control station (command post)	1
P-10 (ASCC-code 'Knife Rest') VHF-band early warning radar (range 75km/47nm)	1
P-12 (ASCC/NATO-codename 'Spoon Rest') C-band acquisition radar (range 250–300km/155–186nm)	1
PRV-10 (ASCC/NATO-codename 'Rock Cake') or PRV-11 ('Side Net') E-band height-finding radar (range 200km/124nm or 240km/(149nm respectively)	1
RSNA-75 (ASCC/NATO-codename 'Fan Song A') E/F/G-band fire-control radar (detection range 140km/87nm; acquisition range 100km/62nm); capable of simultaneously tracking up to six targets, but engaging only one at a time	1
SM-63-I launcher	6
PR-11 transporter-loaders (each with one spare missile)	3

(Continued opposite)

4. maintain four interceptors on every base on constant alert during daylight; and
5. bolster defences of all air bases through deployment of additional anti-aircraft guns.

Except for the idea about maintaining interceptors on constant alert during the daylight, all of this was ignored. Even in the case of recommendation 4, this measure resulted in the air force keeping only 34 MiG-21s at the 'Readiness Rate I' (ready to take-off within five minutes), and another 32 at the 'Readiness Rate II' (ready to take-off within 15 minutes). The command of the ADC promptly objected that, considering that the IDF/AF was near certain to deploy 180 fighter-bombers in its first strike, and that the available radar network was unable to detect these if they approached at low altitude, this measure was hopelessly inadequate. To no avail: Sidqi Mahmoud waved the comments away because his Soviet adviser declared the Egyptian air defence system to be 'sound'.[14]

That is at least what the top Egyptian officers said after the war. At least as important for Sidqi Mahmoud's conclusion were assessments by the DM1. Unaware of Israeli determination, capabilities and intentions, the DM1 assessed that the IDF/AF had about 250 combat aircraft of which around 75 percent were operational on average, and that about 25 percent of these would be held back for the defence of Israel, and another 30 percent for fighting Jordan and Syria. As a result, Egyptian intelligence officers concluded that the IDF/AF would have just 90 aircraft to strike the UARAF. Considering this relatively low number, they expected Israel to attack only air bases in Sinai, and some of ADC's SAM sites, and though it possible that these would destroy about 15–20 percent of forward deployed aircraft.[15]

Such conclusions are particularly surprising considering that in 1966 and early 1967, the same service filed numerous reports about the reconnaissance activity of the IDF/AF, and warned about the Israeli capability to strike air bases both in the Suez Canal Zone,

The RSNA-75 ('Fan Song') fire-control radar was the core of every SA-2 site. It used electro-mechanical scanning to emit a pair of beams from its two perpendicular antennae, which formed a cruciform pattern to determine the height and azimuth of the target. The round antenna on the side was used for missile guidance. (IDF, via Albert Grandolini)

One of six SM-63-I launchers with a V-750VMV (also '11DU') missile of an Egyptian SA-75 Dvina-AK SAM system of the ADC, captured by the Israelis in Sinai during the June 1967 War. (IDF, via Albert Grandolini)

A PR-11 transporter-loader with a spare V-750VMV missile, captured by the Israelis. (IDF, via Albert Grandolini)

and west of it – even if approaching at low altitudes. Indeed, on 25 May 1967, Colonel Ali Mansour of the Intelligence Directorate of the UARAF issued a strong warning with similar content, 'Israel can reach all UAR air bases at the same time, especially if aware about numerous weak spots and the poor low-altitude coverage of our radar network.'[16]

However, all such warnings were ignored: instead, Air Marshal Sidqi Mahmoud massively underestimated the capabilities and intentions of the IDF/AF.

Correspondingly, as of early June 1967, the ADC was existent, but dysfunctional by default and ill-positioned to defend Egypt. Its three air defence brigades (92nd, 93rd, and 94th) each included one radio-technical battalion (operating early warning/surveillance radars) and nine SAM battalions/sites operating SA-2s. Foremost, the force had absolutely no operational control over the UARAF's MiG-21 fleet, nor any of the air defences protecting air bases or the army units deployed in Sinai.

5
IRAQI AIR FORCE

Established in 1931 as the first official military flying branch of any Arab country, during the first decades of its existence the service originally named the Royal Iraqi Air Force was constrained to operating light aircraft only.[1] Certainly enough, the Iraqis did everything possible to equip their De Havilland DH.60Ms, DH.60Ts, DH.60Ms, and DH.80Ms with armament, and the air force saw lots of action against various insurgencies. However, it was only in 1939–1940 that Baghdad felt free enough from British supervision to start purchasing combat aircraft from Italy and the USA. In 1941, following a military coup in Baghdad, the British concluded that Iraqi independence went too far and, exploiting Iraqi attempts to obtain arms from Nazi Germany, reinvaded the country, provoking the Anglo-Iraqi War. The RIrAF offered vigorous, even if largely ineffective resistance and was almost completely destroyed – as were most of the aircraft of the German and Italian air forces belatedly rushed to its aid. The recovery was slow and gained some pace only in late 1946, when Baghdad was granted permission to order 30 Hawker Fury FB.Mk 11 fighter-bombers and two Fury Trainer T.Mk 52s, followed by three Bristol Freighter C.Mk 31 twin-engined transports. The former were delivered through 1948–1949, and the latter in 1950, and formed the backbone of the RIrAF for a number of years, despite the acquisition of Vampire and Venom jet-powered fighter-bombers in 1953–1954. Indeed, Furies were to remain in operational service as fighter-bombers for counterinsurgency operations until replaced by Su-7BMKs in 1967–1968, while the last Freighter was retired only in 1970.

Once Iraq joined the Baghdad Pact in 1957, Washington became keen to help expand the IrAF, help finance the acquisition of 12 Hunter F.Mk 6s, and then decided to donate 36 North American F-86F Sabres. Emboldened, the air force developed a plan to establish three bomber units: when the British proved reluctant to deliver any of their English Electric Canberras, the Americans made offers for their version of the same in the form of the Martin B-57. Eventually, all such designs were cancelled by the coup in Iraq of July 1957, which toppled the British-imposed and -supported monarchy. Instead, Iraq subsequently began purchasing Soviet-made aircraft and placed an order for MiG-15UTIs, MiG-17s, and Il-28s, instead. Indeed, particularly good relations between the contemporary commander of the Iraqi air force and Moscow resulted in Iraq becoming the first Arab air force to operate supersonic interceptors: in 1959, the Soviets delivered no fewer than 50 MiG-19s. As well as the standard MiG-19S variant armed with three NR-30 guns, but lacking radar, these included 10 MiG-19Ps (equipped with the RP-1 Izumrud radar and two NR-30 guns), and 10 MiG-19PMs (equipped with the RP-1 Izumrud radar and four Kaliningrad K-5M [ASCC/NATO reporting name 'AA-1 Alkali'] beam-riding, guided air-to-air

In a little-known affair from the period of good cooperation between Baghdad and Washington, in 1957–1958, the Iraqi Air Force became the first in the Middle East to operate unmanned aerial vehicles in the form of the Radioplane OQ-19 (US Navy designation KDR-2): these were remotely controlled (and inexpensive) target drones, that were widely exported through to the 1980s. (Tom Cooper collection)

Operated by a total of two operational units and an operational conversion unit, the Hawker Hunter F.Mk 59A/B formed the backbone of the Iraqi fighter-bomber fleet as of 1967. This photograph shows serial number 570, shortly prior to delivery to Iraq. (Dr David Nicolle collection)

A pair of IrAF MiG-21F-13s (serial numbers 524 in foreground, and 527 behind) from the first batch acquired by Iraq in 1961–1962 and operated by No. 11 Squadron. (Ahmad Sadik collection)

missiles). However, due to continuous political unrest and several purges, the air force did not accept all of them and instead focused on operating only the 16 gun-armed MiG-19S models. Similarly, instead of expanding the bomber fleet to the planned three units, the IrAF acquired 10 Tupolev Tu-16 medium bombers: the sole unit operating them became operational in 1962. Finally, Iraq became the first Arab country to receive and operate the then brand-new MiG-21F-13s. A total of 16 were delivered by 1962, together with R-3S air-to-air missiles.

In the course of the coup of February 1963, the IrAF suffered significant losses, including between four and six MiG-19S, at least three, possibly four MiG-21F-13s, and at least one MiG-17F. The new government in Baghdad then terminated all military cooperation with the USSR, and in a demonstration of its good will to Nasser, donated surviving MiG-19S models of No. 9 Squadron to the UARAF – while the delivered, but never accepted, MiG-19Ps and MiG-19PMs were all returned to the USSR. Instead, in July 1963, Baghdad returned to the practice of purchasing British fighter-bombers and placed an order for 22 Hunter F.Mk 59s. In early 1964, this was followed by an even bigger order for 12 additional Hunter F.Mk 59As (plus an upgrade of old Hunter F.Mk 6s to the same standard), 12 Westland Wessex HU.Mk 52 helicopters, and 12 (later increased to 20) British Aerospace Corporation Jet Provost T.Mk 52 training jets. Finally, in late 1964, Iraq acquired 13 Hunter F.Mk 59Bs, together with six Hunter T.Mk 66 and T.Mk 69 two-seat conversion trainers. Deliveries of all this equipment were to last into May 1967, and prompted a major reorganisation of the air force, as well as a significant expansion of the Air Force College. Emboldened, the command in Baghdad thus initiated the search for a new supersonic interceptor. The British-made English Electric Lightning was strongly promoted by London and appeared to be a logical successor to the Hunter. However, as of 1965, it still lacked guns and hardpoints for bombs, and thus in April 1966, the Iraqis turned to the USSR again, placing an order for a total of 22 refurbished MiG-21F-13s, 23 radar-equipped MiG-21FLs, and 34 Sukhoi Su-7BMK fighter-bombers. Contrary to the British, the Soviets scrambled to deliver and not only were all of the MiGs in Iraq by the end of the same year (deliveries of Su-7s began in early 1967), but MiG-21FLs arrived equipped with unique (and little-known) Kh-66 radio-command guided air-to-ground missiles – in addition to the usual R-3S missiles. Correspondingly, as of June 1967, the IrAF was organised and equipped as listed in Table 4.

Like the UARAF, and regardless of all the involvement in politics and the resulting purges of the 1950s and 1960s, the IrAF always went to great lengths to train enough pilots and ground personnel to never experience serious shortages of either. Its fliers did lack realistic training, though: for most of the 1950s and early 1960s, Iraqi pilots and crews of combat aircraft were flying 120–160 hours a year, including about 30 hours of tactical training – mainly consisting of air-to-ground gunnery and rocketing, or nocturnal operations. However, experience from the Frist Iraqi-Kurdish War (fought 1962–1970), and the coups of 1963, clearly demonstrated that this was insufficient. Combined with large-scale orders for new aircraft and helicopters, in 1964–1966, this prompted a significant reform of the entire training curriculum. Not only were ever larger groups of cadets accepted to the Air Force College (where they flew Chipmunks and Provosts for elementary training, before converting to Jet Provosts and MiG-15UTIs for advanced training), or sent abroad for conversion training, but pilots in operational units were

Table 4: IrAF Order of Battle, 5 June 1967[2]			
HQ Baghdad C-in-C Major General Jassam Muhammad ash-Shaher			
Unit	**Base**	**Equipment**	**Remarks**
No. 1 Squadron	Hurriyah (Kirkuk)	20 Fury FB.Mk 1, Venom FB.Mk 50	CO unknown; in the process of re-equipping with Su-7BMK
No. 2 Squadron	Firnas (Mosul)	4 Mi-1, 9 Mi-4, 6 O-1A	CO unknown; O-1A serving as Forward Air Controller
No. 3 Squadron	Rashid (Baghdad)	2 Dove, 2 Heron, Freighter	CO unknown
No. 4 Squadron	Rashid	11 Wessex HC.Mk 2	CO Lieutenant Colonel Hassan Sharif; unit deactivated 1962 but reestablished 1965 as a helicopter squadron
No. 5 Squadron			de-activated in December 1963
No. 6 Squadron	Habbaniya	10 Hunter F.Mk 59A/B	CO Lieutenant Colonel Adil Suleimany; two additional Hunters damaged in collision over Habbaniyah in late May 1967 and not repaired by 5 June 1967
No. 7 Squadron	Hurriyah	20 MiG-17F and MiG-17PF	CO Lieutenant Colonel Masroor Bahaedin
No. 8 Squadron	Hurriyah	11 Il-28, 2 Il-28U	CO Lieutenant Colonel Mehdi Mahsun as-Sabbah; unit redeployed to Firnas, 25 August 1967
No. 9 Squadron		MiG-21PFM	working up on MiG-21
No. 10 Squadron	Taqaddum	9 Tu-16	CO Captain Farouk al-Tail
No. 11 Squadron	Rashid	11 MiG-21F-13	CO Lieutenant Colonel Hashem Manhal al-Azawi
No. 14 Squadron		8–9 MiG-21FL/PFM	working up on MiG-21s
No. 17 Squadron	Rashid	8–9 MiG-21FL/PFM	CO Major Durhid Ibrahim Muslim; OCU for crews of Nos 9 and 14 Squadrons
No. 23 Squadron	Rashid	8 An-2, 6 An-12BP	CO unknown
No. 29 Squadron		16 Hunter F.Mk 59A/B	CO Lieutenant Colonel Ismail Wakti
Hunter OCU	Habbaniya	9 Hunter F.Mk 59 and T.Mk 66	CO 'Captain Crow' (British pilot; real name unknown)
Air Force College	Wahda (Shoibiyah)	Chipmunk, Jet Provost, MiG-15UTI	CO unknown

authorised to fly over 200 hours a year, at least a quarter of which consisted of tactical training. Thanks to improved procedures, IrAF airmen thus became particularly good in air-to-ground gunnery, rocketing, and bombing: only air-to-air gunnery remained underdeveloped, principally because only two Ilyushin Il-28BM target-towing aircraft were available.

That said, the IrAF of the mid-1960s was perhaps the best example of a British-influenced air force in this part of the world:

The backbone of the IrAF transport fleet as of 1967 were eight Antonov An-12BP transports operated by No. 23 Squadron. (Tom Cooper collection)

Officers of No. 10 Squadron – the sole Iraqi unit ever to operate Tu-16 bombers – in front of one of their mounts. (via Ali Altobchi)

orientating on RAF training and tactical manuals only, its senior leadership expected to achieve the same level of proficiency as the RAF simply through the acquisition of ever more combat aircraft and provision of similar amounts of training. Indeed, it took great effort to adapt even the Soviet technology to the British training methods. However, with the General Staff in Baghdad always dominated by the army, and the army being the sole body in Iraq conducting serious studies of strategy and tactics, the air force remained dominated by the mindset of the ground forces. Although as British-influenced as those of the air force, army officers saw airpower in a similar fashion to the Soviets: as an intervention force and a tool of providing extended-range close air support, important at the tactical level, but not at the operational or even strategic level.

6

ISRAEL DEFENSE FORCE/AIR FORCE

The origins of the IDF/AF can be traced back to 1947, when a mix of Jewish airmen and foreign volunteers – most of them with combat experience from the Second World War – flew a miscellany of light civilian aircraft and a few transports in support of various Jewish enclaves in Palestine.[1] This changed dramatically soon after the declaration of independence of Israel: within a day of IDF/AF's official establishment on 27 May 1948, it received its first combat aircraft in the form of Avia S.199s – Czechoslovak-manufactured Messerschmitt Bf.109Gs. By the end of the First Arab-Israeli War, it assumed control of about a dozen well-established air bases constructed by the British, built-up an efficient command structure, and operated a total of more than 200 aircraft of 30 different types.

The usual histories of the IDF/AF in the 1950s and 1960s stress an acute shortage of funding, and – as a result – critical shortfalls in acquisition and training. Certainly enough, on its creation, and despite usurping the flourishing economy left behind by ethnically cleansed Palestinians, for nearly 20 years after its establishment, Israel was economically unsustainable. Its two main products were citrus fruits and chemicals dredged from the Dead Sea, the revenues from which provided for only 18–25 percent of the national budget: the remainder was made up of numerous foreign loans, charitable contribution from American and European Jewry, German reparations for the Holocaust, and direct grants-in-aid advanced by the US government.[2] Unsurprisingly, the IDF/AF actually continued growing and if it experienced any kind of major issues then principally they were because all of its early commanders had no aviation background and their influence within the General Staff IDF was minimal. As a result, through the first decade of its existence the service was merely expected to support the ground forces and struggled to obtain any semblance of operational independence.

The IDF/AF was seriously reinforced in 1951, when Israel acquired 63 De Havilland Mosquito fighter-bombers from surplus stocks of the French air force: following overhauls in France, 58 of these reached the IDF/AF, significantly bolstering the fleet of North American P-51D Mustangs, Supermarine Spitfires, and North American T-6 Texans acquired earlier.

In February 1953, Israel became the second nation in the Middle East (after Egypt) to acquire jet fighters in the form of 11 Gloster Meteor F.Mk 8s and four T.Mk 7s from Great Britain: the second batch of seven Meteor FR.Mk 9 reconnaissance fighters and two T.Mk 7s followed in March 1954. During the same year, the IDF/AF also obtained a night fighter capability in the form of six Meteor NF.Mk 13s. Arguably, deliveries of radar-equipped Meteor interceptors were delayed into autumn 1956 – primarily because of the Israeli 'reprisal' raids into Egypt. However, by then, the IDF/AF was already involved in a much more ambitious deal with France – and one that was to raise much attention in Egypt: starting in mid-1953, Tel Aviv initiated efforts to obtain swept-wing fighter jets. Respecting the Tripartite Declaration, the Eisenhower Administration ruled out any sales of North American F-86 Sabres – whether from the USA or any countries manufacturing the type under licence. However, Paris was less reluctant and in August 1954, the French and the Israelis signed a contract for six Dassault MD.452 Mystère II fighters and one Nord 2501 Noratlas transport aircraft (with an option for further nine Mystères and two Noratlases) – delivery of which was scheduled for February–March 1955. Ironically, this fact is ignored by nearly all histories of the Arab-Israeli conflict: on the contrary, the widespread version is that the

Israeli acquisition of Mystères was prompted by the Czechoslovak Arms Deal. Actually, the research and development of the Mystère II encountered significant difficulties and delays, and this was the reason why in 1955 the French had no other option but to offer the Israelis a batch of 12 straight-wing Dassault MD.450 Ouragans as a stop-gap measure. This was a very expensive acquisition, coming at a cost of US$10 million at the time the entire Israeli defence budget was only US$ 65 million. Rather unsurprisingly, the price was prohibitive enough for Tel Aviv to cancel its order for Mystère IIs later the same year and then opt for the more advanced Dassault MD.452 Mystère IVA, deliveries of which were planned for 1956.[3]

PILOT SHORTAGE

If the scale of the Czechoslovak Arms Deal might have caused a 'shock' in Israel and 'dramatically tilted the quantitative and qualitative balance of power in favour of Egypt' – as systematically insisted by Israelis and in the West ever since – any related concerns were forgotten before long. Within just a few months during the military build-up to the Suez War of 1956, the number of Ouragans increased to 30, that of Mystère IVAs to 37, and the IDF/AF had three Noratlas transports: the number of aircraft reached a point where the service found itself hopelessly short of pilots and ground crews for all of them. Therefore, and while wild myths – including one about '200 Soviet pilots flying MiGs to Egypt and fighting for Nasser' – are still making circles in the Western public until this very day, it was the French who introduced the practice of sending not only aircraft but also flight and ground crews to support their allies in the Middle East, not the Soviets, and even less so the Egyptians. In that case, they deployed two squadrons with 30 Mystère IVAs and 18 (US-made) Republic F-84F Thunderstreak fighter-bombers to Israel and provided the pilots necessary to operate jets for which there were not sufficient pilots from the IDF/AF. Due to stringent requirements and a high wash-out rate, the pilot shortage was not entirely solved even as of 1967: instead of having two pilots per aircraft, as desired by Weizman and Hod, the service was at around 1.4 pilots per aircraft.[4]

AIR FRANCE

The further build-up of the Israeli air force experienced a massive acceleration in 1958, when Major General Ezer Weizman took over as commander. In the same year, he supervised the arrival of the first six out of an eventual 42 Dassault SMB.2s fighter-bombers, followed by the twin-engined – and highly expensive – Vautours. The first version of the Vautour to enter service was the IIN, equipped with the DRAC-25AI or DRAC-32AI radar in the nose, the pilot and co-pilot in tandem seats, and armed with four 30mm DEFA guns. Israel acquired a total of seven, and they were seen as necessary to counter UARAF-operated Il-28 bombers. The second variant was the Vautour IIA: this was a fighter-bomber with a two-man crew, and four internally installed DEFA guns, but also had the ability to carry bombs on underwing bomb racks. Finally, Israel acquired four Vautour IIB reconnaissance fighters equipped with US-made Fairchild KA-52 reconnaissance cameras, which proved their worth during multiple long-range reconnaissance sorties over Egypt, Jordan, and Iraq in 1960.

Both the SMB.2 and Vautour were still very much in the process of being introduced to service by the time the Israelis learned about Egyptian and Iraqi requests for supersonic MiG-19s and MiG-21s from the USSR. In 1960, this prompted Tel Aviv to place an order for 24 of the even more expensive Mirage IIICJs, which was subsequently increased to 48 and – by 1967 – to no fewer than 76 of such interceptors, two Mirage IIIRJ reconnaissance fighters, and four Mirage IIICJ two-seat combat trainers. Moreover, during the same period – and as the French air force was withdrawing the type from service – Israel also continued purchasing MD.450 Ouragans until the total number of jets of this type operated by the IDF/AF reached 70.

Meanwhile, in 1962, US President John F Kennedy began encouraging an improvement in relations with Israel and – amongst others – permitted an arms deal worth US$75 million, a third of which was used to finance deliveries of US-made MIM-23A HAWK SAMs. The first battalion of HAWKs became operational in March 1965: by 1967, enough equipment was supplied for five units, but only three of these were operational due to the lack of qualified personnel. Additionally, Israel purchased no fewer than 200 Bofors 40mm L/70 anti-aircraft guns from Sweden, supported by 40 Super Fledermaus fire-control radars.

Thus came into being the fleet of combat aircraft with which the IDF/AF fought not only the Second Water War, but also the June 1967 Arab-Israeli War: this was often dubbed 'Air France', because it almost entirely consisted of French-made fighter jets, transports, training jets, and helicopters.

An MD.450 Ouragan, a 'straight wing' fighter-bomber of the IDF/AF acquired from 1955, seen on finals for landing. Israel eventually acquired 70 jets of this type, more than 60 of which were still operational as of June 1967. (Albert Grandolini collection)

A pair of MD.452 Mystère IVAs of No. 116 Squadron, IDF/AF, seen before the June 1967 War. The jet proved superior in speed and climb to MiG-15s during the Suez War of 1956, but 10 years later was already considered obsolete and relegated to the ground attack role. (Albert Grandolini collection)

One of 200 Bofors 40mm L/70 anti-aircraft guns that Israel purchased from Sweden in the 1960s. Each of the 40 batteries equipped with these guns was supported by one of 40 Super Fledermaus fire-control radars. (Albert Grandolini collection)

As of June 1967, the IDF/AF boasted around 8,000 regular personnel, augmented by around 11,000 reservists when fully mobilised. As of the morning of 5 June 1967, they were equipped with:

- 65 Mirage IIICJ/BJ and IIICJ/R (64 operational)
- 1 MiG-21F-13 (ex-Iraqi example; armed with Israeli-made Shafrir Mk I air-to-air missiles)
- 35 SMB.2 (all serviceable)
- 19 Vautour IIA/N/BR (18 operational)
- 35 Mystère IVA (32 serviceable)
- 51 Ouragan (48 operational)

This was a total of 206 fighter-bombers. The number was further increased through arming and assigning 44 CM.170s to No. 147 Squadron and deploying them for close-air-support purposes. However, because they were slow and vulnerable to any

Table 5: IDF/AF Order of Battle, 5 June 1967

HQ Baghdad
C-in-C Major General Hod

Unit	Base	Equipment	Remarks
Wing 1	Ramat David		
No. 109 Squadron	Ramat David	Mystère IV	16 aircraft (15 operational); at Tel Nov for initial strikes
No. 110 Squadron	Ramat David	Vautour	19 aircraft (18 operational); at Tel Nov for initial strikes
No. 117 Squadron	Ramat David	Mirage IIICJ/BJ	24 aircraft (24 operational)
	Meggido		FOB, No. 100 Squadron Flight B
Base 15	Sde Dov		
No. 100 Squadron	Sde Dov	Cub, Do.27, C-180, Turbo Porter, Rallye	
No. 125 Squadron	Sde Dov	SE.3130, Bell 47	
	Kfar Sirkin		FOB
Base 27	Lod IAP		
No. 107 Squadron	Lod IAP	Ouragan	16 aircraft (15 operational), redeployed from Ramat David
No. 120 Squadron	Lod IAP	B-377M, C-97, C-47	
No. 145 Squadron	Lod IAP	Dart Herald	mostly Arkia personnel
Wing 4	Hatzor		
No. 101 Squadron	Hatzor	Mirage IIICJ/RJ	22 aircraft (21 operational)
No. 105 Squadron	Hatzor	SMB.2	35 aircraft (35 operational)
No. 113 Squadron	Hatzor	Ouragan	35 aircraft (33 operational)
SAR Flight	Hatzor	S-58	
Base 8	Tel Nov		
No. 103 Squadron	Tel Nov	Noratlas	23 aircraft (21 operational)
No. 114 Squadron	Tel Nov	SA.321H	4 helicopters
No. 116 Squadron	Tel Nov	Mystère IVA	20 aircraft (17 operational)
No. 119 Squadron	Tel Nov	Mirage IIICJ/RJ	21 aircraft (21 operational)
No. 123 Squadron	Tel Nov	Bell 47	30 helicopters
No. 124 Squadron	Tel Nov	S-58	26 helicopters
Wing 6	Hatzerim		
No. 147 Squadron	Hatzerim	CM.170	44 aircraft (44 operational); detached from Flying School
Flying School	Hatzerim	Cub, CM.170, Bell 47	(some elements still at Tel Nov)

Unlike the Arab air forces, where training aircraft were relatively scarce and thus rarely used for anything but training purposes, the IDF/AF took care for its Flying School to organise No. 147 Squadron: this was equipped with Fouga CM.170 Magister training jets, armed with machine guns and unguided rockets, and deployed intensively for close air support during the June 1967 War. (Albert Grandolini collection)

kind of damage, very few Magisters were assigned the task of striking the Arab air bases: 16 were involved in attacks on Egyptian radar stations, while six others flew deception sorties over the Mediterranean Sea.

From the descriptions above, and considering reports about shortages of funds, it might appear as if Weizman and Hod were only able to focus on the acquisition of combat aircraft, while ignoring the combat support component of their force and bolstering this through the acquisition of second-hand aircraft. Actually,

SUPPORT INFRASTRUCTURE

Considering all the above-listed acquisitions through the 1950s and 1960s, one is left to wonder how all the aircraft and their equipment were supported by Egypt/UAR, Iraq, Israel, Jordan, and Syria.

As of the 1950s, the only country to actually have an aircraft industry in all of the Middle East was the UAR: Egypt had manufactured a small number of British- and German-designed aircraft in the 1930s. In 1949, the Egyptian Aviation Factory (also Factory 72) in Heliopolis then launched series production of the Gomhouriya T.Mk 1 primary trainer, based on the design of the German Bücker Bü.181D Bestman from the Second World War. Over 400 Bü.181s were eventually produced over the following decades. Around the same time, Egypt also acquired the licence and all the machinery necessary for domestic production of Vampire FB.Mk 52 fighter-bombers. However, London then withdrew its permission and this project was cancelled, despite delivery of all the necessary tooling and machinery. In 1952, Cairo contacted several German experts left jobless after the Second World War – including Professor Ernst Heinkel – to design a fighter jet that would be manufactured in series in Egypt. However, following several differences, and despite an investment of GB£1.515 million, cooperation ended fruitlessly in 1954. Five years later, the UAR then purchased the licence for production of the Hispano Aviacion HA-200 Saetta, a training jet designed by the famous Professor Willy Messerschmitt in Spain. Re-tooled, Factory 72 rolled out the first 10 HA-200Bs – locally designated al-Kahira ('Cairo', but also 'Conqueror' in Arabic) in early 1960. The Egyptians then contracted not only Messerschmitt to continue his work on a Mach 1-capable fighter, but also hired Austrian Professor Ferdinand Brandner – veteran engineer that worked for Junkers Motorenbau during the Second World War and then designed the Ivchenko AI-20L turboprop engine for the An-12 transport and the Kuznetsov NK-12 for the Tupolev Tu-95 bomber while serving as prisoner of war in the USSR – to develop a suitable lightweight turbojet. The result was the engine designated E-200, developed and manufactured at Factories 35, 72, and 135 in Helwan, which entered testing in 1963. Emboldened by Brandner's success, the Egyptians then increased the requirement for the top speed of the new jet to Mach 2, and then to Mach 2.5. Brandner's team re-designed the E-200 into the more powerful E-300, eight prototypes of which were successfully tested by 1965. However, the HA-300 project was lagging by that time, primarily because the Commander-in-Chief of the UARAF, Air Marshal Sidqi Mahmoud and several of his aides were spreading unsubstantiated rumours about corruption, delays and overspending, while favouring additional acquisitions of Soviet-made jets. Ultimately, although making its first flight on 7 March 1965, and HA-300 was incomplete as of June 1967, and cancelled after the next Arab-Israeli War. Nevertheless, Egypt was left in possession of several factories with the know-how and machinery necessary to overhaul Soviet-made aircraft, manufacture drop tanks, and apply various other, minor modifications, like the addition of launch rails for unguided rockets to the wings of MiG-15bis and MiG-17s in UARAF service. This was of particular importance because, regardless of all the Egyptian (and Iraqi, and Syrian) combat experience from the 1950s and 1960s, the Soviets never listened to any of their complaints or requests for modifications of existing aircraft: the Arabs received only exactly what the Soviets were ready to deliver.

Arguably, amongst the latter were the first guided air-to-air missiles ever exported to the Middle East – such as the above-mentioned Kaliningrad K-5Ms delivered to Iraq in 1959, followed by R-3S that arrived in 1962. Indeed, the batch of MiG-21PFMs acquired in Iraq in 1966 arrived equipped with little-known Kh-66 radio-command-guided air-to-ground missiles. However, these proved so cumbersome to operate that the IrAF never deployed any in combat. Much to their dismay, it was only during the June 1967 War that the Egyptians, Iraqis, and Syrians were to realise just how useless the Soviet R-3S missiles installed on their MiG-21s were.

Unlike the Soviets, the French went to great lengths to modify all of their jets to Israeli specifications prior to delivery, and whenever

A Super Mystère B.2 (a.k.a. 'SMB.2') of the sole IDF/AF ever to operate this type: No. 105 'Scorpion' Squadron, as seen in the mid-1960s. (Albert Grandolini collection)

Continued on page 52

Continued from page 51

necessary, they continued to apply fleet-wide modifications to the jets already introduced to service. Correspondingly – and contrary to the general practice of the times, supersonic interceptors armed with missiles and nuclear bombs appeared to be the future of military aviation – not only Mystère IVAs and SMB.2s, but also Vautours and Mirage IIIs were all converted into multi-role aircraft through the installation of underwing hardpoints for air-to-ground ordnance and drop tanks. Indeed, while the original Mirage IIIC was planned to serve as a high-altitude interceptor – including a rocket motor installed under the rear fuselage, an airborne intercept radar, and armed with Matra R.530 semi-active radar homing air-to-air missiles only – the IIICJ variant made for Israel received two DEFA 30mm guns, and a centreline hardpoint with the capacity for two 400kg bombs: as such, it became a multi-role fighter-bomber. Further cooperation between Dassault and the IDF/AF in this field eventually led to the development of the Mirage 5J: a variant with a stretched fuselage for additional fuel. While lacking a radar, it was custom-tailored for ground attack through the addition of two hardpoints under the rear fuselage, and the development of reinforced underwing drop tanks that also served as multiple ejector racks.

In complete ignorance of contemporary practice in the East and the West, and while MiG-21FLs and MiG-21PFMs delivered to Egypt, Iraq, and Syria in 1966–1967 were all armed with R-3S missiles only, the IDF/AF was insistent on retaining guns on its fighter jets. Arguably, 40 Nord 5103 (also 'AA.20') radio-command-guided air-to-air missiles were acquired for SMB.2s, but they never saw operational deployment and were used for practice purposes only. Similarly, the Israelis acquired just 15 highly expensive Matra R.530 air-to-air missiles for their Mirages: while these are known to have been deployed in at least two air combats of 1966, they proved much too cumbersome and largely ineffective. That said, the Israelis eventually did venture into developing their own guided weapons. With French support, in 1959 they initiated the research and development of an infrared homing, short-range air-to-air missile. The resulting Shafrir (later Shafrir Mk I) became available in 1962, when an order was placed for 200, even before all the related testing was concluded. This proved a mistake: although additional adaptations were continued through 1963 and 1964, the weapon proved to have very poor performance and reliability, was much too short-ranged, and was capable of tracking non-manoeuvring targets only. By this time, the company manufacturing them – Rafael – was already working on the much-improved Shafrir Mk. 2.

On the other hand, and contrary to the UAR, Israel was much less successful in regards of initiating domestic production of aircraft: the country lacked the heavy industry and the skilled workforce necessary for such a venture. In the early 1960s, the state-supported company Bedek Aviation acquired the licence for manufacture of French-designed Fouga CM.170 Magister jet trainers, however: only 36 were assembled from knock-down kits delivered by France. The remaining 40 were acquired in flyable condition from Germany. By 1967, Bedek Aviation was capable of conducting overhauls on all types of French-made jets in service with the IDF/AF, and indeed: it was contracted for similar works on SMB.2s of the French Air Force. This is how Bedek was able to reinforce No. 105 Squadron with additional aircraft, only days before the war.

Mirage IIICJ from No. 117 Squadron as seen on take-off in 'clean' configuration. (Albert Grandolini collection)

their approach to the related issues was as logical as opportunistic. For example, in 1962–1963, eight Noratlas transports acquired from France between 1955 and 1959, were augmented by 16 additional examples donated by the German Luftwaffe. Therefore, there was no need to buy more new aircraft from France. Similarly, venerable Douglas C-47 Skytrain/Dakotas were still providing good service and not only formed the backbone of the transport fleet, but also doubled as navigation trainers and electronic warfare platforms. On the other hand, in 1963, Israel experienced no problems with acquiring five Boeing 377 Stratocruiser airliners from Pan Am and purchasing equipment necessary for the Bedek Aviation company to modify them to the KC-97G/F standard: as tanker aircraft and for reconnaissance purposes.

More than transports, it was the helicopter component that was ignored for much too long: although enough Sikorsky S-55 helicopters were acquired in 1958 to form a squadron equipped with them – and this unit quickly proved its worth deploying Sayeret Matkal special forces operators deep in Arab territory – it was only in 1964–1965 that the IDF/AF expanded the fleet into a three-tier branch, with one squadron each of light, medium, and heavy helicopters.

In April 1966, Weizman handed over to Brigadier General Moti Hod to become Chief of Operations IDF. Weizman's protégé for years and an introvert, Hod faced much suspicion early on, before being recognised as a 'team player' and promoted to the rank of Major General. However, he was to prove his worth and be highly successful – also in terms of acquisition of additional combat aircraft: it was during his tenure that the IDF/AF secured orders for 50 Douglas A-4 Skyhawk ground attack aircraft and another for 50 Dassault Mirage 5J fighter-bombers, both of which had been in negotiation for some time but were placed only in early 1967. The first deliveries of both types were scheduled for autumn of the same year, and pilots and ground crews were already in the USA and France for conversion training when the crisis of May 1967 erupted.

7

ROYAL JORDANIAN AIR FORCE

Carved out of the former Ottoman Province of Syria by the pens of British and French 'administrators', during the first 20 years of its existence, the Hashemite Kingdom of Transjordan was heavily dependent upon British financial assistance and administrative advice for its survival. The available budget was too small to support an air force. A flying branch thus came into being very slowly, as a service of the Arab Legion, the country's armed force completely armed and officered by the British. During the late 1940s, it was equipped with a small number of De Havilland Tiger Moths, Dragon Rapides, and Percival Proctor Mk Vs. In 1948, the governments of Great Britain and what had meanwhile been renamed the Hashemite Kingdom of Jordan, concluded a Treaty of Friendship, under the provisions of which the RAF occupied bases at Amman and Mafraq, and provided assistance in founding the Royal Jordanian Air Force (RJAF) as an independent branch of the armed forces. The RJAF was then put under the command of a British officer who also served as Air Adviser to Amman, and a number of other officers and non-commissioned officers (NCOs) were seconded to provide assistance and training. The first group of Jordanian pilots completed their elementary training in July 1951, but not much happened until Crown Prince Hussein ascended the throne in May 1953: having a strong interest in aviation, he purchased several ex-RAF Taylorcraft Auster AOPs, a twin-engined De Havilland Dove VIP transport and, in 1955, two Vampire T.Mk 11 jet-powered, two-seat conversion trainers which became the first fighter jets of the fledgling air force. On 25 September that year, London donated 10 ex-RAF Vampire FB.Mk 9s, which enabled the establishment of No. 1 Squadron (in February 1956), and 10 ex-RAF North American Harvard T.Mk 2Bs, which entered service with No. 6 Squadron, that acted as an operational conversion unit for all available types. Through 1955 and 1956, the RJAF was bolstered through the donation of three Helwan Gomhouria trainers and five Vampire FB.Mk 52s by Egypt.

Crown Prince Hussein (left) with Squadron Leader Jock Dalgleish, who served as Air Adviser to Jordan in the early 1950s, in front of a Vampire jet fighter marked with the crest of the Hashemite Kingdom of Jordan. (Albert Grandolini collection)

In the wake of the Suez War, Amman began signalling interest in intensifying the growth of its air force. Years-long negotiations with London almost ended nowhere before Washington agreed to sponsor a purchase of 12 Hunter F.Mk 6s in late 1958. By 1961, the RJAF initiated the acquisition of Chipmunk trainers and the second batch of 12 Hunter F.Mk 6s as replacements for the Vampires. Correspondingly, by October 1962, when King Hussein ordered his air force to deploy in support of the Kingdom of Saudi Arabia because of the Egyptian military intervention in Yemen, the force included two squadrons of Hunters, one flying Austers for liaison- and reconnaissance purposes, one transport- and one training squadron. However, as mentioned above, the commander of the RJAF exploited this opportunity to defect to the UAR: while all five aircraft they used for this purpose were eventually returned to Amman, most of their pilots continued serving with the UARAF. As a consequence, No. 2 Squadron RJAF was disbanded without replacement, and all remaining aircraft, pilots, and ground personnel reorganised into No. 1 Squadron.

The structure of the air force remained the same for the next five years, although the number of available aircraft and helicopters fluctuated quite some. Surviving Hunters were gradually sent to Great Britain for overhaul and upgrade to the FGA.Mk 9 standard designated F.Mk 73, but by June 1967 the work was completed on only eight of them. Moreover, Washington meanwhile agreed to re-equip the RJAF with 32 Lockheed F-104 Starfighter interceptors, and two TF-104B two-seat conversion trainers returned from a lease to Taiwan: as a result, in late 1966, nearly 50 percent of Jordanian pilots and ground personnel were sent to the USA for conversion training. Consequently, the RJAF of June 1967 was equipped and organised as listed in Table 6.

Generally, with all of its pilots trained in Great Britain, and well-versed in deploying their Hunters both in air combat and for ground attack, the RJAF was widely considered the best-trained Arab air force of the time. With a British-constructed and -equipped radar station at Mount Ajloun, the force was also the only one to have a good view into Israeli airspace, and capable of following major developments there. However, not only had King Hussein been involved in clandestine negotiations with Israel for years, and thus not expecting to become embroiled in a war with Israel, the RJAF's Hunters were few in numbers and – due to the lack of guided air-to-air missiles – considered obsolete for air combat.

Stills from a video showing two of the RJAF Hunters flown to Egypt by defectors in November 1962. Both jets belonged to No. 2 Squadron and were decorated with black and white checkerboards on the ruder and wingtips. (Tom Cooper collection)

Table 6: RJAF Order of Battle, 5 June 1967

Unit	Base	Equipment	Remarks
HQ Amman Commander of the RJAF Major Saleh Kurdi			
The Royal Flight	Amman IAP	Dove, Riley Dove, Herald, Heron, Viking, Alouette III	CO unknown; established 15 April 1950
No. 1 Squadron	King Hussein AB (Mafraq)	19 Hunter F.Mk 6	CO Major Firass Ajlouni; unit slated to re-equip with F-104A/TF-104B
No. 3 Squadron	Amman IAP	Dove, Riley Dove, Herald, Heron, Viking, Ambassador, C-47, Whirlwind, Alouette III	CO unknown; originally established as No. 2 Squadron in mid-1950s, re-designated as No. 3 Squadron in 1959; operating miscellaneous transports and helicopters
No. 4 Training Squadron	Mafraq	Chipmunk	CO unknown; unit established 1960 with Chipmunks but meanwhile inactive

Hunter F.Mk 6 serial number 705, coded F, was one of the aircraft not yet subjected to an upgrade to the F.Mk 73 standard as of June 1967. This photograph from 1966 shows it with both nose and the fin (including horizontal fins) painted in red, along the UAC order from two years earlier, the full crest of No. 1 Squadron on the nose, and white wingtips. (Albert Grandolini collection)

8
SYRIAN ARAB AIR FORCE

Officially established in 1946, the Syrian Arab Air Force (SyAAF) was initially supervised by a small group of British and French advisers, before its first commander contracted two German and five Croat pilots – all veterans of the Second World War – to serve as instructors for the first class of 30 native pilots.[1] Flying a miscellany of light types acquired from Great Britain and the USA, these were qualified to operate 20 T-6 Texans purchased in 1948, just in time to take part in the First Arab-Israeli War. In 1949, the SyAAF purchased 26 Fiat G.55s and four Fiat G.59B-2 fighters from Italy, followed by nine Fiat G.46-1 two-seat conversion trainers. While Syria helped Egypt secure the above-mentioned acquisition of Vampire FB.Mk 52s from Italy, Damascus returned to the practice of ordering military aircraft from Great Britain. Through 1953–1955, it acquired 12 Chipmunk trainers, 10 reconditioned Spitfire F.Mk 22 fighters, 12 Meteor F.Mk 8s, and two Meteor T.Mk 7 two-seat conversion trainers, followed by six Meteor NF.Mk 13s – which arrived without their radars, and were thus used as conversion trainers only. The reason was a similar series of on/off arms embargoes imposed by London, which eventually prompted the Syrians to follow in Egyptian fashion: in 1955, Damascus thus became the third Arab country (after Egypt and the Imamate of Yemen) to place an order for Soviet military aircraft, including a total of 41 MiG-15bis and four MiG-15UTIs. Expecting to make the assembly of these easier, the aircraft were delivered to Egypt, in late 1955 and early 1956, where their crews were undergoing conversion training. However, this process was only about 50 percent complete by the time of the Suez War: while three MiG-15UTIs were evacuated to Syria (via Saudi Arabia), 20 surviving MiG-15s were subsequently donated to Egypt. To replace the MiG-15s, during that conflict Damascus ordered 60 MiG-17F and MiG-17PFs, 12 Il-28s, six Il-14s, 10 helicopters and 20 training aircraft in the USSR. The first of these reached Syria in early 1957, but only a total of 48 MiG-17Fs and MiG-17PFs had arrived by the time Syria and Egypt formed the United Arab Republic in February 1958. When the SyAAF was assimilated into the UARAF, all of its MiG-17PFs and Il-28s were redeployed to Egypt.

Following the dissolution of the UAR, the SyAAF had to be rebuilt almost from scratch: what the Egyptians had left behind were four Il-28R reconnaissance bombers, 40 MiG-17Fs, five each of Mil Mi-1 and Mi-4 helicopters, and a total of seven Il-14s and one C-47. To the Syrian good fortune, during the times of the union the Egyptians – apparently aiming to establish a unit that would train pilots from many different Arab air forces – brought all of their DHC.1 Chipmunk T.Mk 50s to Syria. Together with the survivors from the batch purchased by Damascus in the early 1950s, and refurbished Spitfires, these formed the backbone of the air force's new training

The Syrian MiG-15bis fleet had an unusual career: all 41 from the order placed by Damascus in 1955 were delivered to Egypt where Czechoslovak instructors were to run the conversion training of their pilots and ground crews. This was still incomplete by the time of the Suez War, when half this fleet was destroyed on the ground: the survivors – including these two examples – were then donated to Egypt where they remained in operational service as of June 1967. (Albert Grandolini collection)

Out of four Il-28R reconnaissance bombers left in Syria after the dissolution of the UAR in September 1961, only this one example survived the June 1967 War. It was photographed in 2011, in derelict condition, at Nayrab Airport in Aleppo. Clearly notable is the primary difference to the 'vanilla' bomber variant: the addition of wingtip fuel tanks. (Photo by Erwin Hausmann)

fleet. New combat aircraft were ordered in the form of a contract for 34 MiG-21F-13 interceptors and four MiG-21UM two-seat conversion trainers, signed in Moscow in June 1962: their deliveries began a year later. Constant political unrest and repeated coups resulted in an urgent need for the expansion of training facilities and thus in 1964 Syria became the first non-European customer for the then brand-new Aero L-29 two-seat training jet made in Czechoslovakia: no fewer than 77 of these were acquired over the following years. Prompted by continuous clashes with Israel, the build-up was continued through 1965 and 1966, when orders for a total of 20 MiG-21FLs, 20 MiG-15UTIs, and 40 Su-7BMKs were placed: however, of these, only the MiGs were in the country as of June 1967, and most of their crews were still undergoing conversion training, resulting in an order of battle as listed in Table 7.

Boasting a strength of about 5,000 personnel – including more than 160 pilots qualified to fly fast jets or multi-engined transports – the SyAAF was still a relatively small force. Out of some 45 MiG-17s, 33 were operational, and there were 32 immediately available pilots for them, with another 23 in the advanced stages of conversion training. Similarly, for 55 MiG-21F-13/FLs, there were 47 fully qualified pilots, with another 23 in the advanced stages of conversion training.

The flight operations of the SyAAF were controlled from two unground centres: one in Damascus, responsible for southern Syria (including the capital and the armistice line with Israel), and the other in Hama, responsible for northern Syria. These were provided with information from 22 radar stations, mostly equipped with P-8s: only a few had been reequipped with the latest Soviet P-30s. Exactly as in Egypt, but even more so because of the local terrain in western and south-western Syria, the radar network was almost completely unable to detect aircraft flying at altitudes below 500m. Therefore – and unlike the UARAF – Moukiiad went to some length to develop

When the SyAAF was reestablished in late 1961, not only its cadets, but even Czechoslovak advisers contracted to help rebuild its capability to train pilots were forced to use British-made Chipmunk training aircraft. The type remained in service until the early 1970s. (Albert Grandolini collection)

Table 7: SyAAF Order of Battle, June 1967[2]

Brigade	Base	Equipment	Notes
Air Brigade 3	Mezzeh		CO Colonel Fayez Mansour
No. 1 Squadron	Mezzeh	11 MiG-17F	dispersed to Bley
No. 10 Squadron	Mezzeh	11 MiG-17F	dispersed to Marj Ruhhayl
No. 19 Squadron	Mezzeh	10 MiG-17F	dispersed to T.4 and Hama
No. 40 Flt	Mezzeh	3 Il-28R	
No. 60 Flt	Mezzeh	7 Il-14, 6 Mi-1, 8 Mi-4	
42nd AAA Regiment	Mezzeh	ZPU-4, S-60	
Air Brigade 7	Dmeyr		Brigadier General Muwaffaq al-Assassa
No. 54 Squadron	Dmeyr	22 MiG-21F-13	CO Lieutenant Colonel Naseh Khalid al-Olwany; dispersed to Tsaykal and Dmeyr
No. 70 Squadron	Dmeyr	10 MiG-21FL	CO Lieutenant Colonel Khalid Marwan Zain ad-Dien; dispersed at T.4
No. 77 Squadron	Dmeyr	23 MiG-21F-13	CO Lieutenant Colonel Abdul Razzak
725th AAA Regiment	Dmeyr	ZPU-4, S-60	CO Colonel Duqaq al-Emad
Air Force Academy	Kweres		
Basic Flying School	Kweres	25 Chipmunk T.Mk 50	
Advanced Flying School	Kweres	Yak-11, Yak-18, Spitfire, Meteor, MiG-15UTI	
Jet Flying School		21 L-29	

a network of ground observer-stations, all connected to the two command centres via telephone. This practice had proved its worth already during the Suez War of 1956 when Meteor interceptors of the SyAAF shot down a Canberra reconnaissance bomber of the RAF based solely on telephone reports from ground observers.

On the basis of experience from clashes with Israel in 1963–1967, the SyAAF held a pair of MiG-21s at Readiness Rate I, and another pair at Readiness Rate II during the daylight, and single MiG-21FLs at each of their two bases by night. Similarly, four MiG-17s armed for ground attack were kept at Readiness Rate III (a 30-minute alert). Moukiiad also recognised the vulnerability of his small fleet concentrated on just two air bases, and thus not only developed a plan for their rapid evacuation in the event of a surprise Israeli attack, but also ordered the preparation of numerous dispersal sites around the country. This is why not only the international airport in Aleppo, but also the newly constructed one in Damascus, as well as Marj Ruhhayl, Tsaykal, T.4, Rasin el-Aboud, and Dayr az-Zawr all had runways capable of supporting MiG-17 and MiG-21 operations. Apparently, this plan was set in motion in the second half of April 1967, when MiG-21s are known to have been dispersed to at least four different forward operating bases. Surprisingly enough, and despite their general predilection for innovation and improvisations, the Syrians never decided to adapt their growing fleet of L-29 jet trainers for combat operations.

As clear from Table 7, the SyAAF included its own ground-based air defence units. However, these were primarily responsible for defence of the air bases. The defence of the army's formations in the field was the responsibility of the 9th Brigade, which consisted of nine well-trained battalions equipped with 14.5mm, 37mm, 57mm, 85mm, and 100mm anti-aircraft artillery, and was usually deployed between Damascus and the Golan Heights. Nevertheless, Moukiiad and other commanders were perfectly aware of their poor air defences and thus they advised Salah Jadid to request the delivery of SA-2s

Pilots of No. 70 Squadron – the first SyAAF unit to fly radar-equipped MiG-21FLs – with one of their mounts, seen around the time this unit was officially established in late 1966. (Albert Grandolini collection)

The commander (centre) and pilots of No. 60 Flight, which as of June 1967 flew not only seven Il-14 transports, but all the Mi-1s and Mi-4s of the Syrian Arab Air Force – in front an Mi-1 of their unit. (Albert Grandolini collection)

from Moscow in early 1967. Regardless how supportive of Jadid's regime on the international level, the Soviets refused to do so.

The morale of the force was very high: the SyAAF acknowledged the loss of four jets in the April 1967 clash with the IDF/AF, but claimed five in return, and thus felt victorious. Moreover, many of its pilots possessed combat experience from skirmishes with Israel: through applying the resulting experience to develop their own tactics, the Syrians were convinced they had made progress towards efficiency. However, the SyAAF was badly hampered by the Assad-controlled and sluggish chain of command in Damascus: none of the brigade commanders was permitted to order the scramble of any aircraft without Assad's permission. This meant that the force had minimal capability of immediate response to an attack: indeed, the Israeli experience from clashes in 1963–1967 was that it usually took at least two hours to react. Moreover, although some recently-interviewed Syrian sources indicate that the operations of their Il-28Rs undertaken after 1962 had collected significant amounts of intelligence about the dispositions of several IDF units deployed opposite to the Golan Heights, it remains unknown exactly how much information on the IDF/AF, its capabilities and intentions the SyAAF had as of early June 1967.[3]

9

THE MAY 1967 CRISIS

Early on 15 May 1967, the mobilisation of the Egyptian armed forces was already in full swing. Marching in long columns and full fanfare, two divisions moved down the major roads of Cairo in the direction of the Suez Canal. Exactly as desired by Nasser, the media created the impression that the UAR was now on a war footing. Only hours later, Major General Fawzy returned from another visit to Damascus to report to Amer about yet another meeting with Suweidani. He had requested to see reconnaissance photographs of an IDF build-up along the ceasefire line, but the takes from 12 and 13 May presented by the Syrian showed none at all. Even today it remains unknown if Amer informed Nasser about this fact, or about the fact that only a few hours later the DM1 reported that the Soviet claims about an Israeli invasion were a fabrication: meanwhile, the service was able to collect enough intelligence from informants in Israel to know there was nothing of such activity. Even then it was too late: a withdrawal of the UAR Army would have been a massive embarrassment for Nasser and this was something even Amer was not ready to risk – especially considering the entire mobilisation was envisaged as little more than a demonstration of strength.[1]

In Israel, neither Eshkol nor Rabin were bothered by the Soviet claims: meanwhile, they knew that this was the fourth time Moscow had issued such a warning, that Nasser had no interest in a war, and that even the CIA was reporting that Cairo only planned a demonstration. Understanding that Nasser liked to make grand gestures, Eshkol warned Rabin not to over-react – and the Chief-of-Staff IDF acted correspondingly: he cancelled all provocations in the north, and only increased reconnaissance activities in the south. Indeed, when Rabin recommended mobilising one or two reserve brigades, the Premier only granted authorisation for the dispatch of a few tank companies. Instead, both Eshkol and Rabin then focused on taking part in a military parade staged by the IDF in Jerusalem – not knowing that precisely this was to be misinterpreted as a

An aerial view of T-54s of the 4th Armoured Division, UAR Army, taking a break during their deployment to the Sinai on 15–16 May 1967. Unlike 1960, this time the mobilisation and the movement of the mass of the Egyptian Army to the peninsula were widely publicised. (Albert Grandolini collection)

A view of a supply column for the same unit, consisting of a long column of trucks hauling fuel and spares. (Albert Grandolini collection)

The IDF military parade staged in Jerusalem on 15 May 1967 included few heavy weapons. Nevertheless, amongst those that were shown were these two M-50 self-propelled 155mm howitzers, built on M4 Sherman chassis. (Albert Grandolini collection)

'confirmation of Moscow's warning' by the Arab leaders. Because the Israeli parade included relatively few heavy weapons, the Arab leaders concluded that the Israelis were concentrating these for an invasion of Syria.[2]

FATAL BLOCKADE

By the end of 16 May, AMAN had identified the deployment of two additional Egyptian divisions and two squadrons of fighter aircraft to Sinai. This puzzled Rabin, who was concerned about an attack on the Israeli nuclear complex of Dimona, and eventually persuaded Eshkol to mobilise two reserve brigades. Playing straight into the hands of the General Staff IDF, Nasser – persuaded by Amer – then severely deepened the crisis by ordering the UNEF out of Sinai. Concerned, the commander of the 'Blue Helmets', Indian Major General Indar Jit Rikhye, requested the Secretary-General of the UN, U Thant, to mediate, but there was no response: the Secretary-General reacted only three days later. Meanwhile, the order for withdrawal of the UNEF, prompted the IDF to elevate the alert state of its units and start deploying air defence systems. On 19 May, the Director of AMAN briefed the General Staff IDF that the previous assumption was that there would be no major action by the UAR before around 1970, but that with the deployment of 80,000 troops, 1,000 artillery pieces, and 500 tanks, Nasser's intentions were unclear. Therefore, he recommended calling up 140,000 reservists and warned that this would be a preparation for war. Eshkol granted permission for mobilisation of 80,000 reservists and ordered the General Staff to deploy 300 tanks to Negev, to prepare a plan for reopening the Straits of Tiran by force, and strike UARAF air bases

Also shown in the military parade in Jerusalem on 15 May 1967 was this pair of M197 launchers for MIM-23 HAWK SAMs, each with three missiles. (Albert Grandolini collection)

FISHBEDS OVER DIMONA

Some of the shockwaves caused by the Egyptian overflights of Dimona from May 1967 can be felt to the present day. In recent years scholarly publications concerning this and the following series of overflights of Israel have suggested that the aircraft involved was a Soviet-owned and flown MiG-25R reconnaissance fighter, and that these overflights were undertaken with the aim of preparing some sort of a Soviet attack on Israel, at least a military intervention on the Arab side – set up by Moscow because they were gravely concerned about Israeli nuclear weapons.

While there is little doubt that the Soviets had known about the Israeli project to develop nuclear bombs at least since the early 1960s – and while there is no doubt that it was a fake Soviet report about an 'imminent Israeli invasion of Syria' that sparked the crisis that eventually culminated in the June 1967 War and the catastrophic defeat of the Arab militaries – there is also little doubt that Moscow was doing its best to maintain the status quo in the Middle East, to prevent any kind of armed conflict, and to keep itself non-involved. Foremost, there is no trace of evidence about any deployment of Soviet MiG-25Rs in Egypt at that time: if for no other reason than because as of May 1967 the type was available in prototype form only (designated Ye-266), and still years away from entering operational service. Indeed, the development of the reconnaissance variant of the MiG-25 began only in 1969, the resulting MiG-25R first flew in 1970, and was still very much undergoing testing when actually deployed in Egypt for the first time in 1971. Unsurprisingly, some sort of a 'definitive confirmation' that such aircraft had been deployed in Egypt, and then at an air base as exposed and as relatively primitive as Meliz AB – in the middle of the Sinai desert, only 50 kilometres from the border with Israel – as of May 1967 is less than 'unlikely' to ever become available.[10] This is even more so considering that the aircraft in question were MiG-21F-13s from No. 45 Squadron, UARAF and that their pilots were Egyptians. This point is a matter of fact that has failed to attract the attention of researchers daydreaming about MiG-25s overflying Dimona as of May 1967, primarily because they have never attempted to directly research the Egyptian air force. One of the two pilots involved in the overflight of 17 May was Qadri Abd el-Hamid:

A young pilot joy-riding MiG-21F-13s high over the Israeli nuclear complex in Dimona in May–June 1967, Qadri Abd el-Hamid went on to pursue a distinguished career with the EAF. Amongst others, he claimed at least one Israeli Mirage during the War of Attrition and then a Phantom during the October 1973 War. This photograph was taken when he was flight-testing BAe HAWK training jets in the UK in the mid-1970s. (Qadri Abd el-Hamid collection)

> I was with No. 45 Squadron at Meliz AB in the central Sinai… None of us thought we would really have to fight with Israel, but we felt we were very good… [and thus felt like] …flying above Israel at a flight level above 18km [11 miles]. They shot at us with their HAWK missiles, but because of our height they didn't hit us. We were flying over Israeli territory but stayed over it just a short time, so the (Dassault) Mirage (IIICJ interceptors) couldn't reach us. On 29 May 1967, we had seen Eshkol [on TV] with President [Lyndon B] Johnson in the USA. He was begging for US support because the Egyptians were flying over them every day, and they could not stop us.[11]

It might sound unusual for MiG-21s to fly so high. However, one should keep in mind that this type was originally developed on the basis of experiences from the Korean War, where Soviet-made MiG-15 proved capable of flying *higher* than all types in US and allied service and thus remained a major problem throughout the three years of that conflict. From the standpoint of top Soviet military decision makers of the General Staff of the Soviet Armed Forces – bolstered by reports about the USA developing several types of high-flying strategic bombers – in any

should there be an attack against Dimona – but remained insistent on a diplomatic solution. Rabin reacted by informing the senior leadership of the IDF that he felt Israel was isolated on the diplomatic level, and he was isolated from Eshkol and his government, and the sole solution was a 'pre-emptive' strike.[3]

Even before the Israelis were seriously concerned, Nasser – once again under pressure from Amer, but fully aware this would increase the threat of an Israeli attack – decided to 'enforce' the blockade of the Tiran Straits. The final decision in this regard came during a conference of the Higher Executive Committee on 21 May, when the President of the UAR explained the situation and then asked Amer if the armed forces were ready. The Field Marshal put a hand on his throat while replying: 'My neck is at stake, boss. Everything is in tiptop shape.'[4]

Bearing in mind the condition of the Egyptian Army (which is to be discussed in Volume 2 of this mini-series) was even poorer than that of the UARAF described above, and that not only Amer, but Sidqi Mahmoud must have been aware of this fact, the reason for Amer's fateful answer remains unclear. A definite answer was never provided.

The decision to blockade the Straits of Tiran was announced in public during Nasser's visit to Abu Suweir AB on 22 May – at the same time a battalion of 400 paratroopers commanded by Brigadier Abd al-Moneim Khalil – supported by seven SU-100 tank destroyers, six motor torpedo boats and a destroyer of the UAR Navy – deployed future conflict the Soviet air force would need a fighter flying even higher. Correspondingly, the MiG-21 was designed with flying at altitudes of up to 18,000m (59,055ft) and higher in mind, and (as confirmed not only by those that flew the type in the early 1960s, but also by tactical manuals for this type from the same time) their pilots trained in such operations.[12]

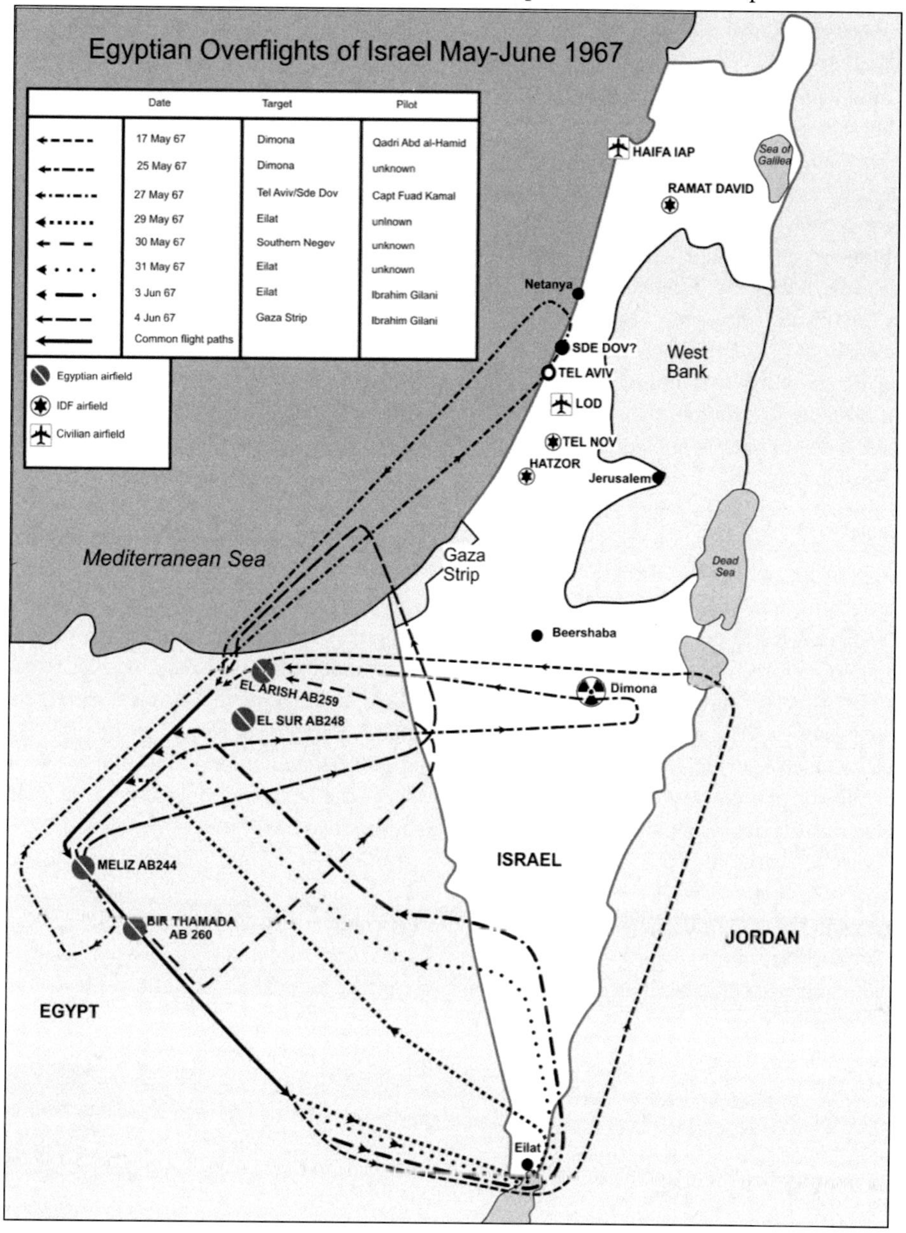

A map illustrating known Egyptian penetrations of Israeli airspace during the second half of May and early June 1967. While causing grave concern within the top ranks of the IDF, as is clear not only from the routes taken by UARAF MiG-21s, but also from descriptions provided by the pilots involved, these operations were undertaken for 'joy-riding' purposes and did not result in the collection of any kind of useful intelligence. (Map by Mark Thompson, based on Shalom, *Like a Bolt out of the Blue* and interviews with involved UARAF pilots)[13]

in Sharm el-Sheikh. That said, Khalil was strictly prohibited from firing upon any Israeli ships, and this was later confirmed during the interrogations of several Egyptian prisoners of war.[5]

ALARM IN TEL AVIV

Meanwhile, the situation was heating up in the sky over the Sinai and the Negev Desert. On 17 May 1967, a pair of Egyptian aircraft launched from Meliz Air Base in central Sinai, passed south of the port of Eilat at an altitude of more than 18,000 metres (59,050ft), before reaching Jordan. After flying north for a while, the jets then turned west and made a pass not only over Israel, but directly over the Dimona complex, this time reaching an altitude of 21,340 metres (70,000ft). The battery of MIM-23 HAWK SAMs deployed to protect the strategically important installation opened fire but failed to shoot down the intruders: they flew above its engagement envelope.[6]

To say that this overflight caused 'consternation' within the Israeli government and the General Staff IDF, would be an understatement: combined with AMAN's reports about the deployment of the Egyptian Il-28 bombers to bases in the Sinai (which turned out to be bogus), it resulted in the IDF/AF being put on alert and its Mirage pilots given the authorisation to cross the border in pursuit of overflying 'MiGs' if necessary.[7]

The sources differ over the date of the next Egyptian overflight of Dimona: according to one version, this took place around midday on 26 May, and included four aircraft: while two returned early, the other two overflew Dimona. According to the other version, it took place only on 3 June. What is certain is that with the General Staff IDF informing Israeli Prime Minister Levi Eshkol about the Egyptians 'possibly preparing a coordinated attack on Dimona including up to 40 aircraft', he then authorised the IDF/AF to promptly hit back against all of the Egyptian air bases in the Sinai should anything of that kind happen. Although some of the Israeli and Western sources stress that this intelligence was substantiated, and that even the later Egyptian Chief-of-Staff Muhammad Fawzy alluded that Egypt was actually planning to open an aerial offensive on Israel on the morning of 27 May – but that this was cancelled by Nasser at the very last moment – the author has never found any kind of evidence for such plans: if they ever existed, they must have remained one of the best-ever protected secrets of Egypt.[8]

Of course, the leadership of the IDF knew that the high-flying MiG-21s were no direct threat to Dimona. Nevertheless, generals like Rabin took nothing for granted. By 28 May 1967, a combined civilian and military team had assembled the first two or three – improvised – nuclear bombs and drawn up a preliminary contingency plan codenamed Operation Shimshon. This envisaged a demonstrative deployment of a nuclear device by two Super Frelon helicopters in a desolate part of eastern Sinai, as the 'last trump card' for the (very unlikely) case that Israel found itself in peril.[9]

While the crisis that eventually led to the June 1967 Arab-Israeli War thus marked the moment in which Israel crossed the nuclear threshold, the available information indicates that these early nuclear weapons assembled as of 28 May were clumsy, spider-like, improvised constructions unsuitable for deployment by platforms such as combat aircraft or ballistic missiles. Moreover, their possible deployment was quickly overtaken by developments.

AMER'S CIRCUS

Perhaps the biggest irony about the crisis and the war of June 1967 is that the UAR armed forces were commanded by a person not supposed to command them. Officially at least, Field Marshal Amer had handed over the post of the Minister of War to General Shams Badran, and that of the chief-of-staff to Major General Fawzy (a supporter of Nasser) in 1963. Nevertheless, he remained in control of the UAR armed forces and continued meddling at every opportunity and level, until no decision could be taken without him. Generally, Nasser, who was only keen in reaping political gains, did not interfere in Amer's decisions, although Amer was able to question or even to reverse his decisions. This was true for almost everything the armed forces did through the second half of May 1967.

Initially, the army deployed following the plan for Operation Conqueror. Finalised on 1 December 1966, this stipulated the defence of Sinai along three well-fortified lines: essentially, the Egyptians expected to drag the IDF into three successive 'killing fields' and weaken it to the degree where they could launch a limited counter-offensive against the Eilat area in southern Israel. However, right from the start of mobilisation, Amer began bypassing not only the Chief-of-Staff of the UAR Army, but nearly all subordinate commanders down to the level of division commanders and lying to them – and nobody dared seriously countering him. As a result, the UAR Army's deployment to Sinai rapidly descended into chaos and confusion.[14]

According to the Operations Directorate of the Army, the realisation of planning for Operation Conqueror required some six months of preparations, including construction of additional fortifications and a better supply system, and careful training and deployment of the units involved. The plan was complex enough for there to also be a requirement for the establishment of a special field army headquarters, subordinated to the General Headquarters in Cairo. Indeed, Amer established such a command node on 15 May, and appointed Lieutenant General Salah ad-Din Mohsen in command. However, to ensure that Nasser would not interfere, and to bypass Fawzy, two days later he then established a separate Front Headquarters under the command of Major General Abdel Mohsen Murtagi, a competent officer recalled for this purpose from Yemen, but entirely unfamiliar with planning for Operation Conqueror. Actually, Amer – fully convinced about the UAR's military superiority to Israel – decided to command on his own, and assured Murtagi that his task was merely that of acting his chief-of-staff. Murtagi shared Amer's confidence: when British Field Marshal Bernard Montgomery visited the UAR on 12 May, and bluntly warned the Egyptians would lose a war with Israel, Murtagi replied that they had the best Soviet equipment.

Meanwhile, Amer replaced all the divisional commanders (except that of the 20th Division), and at least six brigade commanders. While this seems to have been motivated by the need to have combat-experienced veterans of the Yemen War in command, combined with the necessity to replace units redeployed

Field Marshal Hakim Amer talking to a group of MiG-21 and Su-7 pilots at Abu Suweir on 23 May 1967. While not even meant to command the UAR armed forces in May 1967, he micromanaged them into the state of chaos and confusion. (Tom Cooper collection)

to Sharm el-Sheikh by those from the strategic reserve, it completely disrupted the chain of command at a critical point in time: at the point when the UAR had to decide if it wanted to attack or not. Instead, Amer went on ruining the plan for Operation Conqueror through haphazard redeployment of entire divisions ever closer to the armistice lines with Israel. Some interpret this as him drafting offensive plans, however, regardless of how optimistic, he must have known that his units were not ready, and there is no evidence for such intentions. Indeed, although the IDF subsequently captured the almost complete documentation of the UAR Army in Sinai, and although Fawzy, Gamasy and Murtagi did mention plans like Lion (an offensive on Eilat) and Leopard (an offensive in the direction of Tel Aviv), at most, they were developed by Amer in private, without any involvement of the General Headquarters or the Planning Division, no maps or arrangements for communications, support, and logistics. Instead, only the following facts are certain:

- During the famous meeting and press conference with the pilots of Air Group 7 at Abu Suweir on 23 May, Nasser stressed that the UAR would not start a war. When challenged by one of the pilots, he explained that this would mean a war with the United States and that the UAR was neither willing, nor able to fight a superpower.
- Even if not explaining this in public, it is clear that Nasser was searching for a new outlet for his earlier failures. When, for example, Sidqi Mahmoud warned him that the blockade of the Straits of Tiran made war 'inevitable', and demanded an attack on Israel, Nasser refused to consider that option and stressed that a political solution would be found, exactly like in 1960. To no small degree, a factor important to him was that only five Israeli ships had passed the straits over the last 10 years, and not one in 1966 and 1967. Therefore, the conclusion to be drawn is that Nasser used the blockade as a tool to exercise political pressure – and even tied it to a negotiated peace with Israel – without the intention to actually provoke a war.
- While aware of Amer's planning, during a conference with Amer, Fawzy, Gamasy and the service chiefs on 25 May, Nasser not only repeated his rejection of initiating an attack: indeed, he insisted on reinforcing the defences of the Gaza Strip and Sharm el-Sheikh.
- Finally, numerous statements by the members of the General Staff IDF since have made it clear that, actually, Nasser's blockade of the Straits of Tiran played little role in their decision-making as the public perception of UAR armed forces' deployment along the ceasefire lines would have posed a serious threat to the existence of Israel.

Commander of No. 55 Squadron, Major Abdel Moneim el-Shennawy, explaining the then brand-new Su-7BMK fighter-bomber to President Gamal Abdel Nasser during his visit to Abu Suweir Air Base on 23 May 1967. (Tarek el-Shennawy collection)

Correspondingly, if there were really any Egyptian offensive plans all had been abandoned by that point in time, and neither they nor the blockade of the Straits of Tiran were what mattered to the leadership of the IDF – which, as subsequent developments were to show, was the body actually in charge of what was to follow.[15]

GENERAL'S COUP

The Israelis were informed about the blockade of the Straits of Tiran on 23 May, when a meeting was set up between Eshkol, AMAN, and the General Staff IDF. This time, the AMAN director warned that a decisive moment had arrived and Israel either had to attack or face a long-term threat to her existence. Rabin exploited the opportunity to present the options:

a) Operation Atzmon: limited offensive, or
b) Operation Axe: all-out attack on Egypt, followed by a conquest of Sinai and strikes on Jordan and Syria.

Eshkol still hesitated, but Rabin continued insisting until the point where he collapsed under the strain: he did not return to duty for 30 hours, and even once he did, he was not fully recovered. With this, Rabin's deputy Ezer Weizman assumed the position of the chief-of-staff. Without waiting for Eshkol's approval, he ordered the IDF to starting positions for Operation Axe, aiming to initiate an attack on 26 May. Meanwhile, the Northern and Central Commands were to prepare for the event of either Jordan or Syria trying to intervene. However, once again, Eshkol restrained the IDF, demanding that the generals enable his minister of foreign affairs, Abba Eban, to try to find a diplomatic solution.[16]

At an emergency meeting of the Israeli cabinet on 27 May, AMAN reported that the Iraqi 1st and 8th Mechanised Brigades were underway to Damascus, and that the Jordanian and Lebanese armed forces were being mobilised. At least in public, it appeared that Israel was now surrounded by enemies ready to strike and destroy it. Unsurprisingly, this impression resulted in the cabinet splitting over whether to rely upon US diplomatic action or striking first, emboldening the General Staff IDF to act on its own: despite Eshkol's order to demobilise 40,000 reservists, it called up yet more. Facing mounting pressure, on 28 May 1967, Eshkol then decided to address the nation via radio – but this led to a disaster: still recovering from recent treatment for a cataract, and reading from a script with many unreadable, last-minute changes, he began stuttering and rambling, creating the impression of being exhausted and panicking. Rather unsurprisingly, during his next meeting with the senior leadership, frustrated Israeli generals began exercising massive pressure upon Eshkol to authorise an offensive: confident that they had a powerful army and could win a 'decisive, quick and elegant' victory; arguing that if Israel failed to react, its deterrence capacity would suffer 'irremediable damage', that this was a 'historic opportunity' to enlarge the country – even offering to 'invent a pretext' – they demanded that the prime minister give an immediate order to start the war. The eventual result was what Israeli historian Guy Laron termed as 'a very Israeli putsch'. With everybody in agreement that Egypt would have to be knocked out of the conflict first, and although fearful of a possible Soviet reaction, Eshkol gave in: on 1 June 1967, he appointed his political opponent Moshe Dayan as minister of defence.[17]

From that point in time, the only spark necessary to initiate an Israeli attack and accomplish what Dayan, Rabin, Weizman, Hod and other IDF generals had wanted to realise for years, was US permission to do so. Israel's foreign minister Abba Eban travelled to the USA to meet Secretary of State Dean Rusk, however: Washington only announced it would intervene on Israel's behalf if the USSR joined the fighting. Moreover, President Johnson warned Israel not to open hostilities and that Israel would be alone if it decided to act alone. However, Director of Mossad, Meir Emit then returned from consultations in Washington, convinced that the Americans supported an Israeli first strike, and recommending war. At Dayan's request, the cabinet thus met once again, at 08.15hrs of 4 June 1967, and – although Eshkol was still reluctant – reached the final decision to embark on war.[18]

FINAL WARNING

Meanwhile, and much too late, Nasser began comprehending his complete misreading of the Israeli strategy. Even then, to a large degree, it remains unclear how much of such information Nasser ever forwarded to Amer and the other commanders of the UAR armed forces. What is known is that after the meeting of 25 May, Sidqi Mahmoud toured several bases and – in cooperation with Minister of Agriculture Shafeeq al-Qishin – began searching for ways to fortify air bases using sandbags. Although this resulted in some work at Abu Suweir and Cairo West, overall, it proved too little, too late.[19]

On 2 June, the DM1 received a warning that Israel was planning to attack on 4 or 5 June, either from a high-ranking IDF officer whose name is still unknown, or from Refaat Ali Suleiman al-Gammal, its agent performing clandestine operations in Israel. Later during the day, the DM1 also received a warning from the India's Research and Analysis Wing that an Israeli attack would occur on 4 or 5 June. General Sadek discussed this information with Nasser during a meeting on the same day, prompting Sidqi Mahmoud to demand an order for a pre-emptive strike on Israel. However, Nasser refused to commit, leaving the commander of the UARAF to conclude that an opening Israeli strike would be 'deadly'. Having no other choices and trusting intelligence assessments that the IDF/AF was lacking the range to strike bases in the Nile Delta, Sidqi Mahmoud then ordered the evacuation of the mass of aircraft from air bases on Sinai. It was for this reason that as of the morning of 5 June, only seven MiG-17Fs of No. 18 Squadron were left at el-Arish, half of No. 25 Squadron at Bir Thamada, and only a handful of MiG-15s from No. 24 Squadron at el-Sur: only No. 45 Squadron kept all of its MiG-21F-13s and one MiG-15UTI at Meliz AB.

The UARAF's posture was thus reduced to that resembling Nasser: despite verbal hostility and repeated overflights of southern Israel, the air force was forced to think defensively, to hope it could survive the opening Israeli air strike and then to pick the time and place for combat.

10
ONSLAUGHT

During the meeting of the Israeli cabinet on 4 June 1967, there was no discussion at all about Israel's precise aims and objectives: obviously, these were left at the discretion of the General Staff IDF. Once the decision for war was taken, Dayan and Rabin decided H-Hour would be between 07.00 and 07.30hrs the following morning, and then began issuing the relevant orders.[1] However, more was not necessary because the General Staff IDF already had its forces in position and all the planning ready for months.

OPERATION FOCUS[2]

In contrast to the Arab, and particularly Egyptian, war-planning – which was not only based on faulty intelligence but also envisaged a slow, set-apiece air battle – the Israeli war-planning emphasised a massive and concentrated aerial campaign of sustained attacks on enemy air bases at the start of war. Defined as the plan for Operation Focus in mid-March 1967, this envisaged the neutralisation of enemy air forces through damage to runways and destruction of the maximum number of aircraft on the ground by flight-sized formations within two to four hours of orders being issued. Operation Focus was a relatively flexible plan, enabling several scenarios: the most important was Focus A, which prioritised the neutralisation of 13 Egyptian air bases.

This campaign was crucial for the outcome of the entire conflict and was therefore planned as the major effort by Israeli air power. Indeed, it would involve practically every available combat aircraft. The hammer blow it was expected to deliver was aimed at physically destroying the enemy air forces on the ground (in order to establish complete air superiority over the battlefield): correspondingly, it was an all-out effort – very different from the 'sit and wait' position into which the United Arab Republic Air Force had been forced by the decisions of the top political and military leadership in Cairo. It relied on the capabilities of the IDF/AF ground crews to 'turn around' every combat aircraft within seven to eight minutes, thus multiplying the relatively small force of fighter jets available. In fact, the Israelis possessed only 206 fighter-bombers, of which around 197 were operational and 183 were manned as of the morning of 5 June 1967. However, due to the excellent training of their ground crews, most of these were available to be flown – by using different pilots – up to eight times a day.[3]

The net result of this capability was that the planners of Operation Focus concluded that they could put an attack formation over each major Arab air base at intervals of between 10 and 15 minutes, and thus keep their enemy under constant pressure during the crucial first few hours of the war. This important factor is very seldom placed within the proper context in the various studies of the Arab reaction to the Israeli assault. However, when taken together with experience of the US, British and French aircraft carriers that were used for interventions in the Middle East during the 1950s and 1960s, it serves to explain why many Arab leaders of the time, and so much of the Arab public until the present day, remain convinced that Israel was not alone in launching this attack: in the Arab world, it is still widely believed that the Israelis were supported by (at least) British and US aircraft. The fact is that the Arabs were – and remain – stunned by the sheer number of aircraft the Israelis threw into the fray as they were hit by successive waves of IDF/AF fighter-bombers. Thinking in terms of their own insufficient military education and training, the military commanders in Cairo in particular could not imagine that the Israelis could put so many aircraft into the skies over the Egyptian air bases. The pace of Operation Focus was therefore one of the decisive factors, and – considering the chaos it caused within the Egyptian military hierarchy – there is little doubt that the Israeli plan would have succeeded even if the first Israeli attack wave had not achieved the level of surprise it did: as explained above, the fact is that the UARAF was unable to scramble enough fighters to intercept so many incoming Israeli formations.

The final order for Operation Focus envisaged the strike would hit the UARAF at 08.45hrs local time (07.45 in Israel): by then, the usual Egyptian combat air patrols launched at dawn would have returned to base, the morning mist would dissipate, and senior officers would be underway to their offices. However, only the first wave was planned in detail. The planning for all subsequent waves was based on the principles of *Auftragstaktik*: post-strike and intelligence reports concerning enemy activity, plus a considerable degree of improvisation. Unsurprisingly considering the cumbersome Egyptian command and control system, the focus on the UARAF alone, combined with the speed of the execution and severity of the blows inflicted, the aim of the operation was also to paralyse the Egyptian chain of command to a degree where the Israelis were free to act against the slow and ineffective responses from Iraq, Jordan, and Syria: therefore, the number of targets rose to more than 20 during the third wave. By then, the IDF/AF could also count on achieving a more favourable numerical superiority over the other Arab air forces.

The basic principle behind the Israeli planning was simplicity. For navigation to their targets the leaders of the Israeli formations depended on a compass, map, wristwatch, and their own skills and experience. All subsequent reports alluding to various 'traitors' guiding Israeli fighters to their targets remain unsubstantiated and, indeed, highly unlikely.

To ensure operational and tactical surprise, the pilots involved in the first few waves were required to approach their targets along carefully pre-selected routes and at very low level. However, most subsequent operations were undertaken by aircraft flying at medium altitudes, while many formations returned to Israel at high altitude in order to conserve fuel: by then, of course, the Israelis had already achieved surprise and no longer found concealment necessary.

Some of the ingress routes selected for the first wave were over the Mediterranean Sea, but none of the attack formations flew first to the west before attacking from that direction: indeed, many formations flew along routes that were well overland. Exactly as expected by officers of the Egyptian ADC, and except for the opening wave, the Israelis found no difficulty in reaching their targets deep inside Egypt while flying at very low altitude. For their part, knowing that Egypt's low-altitude radar coverage was very poor, the UARAF pilots expected the Israelis to come in at low level – and take them by surprise. However, some formations tasked with targeting very distant bases within Egypt were scheduled to take-off well after the initial attack in order to be able to save fuel and reach their targets by flying at high altitudes. Even if it was to be expected that such formations would be detected by the UARAF relatively early, the IDF/AF could still count on the inertia and chaos that by then reigned in the Egyptian chain of command.

The weapons deployed by the Israelis were also simple: runways were targeted with general-purpose bombs of 50kg, 70kg, 100kg, 250kg, 400kg and 500kg, while aircraft parked on the ground were strafed by 30mm autocannons. Most bombs were equipped with detonators set at 0.1 seconds, but some had delay detonators and were intended to explode long after the actual attack, in order to hamper any runway repair efforts. Unguided rockets of 80mm calibre were deployed only by the slower fighter-bombers in Israeli service. Stories concerning the use of 'infrared homing' rockets and/or missiles to target Arab aircraft on the ground belong to the realm of fantasy. Indeed, even the stories concerning the use of runway-penetration (so-called 'dibber') bombs are much exaggerated: in cooperation with France, the Israelis did develop two types of runway-penetration weapons, however, these were not only in short supply but also proved relatively unreliable. Fewer than 150 such weapons were deployed on 5 June. In contrast, the majority of Israeli fighter-bombers sent to attack the Arab air bases which were capable of supporting heavier aircraft and had particularly hardened runways, were armed with general-purpose bombs equipped with hardened penetration cones.

Most of the Israeli formations consisted of four aircraft. However, technical malfunctions, combat damage and losses regularly reduced these to three or even two aircraft. Even so, it was impressed upon the pilots that they had to reach their targets and accomplish their mission regardless of the price. Every formation was authorised to fly a single bombing run, followed by as many strafing passes as the formation leader found necessary – while keeping in mind the allocated time-over-target, which was usually limited to between 10 and 15 minutes.

As of 1967, the IDF/AF had developed two different schools of thought regarding tactics for airfield attacks – and the final choice was left to squadron commanders. While some insisted on their aircraft operating in pairs that would approach targets from opposite directions, others ordered their formation members to separate before reaching the target and each aircraft to attack from a different direction. There is little doubt that these slight tactical differences added much to the confusion seen at Arab air bases on that morning.

FIRST WAVE

Operation Focus was actually launched on the evening of 4 June, when IDF/AF pilots were briefed about the forthcoming attack. Ground crews were only informed on the morning of 5 June, because there was no necessity for them to know earlier: all the available fighter-bombers were already refuelled, armed and ready for combat. The first to launch on the morning of 5 June was a Boeing KC-97 equipped as an ELINT/SIGINT-gatherer, which took off at 03.25. The crews involved in the first wave were woken at 04.38hrs local time (05.38hrs Cairo time) and ordered to report to briefing rooms where each squadron's assignments were written on blackboards. Formation leaders then began briefing pilots with the help of detailed target folders. The pilots were then driven to their aircraft and after pre-flight checks taxied to their take-off points guided by traffic marshals with big signs, because radio silence was imperative (all aircraft had their receivers on, but kept their transmitters off).

The plan for Operation Focus was constantly updated depending on intelligence, but the first wave of fighter-bombers launched between 07.14 and 08.28 Israeli time (08.14 and 09.28 Egyptian

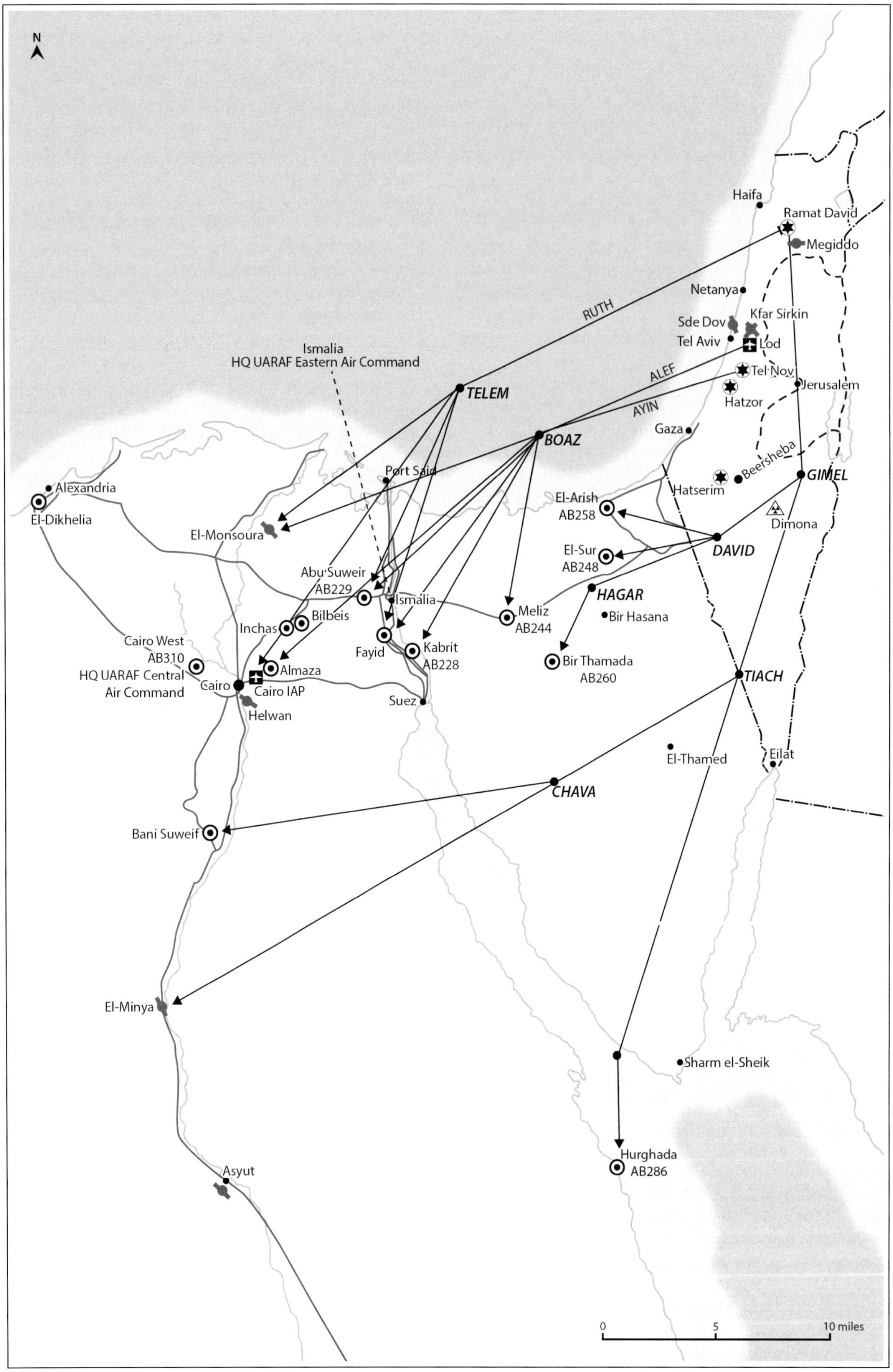

A map of the routes taken by Israeli fighter-bomber formations during Operation Focus to reach air bases in the UAR during the first wave of attacks on the morning of 5 June 1967. As can be seen, only a few routes led over the Mediterranean Sea: none of them as far as often reported. (Map by George Anderson)

time): it included a total of 45 formations with 170 fighters – several of these flying post-strike reconnaissance. They were supported by two C-47s that acted as radio relays; at least one Vautour with Thompson-CSF Calypso stand-off jamming equipment; three Pipers that flew reconnaissance along the Israeli frontiers, and then by a group of six CM.170s that flew a deception sortie over the Mediterranean Sea: departing Hatzerim Air Base, the latter formation simulated a group of fighters, using call signs and scripted radio chatter to imitate a 'normal fighter training mission'.

After take-off, the flights formed and turned in the direction of their targets while underway at altitudes of 30–90m (100–300ft). Although thus remaining unobserved by Egyptian early warning radars, they were detected by the Jordanian radar at Ajlun, where the duty officer – realising the magnitude of dozens of blips taking off and turning west – radioed the code word for war to the HQ of the UAC in Amman. Major General Riyadh promptly forwarded the warning to Cairo: '50 Israeli aircraft will attack Egypt between 08.35 and 08.45. Inab, inab, inab.'[4]

However, the message was ignored because only a day earlier, the Egyptians had changed their codes – without informing anybody. The reality is that even if anybody had tried to warn key commanders within the military hierarchy in Cairo, it would have been too late: they were already on board two Il-14s of No. 11 Squadron that took off from Almaza around 08.15hrs and were underway for Bir Thamada. One carried Amer, Sidqi Mahmoud, numerous other ranking commanders, and the Soviet air force liaison officer in Egypt for an inspection of the troops in Sinai. The second carried the Egyptian Vice-President Hussein el-Shafei, and an Iraqi delegation led by Prime Minister Yahya el-Tahir. Because of their flights, all anti-aircraft batteries protecting Abu Suweir, Fayid, Kabrit, Meliz, el-Sur and Bir Thamada air bases were ordered not to open fire between 08.00 and 09.00hrs. Air defence units protecting Beni Suweif and Cairo West had received similar orders due to other activities – including a flight of four MiG-21s from No. 26 Squadron, and six Il-28s that launched for a mission over Yemen. Finally, in addition to a pair of MiG-17s on a combat air patrol over

Wreckage of MiG-17F serial number 2235 seen after el-Arish was overrun by the IDF. As usual for No. 18 Squadron, the jet had chequered markings on its ruder: in this case, these were applied in blue. (IDF, via Albert Grandolini)

The sole MiG-15bis of No. 18 Squadron caught by Ouragans at el-Arish was the example with serial number 2665, wearing the red insignia of the 'flying panther' on the nose. (Tom Cooper collection)

Wreckage of two of No. 45 Squadron's MiG-21F-13s destroyed at Meliz AB (Bir Gifgafa), during the first seconds of the June 1967 War. Ouragans of No. 113 Squadron destroyed a total of 13 MiG-21s, two Il-14s, and two Mi-6 helicopters. (IDF, via Albert Grandolini)

A post-strike reconnaissance photograph of Meliz AB (taken by one of two Vautour IIBRs of No. 110 Squadron), showing the wreckage of two Il-14s and an Mi-6. (IDF, via Albert Grandolini)

Sinai, and three MiG-15s that had taken off from Cairo West for a training sortie, a formation of six Tu-16 bombers launched from Beni Suweif at 08.40.

BLOWS AND CHAOS

At el-Arish, Israeli fighter-bombers quickly wiped out six MiG-17s and one MiG-15bis of No. 18 Squadron that were still around. Meliz was attacked by four Ouragans from No. 113 Squadron: of four No. 45 Squadron's MiG-21s that attempted to scramble, two were set on fire before they could get airborne; one shot down shortly after take-off, and another disappeared during a dogfight in which an Ouragan also disappeared. Another Israeli jet was shot down by ground fire, while a third made a belly landing back in Israel. Out of No. 45 Squadron's complement of 14, just one damaged jet and that unit's MiG-15UTI survived. At Bir Thamada, the Israelis first destroyed two MiG-17s rolling for take-off, then turned around and finished the other six. Similarly, at el-Sur, all of No. 24 Squadron's MiG-15bis were destroyed in a matter of minutes.

In the Canal Zone, at 08.45hrs, SMB.2s of No. 109 Squadron bombed the runway of Fayid and then strafed eight MiG-21s of No. 47 Squadron, before blowing up four Su-7s from Nos. 1 and 55 Squadrons. Amid the ensuing chaos, large fires and huge clouds of smoke, the Il-14 carrying the Egyptian and Iraqi prime ministers landed, its crew and occupants evacuating the aircraft only seconds before it was hit and set on fire: the wreckage thus blocked the runway. Ground crews and anti-aircraft gunners had barely managed to recover from the shock when four Ouragans appeared at 09.10hrs to repeat the exercise: one of these was shot down and its pilot killed, but in total Air Group 1 lost 12 MiG-21s, two MiG-19s and 10 Su-7s, and both runways were either cratered or blocked by wreckage.

Kabrit came under attack by SMB.2s at 08.45hrs, and then another at 08.55, but managed to scramble a pair of MiG-17PFs

MiG-17PF serial number 2302, piloted by Mustafa Hafez, was badly damaged and 'confirmed' as shot down by the IDF/AF. The Egyptian managed to make a safe landing, and his jet was subsequently repaired. (Mustafa Hafez collection, via Dr David Nicolle)

Another view of the damaged MiG-17PF serial number 2302. Visible in the rear to the left is the MiG-15UTI serial number 2606: that jet was also damaged in Israeli attacks on Kabrit and had to undergo extensive repairs. (Mustafa Hafez collection, via Dr David Nicolle)

Table 8: Operation Focus, First Wave, Summary						
Target	Attacking aircraft	Sorties (aborted)	Aircraft lost	Aircraft damaged	Crew killed	Crew PoW
Abu Suweir	Mirage	12 (1)	-	-	-	-
	Super Mystère	8	1	-	-	1
	Mystère	4	-	-	-	-
	Vautour	4	-	-	-	-
El-Arish	Ouragan	8		1	-	-
Bani Suweif	Mirage	3	-	-	-	-
	Vautour	10	-	-	-	-
Bir Gifgafa	Mystère	4 (1)		2	-	-
	Ouragan	16	2	3	1	1
Bir Thamada	Mirage	3	-	-	-	-
	Mystère	4	-	-	-	-
	Ouragan	7	-	-	-	-
Cairo West	Mirage	22	-	-	-	-
	Super Mystère	4 (1)	-	-	-	-
Fayid	Mystère	12 (2)	1	-	-	-
	Ouragan	13	1	-	1	-
Inchas	Mirage	4	-	-	-	-
	Super Mystère	11 (1)	1	1	1	-
Jebel Libni	Mirage	2	-	-	-	-
Kabrit	Super Mystère	11	-	-	-	-
	Mystère	7	2	-	2	-
Radar stations	Magister	16	1	-	1	-
Total		185 (6)	9	7	6	2

from No. 31 Squadron in between. The IDF/AF credited one of its pilots with a confirmed kill, but actually, the Egyptian pilot managed to land his badly damaged jet safely.

A still from a gun camera film from an SMB.2 of No. 105 Squadron IDF/AF that hit Kabrit on the morning of 5 June, showing hits on a pair of Su-7BMKs from No. 55 Squadron, UARAF. (IDF, via Albert Grandolini)

Housing three squadrons of Il-28s and MiG-21PFMs of No. 26 Squadron, Abu Suweir was one of the primary Israeli targets and the IDF/AF deployed three flights of Mirage IIICJs to attack it within the first 20 minutes. However, their plan had one flaw: the first Mirage flight only bombed the runway, without strafing the parked aircraft. This enabled the scramble of several MiG-21s. While one was shot down while taking off, and its pilot killed, the rear pair heard frantic calls for help from an Il-14 crew that was trying to

Taken after the first wave of Israeli attacks, this reconnaissance photograph of Abu Suweir shows at least five of Air Group 61's Il-28s that survived the initial onslaught. Eventually, all were knocked out before there was a chance to evacuate them. (IDF, via Albert Grandolini)

A view of the underside of an Israeli Mirage IIICJ: a sight that UARAF pilots and ground crews at Abu Suweir, Inchas, and Cairo West certainly saw more often than they would have preferred on the morning of 5 June 1967. (IDF, via Albert Grandolini)

land at Kabrit. They arrived too late: the transport was hit and made an emergency landing in the sand dunes of Sinai. Moments later, the MiGs ran into a pair of SMB.2s and shot down both of them using R-3S missiles. Around 09.20hrs, four MiG-21s were scrambled from Abu Suweir. Two pursued the withdrawing Israelis all the way to el-Arish: on the way back both pilots ran out of fuel before reaching the

This MiG-21FL of No. 43 Squadron survived the onslaught on Inchas with a badly damaged fin. Notable under the wing is a pair of UB-16-57 rocket pods, used for ground attacks. (IDF, via Albert Grandolini)

A scene from Beni Suweif photographed by an Israeli reconnaissance fighter. Visible in the foreground is a Tu-16 burning fiercely. The example in the background appears to remain intact: it was destroyed in a subsequent strike. The IDF/AF eventually claimed its pilots had destroyed 30 Egyptian Tu-16s – which was slightly over the mark: the UARAF had only 23 on the morning of 5 June 1967, and only 17 of these were at Beni Suweif. (IDF, via Albert Grandolini)

Suez Canal and were forced to eject. Of the other two, one landed safely, while the pilot of the other shot down one of four Mystère IVAs from No. 116 Squadron when they approached Abu Suweir around 10.00hrs. However, the successful Egyptian pilot was then killed when his jet hit a bomb crater.

At 08.50hrs, four Mirage IIICJs attacked Inchas AB, destroying or damaging 28 MiG-21s on the ground. Two jets from No. 49 Squadron did manage to scramble and attempted to pursue the Israelis, but both ran out of fuel while returning towards the Suez Canal, leaving their pilots with no option but to eject.

Being the home base of the UARAF's Tu-16 fleet, Cairo West was another priority target for the IDF/AF. A flight of Mirages hit two bombers loaded with KSR-2 air-to-surface missiles at the start of their attack, causing tremendous detonations that sent everybody on the ground into trenches. Eventually, all Tu-16s, two MiG-15UTIs, 12 MiG-17s, both runways and one taxiway, the local radar station, and the nearby SA-2 SAM site were destroyed in successive air strikes.

Overall, the first wave of Operation Focus successfully hit 10 air bases in the UAR. Although suffering a number of aborts due to technical difficulties and – in several instances – facing stiff opposition, it achieved nearly complete surprise and corresponding results. In exchange for nine aircraft and eight pilots, the IDF/AF claimed the destruction of over 100 enemy aircraft. While many of its claims were actually exaggerated – even if subsequently declared as 'confirmed' – there was no doubt about the immense success of this effort: the mass of Egyptian Tu-16 and Il-28 bombers at Beni Suweif and Cairo West, as well as almost all fighter-bombers deployed on air bases in Sinai were wiped out with a single blow, leaving the UARAF with next to no offensive capability. And that was only the very beginning of the June 1967 Arab-Israeli War.

BIBLIOGRAPHY

PRIMARY DOCUMENTS

Manuscripts and photographs from private documentation of following veteran EAF, IrAF, and SyAAF pilots were used:

Mohammad Ahmad (IrAF)
Fayez Baqir (IrAF)
Rabee' Dulaymi (IrAF)
Fikry el-Gindy (EAF/UARAF)
Gabr Ali Gabr (EAF/UARAF; 'Notes')
Magd el-Din Rifaat (EAF/UARAF; 'The Diary of a Mirage Pilot in the October War', 'Memoirs of Major General Magd el-Din Rifaat')
Jameel Salwan (IrAF)
Mohammad Saaydon (IrAF; 'Pilot Memoir', privately published document from 2005)
Mohammad Salman (IrAF)
Haytham Khattab Omar (IrAF; 'Memoirs of the Commander of the Iraqi Air Force')
Tahseen Zaki (EAF/UARAF; 'Testament')

Air Ministry (UK), files as listed in endnotes.
British Defence Attaché in Iraq (UK), files as listed in endnotes.
Foreign Office (UK), files as listed in endnotes.
Foreign Technologies Division (USAF), *Fishbed C/E Aerial Tactics* (tactical manual for MiG-21F-13, MiG-21PF, MiG-21FL and MiG-21PFM, obtained from Iraq in 1963 and translated to English by the Foreign Technologies Division USAF, in 1964)
Iraqi Air Force Martyrs Website, 1931–2003, *iraqiairforcememorial.com*
Ministry of Defence of the United Arab Republic, Commission headed by the Supreme Military General Hassan Metawea, *Document No. 44: Inquiry into Circumstances that led to the Disaster of 5 June, 1967* (in Arabic), (Cairo, Ministry of Defence UAR; date of issue unknown; listed in endnotes as 'Document 44')
Office of Naval Intelligence (USA), files as listed in endnotes.

INTERVIEWS

As well as the officers mentioned in the Acknowledgements, the following officers and other ranks of the SyAAF, whose names I do not feel free to reveal for concerns related to their safety and that of their families, have been interviewed for this project over time:

'Adad' (retired Su-7/20/22 pilot, SyAAF), interview, May 1996
'Boudros' (retired MiG-21 pilot, SyAAF), interviews in October 2001, March 2007, October 2008, November 2015, February 2016, April 2018, March 2021
'Hussam' (retired MiG-21 and MiG-25 pilot, SyAAF), interview, October 2016, April 2018
'Duha' (retired SyAADF officer), interviews, August 2004, March 2007, July 2013, November 2015, February 2016, April 2018
'E. R.' (veteran of the IDF), interviews, July 2012
'Hashim' (retired SyAADF officer), interviews, March 2005, March 2006, July 2013, November 2016
'Ismael' (retired SyAAF MiG-21/Su-22/Su-24 pilot), interview, November 2015
'Jabbar' (retired officer of Syrian Military intelligence), interviews, June 2003 and March 2006
'Nabil' (SA-6/11/17 operator, SyAADF), interviews, April 2001, March 2007, October 2007, July 2013, November 2016
'Mouhannad' (MiG-21 and Su-22 pilot, SyAAF), interview, August 2004, June 2011, July 2013, December 2016, April 2018
'Talal' (CO SAM-brigade, SyAAF/SyAADF), interviews, April 2001, August 2004, March 2005, March 2006, March 2007, October 2007, October 2008, December 2012, July 2013, November 2015, December 2016, April 2018

SELECTED BIBLIOGRAPHY

Alawi, A. A., *Faisal I of Iraq* (Yale: Yale University Press, 2014)
Alexander, Martin S. (Editor), *Knowing Your Friends: Intelligence Inside Alliances and Coalitions from 1914 to the Cold War* (London: Frank Cass, 1998)
Almog, O., *Britain, Israel, and the United States, 1955–1958: Beyond Suez* (London: Frank Cass, 2003)
Ameri, H. A. 'Water War in the Middle East: a Looming Threat', *The Geographical Journal*, No. 168
Asher, D., *The Egyptian Strategy for the Yom Kippur War: An Analysis* (Jefferson, NC: McFarland & Co. Inc., 2009)
Awardi, A al-, *History of the Iraqi Armed Forces, Part 17: Establishment of the Iraqi Air Forces and its Development* (in Arabic, translation by Ali Tobchi) (Baghdad: Ministry of Defence, 1988)
Badri, H. el-, Magdoub, T. el-, Zohdy, M. D. el-Din, *The Ramadan War, 1973* (Dunn Loring: T. N. Dupuy Associates, 1978)
Baker, R., *King Hussain and the Kingdom of Hejaz* (The Oleander Press, 1979)
Bar-Joseph, U., 'Rotem: The Forgotten Crisis on Road to the 1967 War', *Journal of Contemporary History*, Vol. 31 (1996)
Bar-Noi, U., *Revelations From the Polish Archives*, Cold War International History Project at the Woodrow Wilson International Center for Scholars, e-Dossier No. 8 (based on 'On Soviet Policy Following the Israeli Aggression in the Middle East', by Comrade L. I. Brezhnev to the Plenum of the Central Committee of the CPSU, 20 June 1967, Archiwum Akt Nowych – a Polish document describing the speech given by Brezhnev to the Plenum of the Central Committee of the Communist Party of the Soviet Union on the actions undertaken by the Soviet leadership before and during the 1967 Arab-Israeli War)
Bar-on, M., 'The Generals' Revolt: Civil-Military Relations in Israel on the Eve of the Six Day War', *Middle Eastern Studies*, Vol. 48 (2012)
Barak, E., 'Caught in the Middle: The United Nations Emergency Force, Israel, and the 1960 Rotem Crisis', *Diplomacy & Statecraft*, Vol 17 (2006) Issue 2 pp. 393–414
Barr, J., *A Line in the Sand: Britain, France and the Struggle that shaped the Middle East* (London: Simon & Schuster UK Ltd., 2011)
Beauffre, André, *The Suez Expedition 1956* (New York, Praeger, 1969)
Bowen, Jeremy, *Six Days: How the 1967 war shaped the Middle East* (London, Simon & Schuster UK Ltd, 2003)
Brandner, Prof. F., *Life between the Front Lines: an Engineer in the Line of Fire* (Wels-München: Verlag Welsermühl, 1973) (in German)
Burns, W., *Economic Aid and American Policy towards Egypt* (New York: State University of New York Press, 1985)

Centre for Military Studies, *The History of the Syrian Army* (Damascus: Centre for Military Studies, 2001–2002) (in Arabic)

Childers, Erskine B., *The Road to Suez* (MacGibbon & Kee, London, 1962)

Cobban, H., *The Palestinian Liberation Organisation: People, Power, and Politics* (Cambridge: Cambridge University Press, 2008)

Cohen, Colonel E. 'Cheetah', *Israel's Best Defence* (Shrewsbury: Airlife Publishing Ltd., 1993)

Cooley, J. K., 'The War over Water', *Foreign Policy* (Spring 1984), pp. 3–26

Cooper, T. & Salti, P., *Hawker Hunters at War: Iraq and Jordan, 1958–1967* (Solihull: Helion & Co., 2016)

Cooper, T., *Hot Skies over Yemen, Volume 1: Aerial Warfare over the Southern Arabian Peninsula, 1962–1994* (Solihull: Helion & Co., 2017)

Cooper, T. & Santana, S., *Lebanese Civil War, Volume 1: Palestinian Diaspora, Syrian and Israeli Interventions, 1970–1978* (Warwick: Helion & Co., 2019)

Cooper, T. & Emran, A., *1973: The First Nuclear War, Crucial Air Battles of the October 1973 Arab-Israeli War* (Warwick: Helion & Co., 2019)

Crosbie, S., *A Tacit Alliance: France and Israel from Suez to the Six Day War* (Princeton: Princeton University Press, 1974)

Creveld, M. van, *The Sword and the Olive: A Critical History of the Israeli Defense Force*, (New York: BBS Public Affairs, 2002)

Dimitrijevic, B., *UNEF: The Yugoslav Contingent; Yugoslav Army Contingent in the Sinai Peninsula, 1956–1967* (Warwick: Helion & Co., 2019)

Dupuy, Col. T. N. & Blanchard, W., *The Almanac of World Military Power* (New York: T. N. Dupuy Associates, 1972)

Farr, Lt-Col Warner D., 'The Third Temple's Holy Of Holies: Israel's Nuclear Weapons', *The Counterproliferation Papers Future Warfare Series No. 2*, USAF Counterproliferation Center, Air War College Air University Maxwell Air Force Base, Alabama, September 1999

Fawzy, Major General M., *The Three-Years War* (Beirut: Dar Mustakbal al-Arabi, 1998) (in Arabic)

Ferris, J., 'Soviet Support for Egypt's Intervention in Yemen, 1962–1963', *Journal of Cold War Studies*, Volume 10, Number 4, Fall 2008, pp. 5–36 (Article)

Flintham, V., *Air Wars and Aircraft: A Detailed Record of Air Combat, 1945 to the Present* (London: Arms and Armour Press, 1990)

Gamasy, FM M., A., G., el-, *The October War: Memoirs of Field Marshal el-Gamasy of Egypt* (Cairo: The American University of Cairo Press, 1993)

Gat, M. *Britain and the Conflict in the Middle East, 1964–1967: the Coming of the Six-Day War* (Westport: Praeger Publishers, 2003)

Gat. M., 'On the Use of Air Power and its Effect on the Outbreak of the Six Day War', *The Journal of Military History*, Volume 687, Number 4, October 2004, pp. 1187–1215

Green, S., *Taking Sides: America's Secret Relations with a Militant Israel, 1948/1967* (London: Faber and Faber Ltd, 1984)

Green, S., *Living by the Sword: America and Israel in the Middle East* (Brattleboro: Amana Books, 1988)

Green, W., and Fricker, J., *The Air Forces of the World* (London: MacDonald, 1958)

Gindy, F. el-, *Egyptian Eagles over the Golan* (Cairo: al-Hay'ah al-Misriyah al-'Ammah lil-Kitab, 1992) (in Arabic)

Gunston, B., *An Illustrated Guide to Modern Fighters and Attack Aircraft* (London: Salamander Books Ltd., 1980)

Gunston, B. & Spick, M., *Modern Air Combat: The Aircraft, Tactics and Weapons Employed in Aerial Warfare Today* (London: Salamander Books Ltd., 1983)

Gurov, I. M., *Ground-based Air Defence Systems at Wars in Vietnam and the Middle East* (Moscow: Ministry of Defence of the USSR, 1980; published for internal use as a training tool) (in Russian)

Hammel, E., *Six Days in June: How Israel won the 1967 Arab-Israeli War* (New York, Charles Scribner's Sons, 1992)

Heykal. H. M., *Cutting the Lion's Tail: Suez Through Egyptian Eyes* (London, Deutsch, 1986)

Heykal, H. M. *The 30 Years War* (Cairo: el-Ahram Publishing & Translation Centre, 1990) (in Arabic)

Hinnebusch, R., *Syria: Revolution from Above* (Taylor & Francis: 2001)

Hughes, M., 'The Banality and Brutality: British Armed Forces and the Repression of the Arab Revolt in Palestine, 1936–1939', *English Historical Review*, Vol. CXXIV, No. 507

Jawadi, Dr M. al-, *In Between the Catastrophe: Memoirs of Egyptian Military Commanders from 1967 to 1972* (Cairo: Dar al-Khiyal, 2001) (in Arabic)

Khalil, M., *The Fall of the Golan* (Cairo: Dar al-Itisam, 1980) (in Arabic)

Khalidi, R., *The Hundred Years' War on Palestine: A History of Settler Colonial Conquest and Resistance, 1917–2017* (Profile Books: 2020)

Konzelmann, G., *Damaskus: Oase Zwischen Hass und Hoffnung* (Frankfurt/Main: Ullstein Buch, 1996)

Kotlobovskiy, A. B., *MiG-21 in Local Wars* (Kiev, ArchivPress, 1997) (in Russian)

Konzelmann, G., *Damaskus: Oase zwischen Hass und Hoffnung* (Frankfurt/Main: Ullstein Buch, 1996)

Kerr, Malcom H., *The Arab Cold War: Gamal 'Abd al-Nasir and His Rivals, 1958–1970* (Oxford, Oxford University Press, 1971)

Kyle, Keith, Suez: *Britain's End of Empire in the Middle East* (I.B. Tauris, London, 2003)

Langeron, J.M., *F-4 Phantom II Flight Model Identification* & *Compared Air Combat Performances Analysis: MiG-21 versus F-4 Phantom II* (Parts 1, 2 and 3). These privately published assessments are based on following documents:

- *Flight Manual F-4C,/D,E-1-S, T.O. 1F-4C-1*, 15th August 1973, Change 1
- *Performance Data Manual F-4C, D, E-1-1-S, T.O. 1F-4C-1-1*, 15 July 1969, Change 1
- *Flight Manual F-4E, T.O. 1F-4E*, 1 February 1979
- *NATOPS Flight Manual MiG-21M*
- *NATOPS Flight Manual MiG-21MF*
- *NATOPS Flight Manual F-4D blk37*
- *NATOPS Flight Manual F-4E blk31*
- *NATOPS Flight Manual F-4E blk41*
- *NATOPS Fight Manual F-4E blk46 To.556*
- *NATOPS Flight Manual F-4E blk50*
- Robert K Heffley & Wayne F Jewel, NASA CR-2144: *Aircraft Handling Qualities Data*, NASA, December 1972
- Joseph R Chambers & Ernie L Anglin, NASA TN D-5361: *Analysis of lateral-directional stability characteristics of a twin-jet airplane at high angles of attack*, NASA, August 1969.

Laron, G., 'Stepping Back from the Third World: Soviet Policy towards the United Arab Republic, 1965–1967', *Journal of the Cold War Studies*, Vol. 12, No. 4, Fall 2010, pp. 99–118

Laron, G., *The Six-Day War: The Breaking of the Middle East* (New Haven: Yale University Press, 2017)

Lucas, S., *Britain and Suez: The Lion's Last* Roar (Manchester: Manchester University Press, 1996)

Luttwak, E., Horowitz, D., *The Israeli Army* (Allen Lane, 1975)

Menahim, Major General K. al-, *Egyptian Wars in Modern History* (Beirut: Dar Mustakbal al-Arabi, 1990) (in Arabic)

Meyer, K. E. & Brysac, S. B., *Kingmakers: The Invention of the Modern Middle East* (W. W. Norton & Co. 2009)

Michel, M. L., *Clashes: Air Combat over North Vietnam, 1965–1972* (Annapolis: Naval Institute Press, 1997)

Morris, B., *Israel's Border Wars, 1949–1956: Arab Infiltration, Israeli Retaliation, and the Countdown to the Suez War* (Oxford: Oxford University Press, 2005)

Morris, B., *Israel's Secret Wars: A History of Israel's Intelligence Services* (London: Grove Press, 1992)

Moukiiad, Major General M. A., *My Life* (Damascus: az-Zakhira, 2005) (in Arabic)

Mustafa, General H., *The June War, 1967, Part II* (Beirut: Establishment for War Studies, 1970) (in Arabic)

Nicolle, Dr D., Gabr, AVM G. A., *Air Power and the Arab World 1909–1955, Volume 1, Military Flying Services in the Arab Countries, 1909–1955* (Warwick: Helion & Co., 2019)

Nicolle, Dr D. & Gabr, AVM G. A., *Air Power and the Arab World 1909–1955, Volume 2, Military Flying Services in the Arab Countries, 1909–1955* (Warwick: Helion & Co., 2020)

Nicolle, Dr D. & Gabr, AVM G. A., *Air Power and the Arab World 1909–1955, Volume 3, Colonial Skies, 1918–1936* (Warwick: Helion & Co., 2020)

Nicolle, Dr D. & Gabr, AVM G. A., *Air Power and the Arab World, 1909–1955, Volume 4, The First Arab Air Forces, 1918–1936* (Warwick: Helion & Co., 2021)

Nicolle, Dr, D & Gabr, AVM G. A. *Air Power and the Arab World, 1909–1955, Volume 5* (Warwick: Helion & Co., 2021)

Nicolle, Dr D., Cooper, T., Air Vice Marshal Gabr Ali Gabr, *Wings Over Sinai: The Egyptian Air Force During the Sinai War 1956* (Warwick, Helion & Company, 2017)

Nicolle, Dr D. & Cooper, T., *MiGs in the Middle East, Volume 1: Soviet-Designed Combat Aircraft in Egypt, Iraq, and Syria, 1955–1963* (Warwick, Helion & Company, 2021)

Nicolle, Dr D. & Cooper, T., *MiGs in the Middle East, Volume 2: Soviet Designed Combat Aircraft in Egypt and Syria, 1963–1967* (Warwick, Helion & Company, 2021)

Nordeen, Lon and David Nicolle, *Phoenix Over the Nile: A History of Egyptian Air Power 1932–1994* (Washington DC, Smithsonian Institution Press, 1996)

Norton, Bill, *75 Years of the Israeli Air Force. Volume 1: The First Quarter of a Century 1948–1973* (Warwick, Helion & Co, 2020)

Okasha, Maj Gen Mohammed Abdel Moneim Zaki, *Conflict in the Sky: the Egyptian-Israeli Wars, 1948–1967* (Cairo: Ministry of Defence, 1976) (this book is largely based on an internal study on the UARAF performance in 1967, undertaken in cooperation between the author and the then Chief-of-Staff Egyptian Air Force, Hosni Mubarak, in 1976. As such, it is de facto the only 'official' Egyptian history of the June 1967 Arab-Israeli War)

Okasha, Major General Mohammed Abdel Moneim Zaki, *Soldiers in the Sky* (Cairo: Ministry of Defence, 1976) (in Arabic)

Okasha, Major General Mohammed Abdel Moneim Zaki, *Operation Spark: I Wave* (Cairo: Ministry of Defence, 2011) (in Arabic)

Okasha, Major General Mohammed Abdel Moneim Zaki, *69 Squadron at War* (Cairo: Ministry of Defence, 2012) (in Arabic)

Oren, M. B., *Six Days of War: June 1967 and the making of the modern Middle East* (Oxford: Oxford University Press, 2002)

Ovendale, R., *The Origins of the Arab-Israeli Wars* (Harlow: Longman Group UK Ltd, 1984)

Pappe, I., *The Ethnic Cleansing of Palestine*: (Oxford: Oneworld Publications, 2006)

Perlmutter, A., *Politics and the Military in Israel 1967–77* (London: Frank Cass and Company, 1978)

Parker, Richard B., 'USAF in the Sinai in the 1967 War: Fact or Fiction?', *Journal of Palestine Studies*, XXVII, No 1 (Autumn 1997) pp. 67–75

Pollack, K. M., *Arabs at War: Military effectiveness 1948–1991* (Lincoln: University of Nebraska Press, 2002)

Raspletin, Dr A. A., 'History PVO' (website in Russian: *historykpvo.narod2.ru*) (2013)

Rathmell, A., 'Brotherly Enemies: The Rise and Fall of the Syrian-Egyptian Intelligence Axis', 1954–1967, in Martin S. Alexander's *Knowing Your Friends*, pp. 230–253

Riad, M., *The Struggle for Peace in the Middle East* (Consett: Quartet Books, 1981)

Safran, N., *From War to War: the Arab-Israeli Confrontation*, 1948–1967 (New York: Pegasus Books, 1969)

Sampson, A., *Die Waffenhändler: Von Krupp bis Lockheed, Die Geschichte eines tödlichen Geschäfts* (Reinbek bei Hamburg: Rowohl Verlag GmbH, 1977)

Sayigh, Y., *Armed Struggle and the Search for State: The Palestinian National Movement, 1949–1993* (Washington: Institute for Palestine Studies/Oxford University Press, 1997)

Schmidt, D. A., *Yemen: The Unknown War* (London: The Bodley Head Ltd. 1968)

Segev, T., *1967: Israel, the War, and the Year that Transformed the Middle East* (Abacus: 2008)

Shalom, D., *Like a Bolt out of the Blue: 'Moked' Operation in the Six Day War, June 1967* (Rishon Le-Zion: BAVIR Aviation Publications, 2002) (in Hebrew)

Shevchuk, D., *The Soviet-Israeli War* (in Russian; unpublished manuscript)

Shlaim, A., *The Iron Wall: Israel and the Arab World* (W. W. Norton & Company, 2001)

Shlaim, A., *Lion of Jordan: The Life of King Hussein in War and Peace* (Vintage Books: 2009)

Shukairy, A., *The Great Defeat; Major Defeat of Kings and Presidents* (Cairo: Arab Foundation for Publishing and Distribution, 2005)

Sipos, M. & Cooper, T., *Wings of Iraq, Volume 1: The Iraqi Air Force, 1931–1970* (Warwick: Helion & Co., 2020)

Sipos, M. & Cooper, T., *Wings of Iraq, Volume 2: The Iraqi Air Force, 1970–1980* (Warwick, Helion & Co., 2022)

Smisek, M., *Czechoslovak Arms Exports to the Middle East, Volume 1: Israel and Jordan* (Warwick, Helion & Co. 2021)

Smisek, M., *Czechoslovak Arms Exports to the Middle East, Volume 2: Syria, 1948–1994* (Warwick, Helion & Co. 2022)

Smisek, M., *Czechoslovak Arms Exports to the Middle East, Volume 3: Egypt, 1948–1989* (Warwick, Helion & Co. 2022)

Sokolov, A, 'PVO in Local Wars and Armed Conflicts: The Arab-Israeli Wars', *VKO*, No. 2 (2), 2001

Sorby, Jr., K., 'The Army's Growing Influence in Iraqi Politics (1937–1939)', *Yearbook of Oriental Studies* (in Slovak), T. LXVIII, Z. i. 2015, 20–36, (Bratislava, 2015)

Sorby, Jr., K., *Iraq Under the Rule of 'Abdassalam 'Arif (1963–1966)* (Bratislava: Institute of Oriental Studies, Slovak Academy of Sciences, 2010)

Sorby, Jr., K., *Iraq: The Rule of Abdarrahman Arif and Its End (1966–1968)* (Bratislava: Institute of Oriental Studies, Slovak Academy of Sciences, 2011)

Stafrace, C., *Arab Air Forces* (Carrolton: Squadron/Signal Publications Inc., 1994)

Stuart-Paul, Air Marshal Sir R., *The Royal Saudi Air Force: A Legacy of His Majesty King Abdul Aziz Ibn Saud* (BAE Systems, in association with Stacey International)

Tessler, M. A., *A History of the Israeli-Palestinian Conflict* (Bloomington and Indianapolis: Indiana University Press, 1994)

Teterin, O., *In Egypt and in Zanzibar: Memoirs of Soviet Military Translators, 1960–1966* (Moscow: Memories Publishing, 2011) (in Russian)

Thompson, Sir R. E., (editor), *War in Peace: An Analysis of Warfare since 1945* (London: Orbis Publishing, 1981)

Thornhill, 'Britain, the United States and the Rise of an Egyptian Leader', *English Historical Review*, Volume CXIV, Issue 483, September 2004, pp. 893–894

Rikhye, Major General I. J., *The Sinai Blunder: Withdrawal of the United Nations Emergency Force leading to the Six-Day War of June 1967* (London: Frank Cass, 1980).

Saikal, A., *Modern Afghanistan: A History of Struggle and Survival* (London: I.B. Tauris, 2006)

Stephens, Robert, *Nasser: A political biography*, Allen Lane (London: The Penguin Press, 1971)

Teveth, S, *The Tanks of Tammuz* (London: Weidenfeld and Nicolson, 1968).

Thompson. Sir R., (editor), *War in Peace: An Analysis of Warfare since 1945* (London: Orbis Publishing, 1981).

Williams, A. G. & Gustin, Dr E., *Flying Guns: the Modern Era* (Ramsbury: The Crowood Press Ltd., 2004)

Zidek, P., Sieber, K., *Czechoslovakia in Middle East of the Years 1948–1989* (Prague, Ustav mezinarodnich vztahu, 2009) (in Czech)

Zidek, P., 'Vyvoz zbrani z Ceskoslovenska do zemi tretiho sveta, 1948–1962', *Historie a vojenstvi*, 3/2002.

Zolotaryov, Maj Gen V. A., *Russia in Local Wars and Military Conflicts in the Second Half of the 20th Century* (Moscow: Institute of Military History, Ministry of Defence of the Russian Federation, 2000) (in Russian)

NOTES

Chapter 1

1 For details of Israeli deployment of chemical weapons against the native population of Palestine, and the civilians in neighbouring countries in 1948–1949, see Ofer Aderet, 'Place the Material in the Wells': Docs point to Israel Army's 1948 Biological Warfare, *Haaretz*, 14 October 2022.

2 Yazigh, p. 37

3 Green, pp. 20–21, based on 'Top Secret', JCS paper 1684/11, dated 31 March 1948, copy in Decimal File 1946–1948, Plans and Operations Division, 091 Palestine TS (Section IIA, Case 6), Record Group 319, National Archives; Morris, *Righteous Victims*, p. 83.

4 For additional details about top Israeli military and political leaders' expression of expansionist intentions in public, see, for example, Green, *Taking Sides*, p. 35.

5 Laron, Chapter 9.

6 Munther J Haddadin, 'Water Resources in Jordan', *Resources for the Future* (2006), pp. 237–238.

7 Haddadin, p. 239

8 'Chief-of-Staff from Major General A. R. Bolling', 4 April 1951, Army Chief-of-Staff Decimal File, 1951–1953, File 092 Israel, Record Group 319, Records of the Army Staff, National Archives (USA); Kobori, I., Glantz, M. H., Aaron T., *Central Eurasian Water Crisis: Caspian, Aral and Dead Seas* (United Nations University Press, 1998), pp. 129, 131.

9 Green, *Taking Sides*, pp. 76–83.

10 Green, *Taking Sides*, pp. 76–83 and Masahiro Murakami, *Managing Water for Peace in the Middle East: Alternative Strategies* (United Nations University Press, 1995), Appendix C; Moshe Gat, *Britain and the Conflict in the Middle East, 1964–1967* (Westport: Praeger Publishers, 2003) p. 101.

11 By the early 2000s the lake had lost about 33 percent of its surface area.

12 Zafrir Rinat, 'Israel's National Water Carrier: Both Boom and Bane', *Haaretz*, 26 June 2014; Green, *Taking Sides*, pp. 78–83. Notably, as of 1951–1953, the USA were sponsoring Israel with US$150 million annually – which in turn made between 80 and 90 percent of Israel's annual budget.

13 For Nasser's background, see Oren, *Six Days of War*, pp. 2–18. For Egyptian political and economic developments in 1957–1967, and for the benefits of improved education upon Egyptian society, see Stephens, pp. 322–330, 375–376, and Nicolle et al, *MiGs in the Middle East* Vols. 1 and 2.

14 For details of Egypt and its armed forces, and relations between Nasser and his aides, before, during and after the Suez War, see Nicolle et al, *Wings over Sinai* & *MiGs in the Middle East*, Vols. 1 and 2 (see bibliography). For a detailed reconstruction of military cooperation between Czechoslovakia and Egypt from 1958 until 1989 – including details of the Czechoslovak Arms Deal, see Smisek, *Czechoslovak Arms Exports in the Middle East, Volume 3.*

15 For details on the Yugoslav contingent of the UNEF, see Dimitrijevic, *UNEF.*

16 See Michael B. Oren, *Six Days of War*, pp. 11–12, 67; Stephens, *Nasser* pp. 441–442 & Nicolle et al, *Wings over Sinai.*

17 For details on related affairs, see Laron, Chapter 5 and Nicolle et al, *Wings over Sinai* and *MiGs in the Middle East*, Vols. 1 and 2.

18 Stephens, *Nasser*, pp. 303–320; Nicolle, *Sinai* and *MiGs in the Middle East*, Vols. 1 and 2; Oren, *Six Days of War*, p. 39.

19 Hillman, *Storm in a Tea-cup*, pp. 21–22 (and, for a more general view, Kerr, *The Arab Cold War*); Nicolle et al, *MiGs in the Middle East*, Vols. 1 and 2; Sipos et al, *Wings of Iraq*, Vol. 1.

20 For the background to the formation of the UAR see Stephens, *Nasser*, pp. 268–300, 384. For the influential role of the intelligence organisations in creation of the UAR see Rathmell's article 'Brotherly Enemies' in Alexander's *Knowing Your Friends*, pp. 232–236. Notably, a month after the United Arab Republic was created, Muhammed al-Badr, the son of the ruler of Yemen, pledged adherence to the UAR, provided his father, Imam Ahmed bin Yaha remained the ruler. Nasser accepted these terms although Yemen was the antithesis of everything for which he stood: in turn, the Crown Prince's association with the Egyptian leader made him profoundly unpopular with religious leaders and other conservatives at home. Ultimately, this alliance was over as soon as it began: in June 1960, the Iman's justified fear of Nasser's influence led him to end his 'membership' in the UAR, and he turned vitriolically anti-Nasser.

21 Laron, *The Six-Day War*, p. 58 and Nicolle et al, *MiGs in the Middle East*, Vol. 2. According to Bowen (*Six Days*, p. 13), Amer and his cronies used transports of the air force to smuggle goods from Syria.

22 Stephens, *Nasser*, p. 321.

23 Uri Bar-Joseph, 'Rotem: The Forgotten Crisis on the Road to the 1967 War', *Journal of Contemporary History*, Vol. 31, No. 3 (July 1995), pp. 547–549 and *The History of the Syrian Army* (see bibliography for details).

24 Uri Bar-Joseph, 'Rotem: The Forgotten Crisis on the Road to the 1967 War', *Journal of Contemporary History*, Vol. 31, No. 3 (July 1995), pp. 551–552

25 Uri Bar-Joseph, 'Rotem: The Forgotten Crisis on the Road to the 1967 War', *Journal of Contemporary History*, Vol. 31, No. 3 (July

1995), pp. 555–560; Nicolle et al, *MiGs in the Middle East*, Vol. 1, pp. 45–46.

26 For details on the situation in Yemen of 1958–1962, see Cooper, *Hot Skies over Yemen*, Vol. 1, and Nicolle et al, *MiGs in the Middle East*, Vol. 2.

27 Stephens, pp. 409–410, 426.

28 Oren, p. 302.

29 Creveld pp. 171–172. Shortly before his death, the former Chief-of-Staff and Defence Minister Dayan in June 1967 claimed that 80 percent of the 'border incidents' from 1949 to 1967 were deliberately provoked by Israel.

30 Unless stated otherwise, based on Sayigh, pp. 58–70, and Cobban, pp. 34–55, with additional details from Bowen, pp. 21–22; Laron, pp. 77, 131–141, and Stephens, pp. 448–454.

31 According to 'standard' sources of reference (for example Martin Gilbert's *The Routledge Atlas of the Arab-Israeli Conflict*), no fewer than 967 Israelis were killed in 'Arab terrorist attacks' between 1951 and 1955. In comparison, Benny Morris (p. 101) declared such figures to be 'pure nonsense' and 'based on a 1956 speech by David Ben-Gurion in which he used a phrase for casualties in their broad sense' (i.e. both dead and wounded), and concluded that such figures were 'three to five times higher than the figures given in contemporary Israeli reports'.

32 Almog, p. 20. Almog quoted Yeshoshfat Harkabi, former head of Israeli military intelligence who stated that, '...these early infiltrations were limited incursions, motivated by economic reasons, such as Palestinians crossing the border into Israel to harvest crops in their former villages'. Furthermore, Shlaim (in *Iron Wall*, pp. 84–85), wrote:

There is strong evidence from Arab, British, American, UN and even Israeli sources to suggest that for the first six years after the [1948] war, the Arab governments were opposed to infiltration and tried to curb it. The Lebanese ... effectively sealed the border with Israel. The Syrian authorities also exercised strict control over their border with Israel, and infiltration was rarer. The Egyptian authorities ... pursued a consistent policy of curbing infiltration until 1955 ... Secret Jordanian documents captured by the Israeli army during the June 1967 war ... reveal strenuous efforts on the part of the Jordanian military and civilian authorities ... to keep [infiltrators] from crossing [the Israeli border].

Further evidence contrary to common Israeli insinuations about infiltrations being 'sponsored, inspired, guided, or at least utilised' by Arab governments, was provided by Benny Morris, who (in *Israel's Border Wars*, p. 67) quoted an Israeli Foreign Ministry official:

[W]hen (we) asked (the IDF for) ... some clear documentary proof of the (Arab) Legion's complicity (in the infiltrations) ... no clear answer came from the army. Finally, Fati (Deputy Minister of Internal Affairs, Yehoshafat Harkabi) told Leon (Savir, senior Foreign Ministry official) and myself, on two separate occasions, that no proof could be given because no proof existed. Furthermore, Fati told me that having personally made a detail study of infiltrations, he had arrived at the conclusion that Jordanians and especially the Legion were doing their best to prevent infiltrations, which was a natural decentralised and sporadic movement. In fact, listening to Fati or his colleagues these days, one could almost mistake them for British Foreign Office (which consistently argued in this vein).

33 Green, p. 99; Shlaim, pp. 128–129; Konzelmann, pp. 287–293; Dupuy et al, *Flawed Victory*, pp. 25–27 and Dahl, p. 41. Notably, Shlaim stressed: 'Records show that until the Gaza raid, the Egyptian military authorities had a consistent and firm policy of curbing infiltration ... into Israel ... and that it was only following the raid that a new policy was put in place, that of organising the fedayeen units and turning them into an official instrument of warfare against Israel.'

34 Gamasy, p. 18 and Hinnawy, interview with David Nicolle, 03/1989.

Chapter 2

1 For additional examples of such intelligence assessments, see CIA, Foreign Relations of the United States, 27 July 1948, Volume 5, pp. 1240–1248 or 'Military Capabilities of Israel and the Arab States', Document No. 50, Case NLJ 04-53, Lindon Baines Johnson Library, from early 1967 and Bowen, pp. 52–53.

2 Unless stated otherwise, conclusions expressed in this chapter are based on Astrabadi, interviews, 03/2005, 03/2006, 03/2007 and 10/2007; Morris, *Israel's Secret Wars*, pp. 207–209; and research for Nicolle et al, *MiGs in the Middle East Volumes 1 and 2*, Cooper, *Hot Skies over Yemen, Volumes 1* and 2, and Cooper et al, *Wings of Iraq, Volumes 1* and 2.

3 Perlmutter, pp. 40, 43; Oren, p. 260.

4 Creveld, pp. 157–159, 169; Hammel, pp. 60–63, 69, 89, 108–112, 121; Luttwak et al, pp. 137, 172–175.

5 Creveld, p. 164.

6 Creveld, p. 164, 166; Luttwak et al, pp. 19–20, 72, 177–179.

7 Luttwak et al, pp. 177–179.

8 Brower, p. 29; Oren, pp. 25.

9 Astrabadi, interviews, 03/2005, 03/2006, 03/2007 and 10/2007; Morris, *Israel's Secret Wars*, pp. 207–209 and Saydoon, *Pilot Memoirs*. Notably, the Mossad agent that 'convinced' Ruefa/Redfa to defect, and 14 of his accomplices, were all arrested by the Iraqi Air Force Intelligence Department (which was thus able to reconstruct the entire Israeli operation), sentenced to death and executed.

10 Tali Yahalom, 'Timeline: Israeli Prisoner Exchanges', *Financial Times*, 16 July 2008, and Moshe Rom, 'Uri Ilan – Message Notes', *Haaretz* (online article in Hebrew, retrieved from www.haaretz.co.il in 07/2008).

11 Offer Drori, 'Operation Kachal' (retrieved from www.global-report.com in 09/2009), and Cohen, *Israel's Best Defence*, p. 166.

12 Astrabadi, interview 03/2005, concluded that it is very likely that the AMAN intercepted even Field Marshal Amer's call to Air Marshal Sidki Mahmoud, on 4 June 1967, when the former ordered the UARAF to prepare two Ilyushin Il-14 transports to take him and his entourage on an inspection of defences in the Sinai Peninsula, the following morning. Many other Arab veterans interviewed over time stress the major advantage provided to Israel by the fact that Egyptian air defences were more concerned with not opening fire on FM Amer's aircraft than offering protection to crucially important airfields. Whether the Israelis set up the timing of their attack accordingly remains unknown, but they obviously took the flight of these two Il-14s into account. Furthermore, Astrabadi stressed that similar Israeli tapping operations were undertaken at later dates as well, for example in preparation for the IDF/AF attack on the Iraqi nuclear complex in Tuwaitha, near Baghdad, in June 1981. According to him, in the course of subsequent investigation, the IrAF Intelligence Department detected and unearthed a tapping device installed by the Israelis on the communications cable connecting al-Wallid AB in Western Iraq with IrAF HQ in Baghdad.

13 Unless stated otherwise, based on Jawadi, *In Between the Catastrophe*, Chapter 2 (containing memoirs of General Mohammed Sadek, Director of DMI from late 1966 until 1967).

14 Boudros, interview, 11/2014.

15 Fawzy, Chapter 8 (containing extensive discussion of Egyptian intelligence reports through May 1967).

Chapter 3

1 Gat, pp. 1098–1099 and Zeev Elron, 'Remarks on Air Power and the Six-Day War', *The Journal of Military History*, Volume 69, Number 3, July 2005, pp. 811–817. According to Elron, the IDF/AF flew a total of 171 combat sorties that day, including 84 ground attacks, and deployed 65,000kg of bombs.

2 Boudros, interviews 10/2001 and 03/2007.

3 Gat, 'On the Use of Air Power', pp. 1200–1201.

4 Bowen, p. 21.

5 Bowen, p. 102.

6 Laron, Chapter 6.

7 For details on this clash, see Cooper et al, *MiGs in the Middle East, Volume 2*, pp. 44–45.

8 Bowen, p. 22; Laron, pp. 141–144.

9 Bowen, pp. 26–30. For details of the Air Battle of Samua, see Cooper et al, *Hawker Hunters at War*, pp. 26–30.

10 Mutawi, pp. 79–85.

11 Danish, interview, 06/2011. Notably, while most published Israeli accounts accuse the Egyptians of an 'attack on a Piper just inside

the Israeli border', in an interview with a British officer and military theoretician Peter Young, in late 1966, Weizman explained that, 'neither by accident nor design had a single Egyptian plane strayed over the Israeli border ever since 1956' (Young, p. 87).

12 Unless stated otherwise, this sub-chapter is based on Gluska, pp. 100–102; 'Confidential, Priority Damascus to Foreign Office', Tel. No. 212, 10 April 1967, addressed to Foreign Office telegram No. 212 of 10 April, Repeated for information to MoD (D14), Tel Aviv, Amman, Beirut, JIG Cyprus, UKMIS New York and Saving to Washington; *The History of the Syrian Army*, Chapter 7; 'Confidential, Priority Damascus to Foreign Office', Tel. No. 212, 10 April 1967.
13 Bowen, pp. 33–34 and Jawadi, *In Between the Catastrophe*, Chapter 2.
14 Bowen, pp. 32–33; Laron, pp. 141–144; Stephens, pp. 466–471.
15 Gamasy, pp. 20–21.
16 Gamasy, pp. 20–21 and Laron, Chapter 6.
17 Uri Bar-Noi, *The Soviet Union and the Six-Day War: Revelations From the Polish Archives*, Cold War International History Project at the Woodrow Wilson International Center for Scholars, e-Dossier No. 8, based on 'On Soviet Policy Following the Israeli Aggression in the Middle East', by Comrade L. I. Brezhnev to the Plenum of the Central Committee of the CPSU, 20 June 1967, Archiwum Akt Nowych. (Polish document describing the speech given by Brezhnev to the Plenum of the Central Committee of the CPSU on the actions undertaken by the Soviet leadership before and during the 1967 Arab-Israeli War.)

Chapter 4

1 For details on the Egyptian and then the United Arab Republic Air Force through the 1950s and 1960s, see Nicolle et al, *Air Power and the Arab World*, Volumes 1–9; Nicolle et al, *Wings over Sinai* and Cooper et al, *MiGs in the Middle East* Volumes 1 and 2 (details in Bibliography).
2 *Department of State Bulletin*, Vol. 22, p. 886.
3 For details on the first decades of the Egyptian Air Force, see Nicolle et al, *Air Power and the Arab World* mini-series.
4 Gindy, interview with David Nicolle, 02/1999 (this and all subsequent quotations from Fikry el-Gindy are based on transcription of the same interview).
5 Bowen, pp. 15–16, 19–20; Stephens, pp. 460–461.
6 EFM, Document No. 44, pp. 1060–1062. Notably, in *Conflict in the Sky*, Chapter 3, Okasha provided slightly different figures, as follows:
- MiG-21s: 91, of which 76 were operational and 15 non-operational
- Su-7s: 16, of which 15 were operational; 16 additional in the process of assembly
- MiG-19: 19, of which 7 were operational
- MiG-17: 69, of which 47 were operational and 22 non-operational
- MiG-15: 14, of which 12 were operational
- Il-28: 27, of which 23 were operational
- Tu-16: 23 (all operational)
- Il-14: 43, of which six were operational
- An-12: 21 operational and 1 non-operational
- Helicopters: 34 in total, of which 8 were non-operational

However, it is unclear which document was used to put together that summary.
7 EFM, Document No. 44, pp. 1060–1062.
8 Raspletin, *SAM Exports*. Notably, the same source details two additional systems delivered to Egypt in 1967, but without an exact date. It is possible that they were actually delivered only after the war of June that year, as attrition replacements.
9 Document 44, pp. 1047–1048 and Taher Zaki, interview, 02/1999.
10 Ayman Sayed Ahmad Hob el-Din (CO 418th Air Defence Battalion, ADC), interview, 11/2012.
11 Document 44, p. 1044; Taher Zaki, interview, 02/1999; Gahramy, interview, 03/2003 and al-Jawadi, *In Between the Catastrophe*, Chapter 1; 'Israel: An open Space for our Fighters', *Binaa al-Watan* (in Arabic), 1 December 1965.
12 Document 44, p. 1046.
13 Document 44, pp. 1054–1055.
14 Gahramy, interview, 03/2003 and Al-Jawadi, *In Between the Catastrophe*, Chapter 1
15 Document 44, p. 1055.
16 Document 44, p. 1058. Rather characteristically, in the same report, Mansour also warned about the Israeli purchase of, '50 A-4 Skyhawk fighter-bombers from the USA', and that these 'have to be considered in all assessments of the Israeli air power'. Actually, at the time Israel was still nearly a year away from receiving any A-4s.

Chapter 5

1 For details on the Iraqi air force through the 1950s and 1960s, see Nicolle et al, *Air Power and the Arab World*, Volumes 1–9; Cooper et al, *MiGs in the Middle East* Volumes 1 and 2; and Cooper et al, *Wings of Iraq, Volume 1* (details in bibliography).
2 Based on *History of the Iraqi Armed Forces, Part 17* (various chapters).

Chapter 6

1 For details on the Israel Defense Force/Air Force in the 1950s and 1960s, see Norton, 75 Years of the *Israeli Air Force, Volume 1* (details in bibliography).
2 Green, p. 80.
3 Burns, p. 11.
4 Norton, pp. 25–26.

Chapter 7

None

Chapter 8

1 For details on the Syrian air force through the 1950s and 1960s, see Nicolle et al, *Air Power and the Arab World*, Volumes 1–9; Nicolle et al, *Wings over Sinai* & Cooper et al, *MiGs in the Middle East Volumes 1* and *2* (details in bibliography).
2 Based on cross-examination of all available sources (see Acknowledgements and Bibliography). Notably, Moukiiad recalled the 42nd Air Defence Regiment as responsible for the protection of Dmeyr AB and the 725th Air Defence Regiment as responsible for the protection of Mezzeh AB, but Boudros provided a more detailed recollection in this regard. Of further interest is that until this very day, Egyptian veterans dispute the Syrian capability to operate the four Il-28Rs left by the UARAF in Syria after the dissolution of the Union in 1961. On the contrary, the Israelis seem to have assessed these four jets as 'bombers', rather than reconnaissance aircraft, which is how the Syrians saw them.
3 Boudros, interview 02/2016 and 03/2021; Duha, interview 04/2018; Jabbar, interview, 03/2006.

Chapter 9

1 Gamasy, p. 72 and Laron, Chapter 6.
2 Bowen, pp. 34–35, 38, 40–41 and Laron, Chapter 6.
3 Bowen, pp. 43–44; Laron, pp. 88–95 and Gluska, pp. 130–140. Had Nasser acted through the United Nations, he would have little trouble in ascertaining support not only from all over the Middle East, the USSR and members of the Warsaw Pact, but much of Asia and Africa, where the UAR's actions were widely popular.
4 Gamasy, p. 26.
5 Bowen, pp. 46–47 and Gamasy, p. 26.
6 Bar-Noi, 'The Soviet Union and the Six-Day War'.
7 Cohen, *The 1967 Six-Day War: New Israeli Perspective.*
8 Cohen, *The 1967 Six-Day War: New Israeli Perspective.* Notably, Ginor et al (p. 124) state that the Israeli Military Censor prevented Danny Shalom from publishing the captured copy of Amer's 'Battle Order #4', which, 'apparently', related 'specifically' to an attack on the nuclear complex in his book *Like a Bolt out of the Blue*. For the full content of UARAF plans for air strikes on Israel captured during the June 1967 Arab-Israeli War, and released by the Israeli Military Censor, see Cooper et al, *Arab MiGs, Volume 2*, pp. 194–200. For Fawzy's statement, see Fawzy, Chapter 1, and for Soviet warnings to Egypt and Israel see Gluska, *The Israeli Military and the Origins of the 1967 War*, pp. 184–185.
9 Cohen, *The 1967 Six-Day War: New Israeli Perspective*, based on the recollection of former Brigadier General Yitzhak Ya'akov (in charge of weapons development, and the chief liaison officer between the IDF and all the civilian defence industries – including the nuclear project – as of 1967), and testimony by the former

Chief of General Staff IDF, Zvi Tzur (chief aid to Moshe Dayan as of 1967).

10 Bar-Noi, *The Soviet Union and the Six-Day War* and Ginor et al, *Foxbats over Dimona.*

11 Abd el-Hamid, interview with Dr David Nicolle, 02/1999; this and all subsequent quotations from Abd el-Hamid are based on a transcription of the same interview.

12 *Fishbed C/E Aerial Tactics*, pp. 108–110. As explained not only in that manual, but also demonstrated by Abd el-Hamid and colleagues, these early variants of the MiG-21 could actually fly even higher than 18,000m – at so-called 'dynamic altitudes', though only if flown along a near-ballistic trajectory. Indeed, the same manual provided detailed instructions for operations at up to 24,000m (78,740ft) and speeds of up to Mach 2.4.

13 This map is based on one published in Shalom, *Like a Bolt out of the Blue*, and on interviews by Lon Nordeen with Egyptian pilots Qadri Abd el-Hamid and Fuad Kamal, in 02/1999.

14 Gamasy, pp. 20–21.

15 While this reconstruction is based on cross-examination of recollections provided by Gamasy (for example pp. 29, 42–44), Fawzy, and Murtagi, and commentary by Gawrych (pp. 77–78), but especially Oren (pp. 66, 92, 97, 119–121), Shlaim et al, and Segev – and will be discussed in more detail in Volume 2 – the current stance is that the sheer existence of any kind of serious offensive planning by the UAR armed forces remains unsubstantiated with documentary evidence, and hotly disputed. If nothing else, and contrary to Oren's claims, not one of dozens of Egyptian military pilots of the time has ever recalled being ordered to strike Israel on 27 May, and/or any such operation being cancelled at the last minute.

16 Bowen, pp. 50–51; Laron, pp. 158–159; Oren, pp. 61–63, 80, 90–92.

17 Bowen, pp. 63–64; Laron, pp. 277–280; Oren, pp. 121–126.

18 Ironically, by early June, intensive diplomatic efforts were initiated to de-escalate the crisis. Ironically, these differed significantly from what was reported to the public. For example, while publicly asserting Israel's peaceful intentions, and calling for international mediation, privately, Prime Minister Eshkol was sending secret messages to Nasser, urging de-escalation. While US President Johnson publicly rebuked Nasser, privately he sent him a reassuring letter, and delayed several arms shipments to Israel that were due for delivery. In turn, Nasser publicly warned that any US-led attempt to break the blockade of the Straits of Tiran would lead Egypt to attack Israel, but privately assured he sought peace, and his action was a matter of national prestige. However, nothing of this could influence the General Staff IDF's thinking any more, and even if: because of very negative experiences with intelligence assessments about Indo-China, Johnson was sceptical about the US intelligence assessments emphasising Israel's military superiority compared to its neighbours – even more so in the light of Israeli 'warnings' that they were facing 'overwhelming odds' and 'had no other options but to attack first'. Even then, and despite a few setbacks, he was willing to continue negotiating and thus the US diplomacy began making some progress, both within the UN Security Council and in Cairo: it was only U Thant who came in between by deciding to adjourn related discussions until Monday 5 June. For details, see Bowen, p. 55–63, 81–83 and Oren, pp. 100–116, 145–147.

19 Al-Jawadi, Chapter 3, Fawzy, Chapter 8.

Chapter 10

1 Bowen, pp. 87–88, 90; Laron, pp. 281–284; Teveth, pp. 97–106.

2 Unless stated otherwise, this sub-chapter is based on Shalom, *Like a Bolt out of the Blue.*

3 Countless Western reports detailing Israeli pilots flying up to seven or eight combat sorties every day during the June 1967 War have all proven unrealistic. More recent Israeli publications indicate that the majority of the 277 available jet fighter pilots (this figure included 42 Magister pilots) flew three or four sorties on 5 June, with only a handful of exceptions – i.e. pilots that flew five or six sorties (the last of which took place in the night from 5 June to 6 June and concerned operations other than attacks on Arab air bases). The operational tempo was relaxed the following day, with most pilots flying three sorties or fewer. Additionally, it should be kept in mind that the availability of IDF/AF fighter-bombers decreased due to losses and combat damage. Despite the hard work of the Israeli ground crews, a number of aircraft damaged in the course of attacks on Egyptian and other air bases on 5 June could not be returned to service before the end of the war.

4 Mutawi, p. 122. The word 'Inab' repeated three times meant that a war was imminent.

ABOUT THE AUTHOR

Tom Cooper is an Austrian aerial warfare analyst and historian. Following a career in the worldwide transportation business – during which he established a network of contacts in the Middle East and Africa – he moved into narrow-focus analysis and writing on small, little-known air forces and conflicts, about which he has collected extensive archives. This has resulted in specialisation in Middle Eastern, African and Asian air forces. As well as authoring and coauthoring 560 books and over 1,000 articles, he has coauthored the Arab MiGs book series – a six-volume, in-depth analysis of the Arab air forces at war with Israel, in the 1955–73 period. Cooper has been working as editor of Helion's five @War series since 2017.